Am I a Jew?

Am I a Jew?

LOST TRIBES, LAPSED JEWS,
AND ONE MAN'S
SEARCH FOR HIMSELF

Theodore Ross

HUDSON
STREET
PRESS

HUDSON STREET PRESS
Published by Penguin Group
Penguin Group (USA) Inc., 375 Hudson Street, New York, New York 10014, U.S.A. ◆ Penguin Group (Canada), 90 Eglinton Avenue East, Suite 700, Toronto, Ontario, Canada M4P 2Y3 (a division of Pearson Penguin Canada Inc.) ◆ Penguin Books Ltd., 80 Strand, London WC2R 0RL, England ◆ Penguin Ireland, 25 St. Stephen's Green, Dublin 2, Ireland (a division of Penguin Books Ltd.) ◆ Penguin Group (Australia), 250 Camberwell Road, Camberwell, Victoria 3124, Australia (a division of Pearson Australia Group Pty. Ltd.) ◆ Penguin Books India Pvt. Ltd., 11 Community Centre, Panchsheel Park, New Delhi – 110 017, India ◆ Penguin Books (NZ), 67 Apollo Drive, Rosedale, Auckland 0632, New Zealand (a division of Pearson New Zealand Ltd.) ◆ Penguin Books (South Africa) (Pty.) Ltd., 24 Sturdee Avenue, Rosebank, Johannesburg 2196, South Africa

Penguin Books Ltd., Registered Offices: 80 Strand, London WC2R 0RL, England

First published by Hudson Street Press, a member of Penguin Group (USA) Inc.

First Printing, September 2012
10 9 8 7 6 5 4 3 2 1

Copyright © Theodore Ross, 2012

Excerpt from "An Open Letter from Erin Hershberg, *Heeb* Editor-in-Chief." Copyright Erin Hershberg, *Heeb*, 2011. Used by permission.

Portions of this book first appeared in *Harper's Magazine*, *Tablet*, and *Jewcy*.

H   REGISTERED TRADEMARK—MARCA REGISTRADA
HUDSON
STREET
PRESS

LIBRARY OF CONGRESS CATALOGING-IN-PUBLICATION DATA
Ross, Ted (Theodore).
  Am I a Jew? : lost tribes, lapsed Jews, and one man's search for himself / Theodore Ross.
    p. cm.
  Includes bibliographical references and index.
  ISBN 978-1-59463-095-8
  1. Jews—Identity. 2. Crypto-Jews—United States. 3. Jewish Christians—United States. 4. Jews—Return to Orthodox Judaism. 5. Jews—United States—Interviews. 6. Ross, Ted (Theodore). I. Title.
  DS143.R585 2012
  305.892'4073092—dc23   2012010160

Printed in the United States of America
Set in Adobe Jensen Pro Regular

PUBLISHER'S NOTE
While the author has made every effort to provide accurate telephone numbers and Internet addresses at the time of publication, neither the publisher nor the author assumes any responsibility for errors, or for changes that occur after publication. Further, the publisher does not have any control over and does not assume any responsibility for author or third-party websites or their content.

BOOKS ARE AVAILABLE AT QUANTITY DISCOUNTS WHEN USED TO PROMOTE PRODUCTS OR SERVICES. FOR INFORMATION PLEASE WRITE TO PREMIUM MARKETING DIVISION, PENGUIN GROUP (USA) INC., 375 HUDSON STREET, NEW YORK, NEW YORK 10014.

Penguin is committed to publishing works of quality and integrity.
In that spirit, we are proud to offer this book to our readers;
however, the story, the experiences, and the words
are the author's alone.

ALWAYS LEARNING   PEARSON

For Diane Ross

CONTENTS

Part VII

Part VIII

Part IX

Part I

HIDDEN JEW

At times the truth shines so brilliantly that we perceive it clear as day. Our nature and our habit then draw a veil over our perception, and we return to a darkness as dense as before. We are like those who, beholding frequent flashes of lightning, still find themselves in the thickest darkness of night.

—Maimonides, *The Guide for the Perplexed*

I.

I was nine years old when my mother forced me to convert to Christianity. We had just moved from New York City to a small southern town whose local hospital had recruited her to open a medical practice. My new faith was a ruse—I never formally converted—but if anyone asked, I was instructed by my mother to say I was Unitarian. She also required me to keep these sectarian machinations secret from my father, who was still in New York and who would have filed a court order demanding custody if he had the slightest notion of what she was up to. Meanwhile, I was enrolled at the Christ Episcopal Day School, where I studied the Bible, attended church each week, received Communion, and even sang in the choir. For the years of my childhood in Mississippi, I lived a minor sort of double life: fake Christian in Mississippi and secular Jew in Manhattan, where I returned for holidays and summer break.

Understand, please, that I love my mother, and know that she had her reasons. In retrospect, her belief that our town would reject a divorced, Yankee, female doctor who was also Jewish seems far from absurd. Yet let no one mistake her either for a friend of the Jews. She was convinced that the ceaseless shtick that defines Judaism in this country—the wry exceptionalism, the ironic fatalism, the false socialism, the Zionist apologetics, the Yiddish jargoning, the hand-wringing over the Holocaust—barred her from the full American experience. For her, being a Jew meant being cheated of a piece of this country's restless, rootless anonymity. She didn't hate Jews or Judaism, and she certainly didn't want to hurt me. She just wanted to be one of *us*.

Neither of my parents came from an observant background: no kashrut, no *Shabbos*, no yarmulkes, no fasting for the sins, no autumnal New Year. Christmas trees stood next to the menorahs in the homes of our families. Religious iconography like the *chai* and the Star of David disappeared permanently with the demise of disco, replaced with popular-cultural or sporting figures of worship (*and* G_d *said*, "Bless the Knicks."). An American Diaspora saw our relatives willingly exiled to white-bred enclaves in Minnesota, Arizona, New Jersey, and California. Then came the inevitable passing of the family patriarchs and matriarchs—the Hebrew and Yiddish speakers, the shtetl descendants, the mumblers of prayers, the pious head-bobbers—survived by offspring who wed non-Jewish spouses. For my family, as for many modern-day American Jews, the faith was no faith, but rather a culture, a sensibility, a form of humor, an array of tastes, a canon of literature, a philosophy of work and education; it crossed over into practice only at Passover and Hanukkah, if then. As such, I knew as a child that my Christianity was a lie but it rarely felt like a pose. Even if we hadn't moved to Mississippi, my mother could have easily disposed of our Jewish identity. It was, put simply, just what you do.

My mother and her equally ambivalent coreligionists have no natural claim to this history, of course. What cohort of postwar Americans, Jewish or otherwise, hasn't confronted such an evolution? That said, not every child of the fifties ended up moving his or her family to the Bible Belt and living as a false Christian. A lapsed Jew is a Jew, whereas a woman who forces her kids to pretend to be Unitarian, sends them to Episcopal school, marries a Catholic man, and publicly denies the religion of her birth—that's a far sight more radical. This, I imagine, requires some explanation.

My mother's mythology on this subject works as follows. She first traveled to Mississippi in the late sixties on a college road trip. Driving a rutted southern highway in her obligatory VW Beetle, this nice Jewish girl from Queens surveyed the antebellum mansions, the Spanish moss, the clouds heavy with the afternoon downpour and, for reasons she finds impossible, even now, to parse in any rational fashion, determines to live there. A life in this place would offer an egress from the specificity of her birth, a release from the responsibilities of history, a new home in which to become the Somebody of her own invention, or better yet, the Nobody of her fantasies. After two children, a divorce, and a failed Manhattan medical practice, she was finally able to fulfill the requirements of the myth and was reborn.

By the time I had reached adulthood, the importance of my forced conversion had seemingly receded. It was another dissociated artifact of my childhood, half myth, half a character trait in someone else's novel. It's not that I *never* thought about Judaism. I did. I even wrote about it on occasion, albeit in a tangential fashion. I published a story about the "Modern Orthodox" Jews who build imaginary homes from fishing line and telephone poles; about a rock band with Jewish singers performing Cambodian pop tunes; about Jewish sex (I was asked by a magazine to write a reader's survey on the topic that was killed, thankfully, before publication). The problem was that nothing I did brought me closer to understanding my identity or even inquiring about it in a serious way. If anything, it made assessing my connection to my birth religion more difficult. I had no stake in these stories. It was Judaism-as-play, an identity that happened to someone else.

As I dabbled in these matters I began to realize just how uncomfortable I am with most practitioners of my birth religion. I worry that if they knew of my past they might not accept me as Jewish, and, with some of my mother's scorn cutting through the unease, I wonder why I would want their acceptance in the first place. The result has been a furtive fascination with Judaism, one that compels and repels in equal measure. Moreover, with the distance that my experiences have put between me and the Judaism of my forebears, I find myself forced to ask a simple question: Am I a Jew?

There is, admittedly, a certain Hebraic quality in even asking such a question. What other faith conjures up so much doubt in its adherents? It is fundamental to the religion itself. Do you speak Hebrew? Great if you do, but if you don't, you can still be a Jew. Were you bar mitzvahed? Nice (such a good boy!), but plenty of Jews weren't. Kosher, not kosher; kosher at home; kosher only if there are no Catholics around; kosher except for bacon, except for shrimp, except for cheeseburgers, only on the good china, never in school, never when it's embarrassing. Have you been to Israel? Did you wail at the Wailing Wall? Do you consider Israel a fascist state? Was your mother Jewish? When was the last time you went to temple? Quick—what's the difference between the Talmud, the Mishnah, and the Gemara? (Hint: It's a trick question.) Do you believe in God? Are you a Jew for Jesus? A Crypto-Jew? Are you a cultural Jew, and if so, what is your opinion of Woody Allen's latest film? Do you find *Heeb* magazine amusing? Sammy Davis Jr.? Were you born Jewish? Did you convert? Did the rabbi send you away three times before he gave you the secret codes to the international bank accounts? Where do you get a bagel in this town?

Am I a Jew? It's an obvious question but one that even the most sophisticated minds struggle to answer. It's a silly question except millions have lost their lives depending on their response. It's a religious question except when an atheist asks it. It's a question as ancient as the First Temple and as contemporary as this week's bestseller. Jewish writers and thinkers from Maimonides to Walter Benjamin to Philip Roth have asked it of themselves and others. Hitler wanted to know, Israel's immigration authorities reserve the right to their own definition, and Jesus had some thoughts on the matter that are worthy of consideration. This book chronicles my efforts to provide my own response.

My first abortive experiment in defining myself in Judaic terms took place in college. I wrote an anthropology term paper under the name Theodore Rosenzweig that included these facts regarding the American history of the Family Ross: In 1945 my paternal grandfather, David, following a brief stint in the navy (he was discharged after a month due to poor eyesight), moved from New York City to Lynchburg, Virginia, to serve as manager of a dry goods store. The charms of the South in that era were such that he chose, like my mother forty years hence, to conceal his identity, shortening his surname from Rosenzweig to Ross. Grandpa David, who died several months before I was born, returned to New York in 1951. He never went back to his old surname.

For his efforts, Theodore Rosenzweig earned a rather lenient B– (we were supposed to write about kinship relations of a less personal sort). Theodore Ross, who never officially completed the assignment, received an F, and by midterms he was back to his given surname.[1]

After college I started telling people about my childhood in Mississippi. *When I was a kid I pretended not to be Jewish.* Powerful words, these. There was something liberating as well in uttering them as an adult, away from the South and the people who knew me there. I chose to excise from my tales any hint of putative childhood trauma, focusing instead on the Chaplinesque character of my years as a bumbling apostolic outsider. (Typical example: *So I went to this kid's house for a sleepover and his mother cooked us a gorgeous dinner of burgers and fries. I was a glutton at that age and piled in without thinking. The boy's mother, this tautly strung Stepford type*

---

1. My professor had a sense of humor: he put both grades on the paper, one next to the other.

with big, white teeth and a slow, unctuous drawl, she looks at me and says, "Tayed, I'm not sure about your home, but in ours we ask the Lord's Blessing before we eat.") Eventually, though, the excitement of "going public" faded. The reaction to these stories seemed to correlate less with the dynamics of my childhood than to stereotypes about the backwardness and absurdity of the South. Even less effective were my attempts to shock my Mississippi friends with "the truth." None seemed overly surprised, having already conflated my inherent abrasiveness with a generic Jewish identity—making all New Yorkers Jewish, even those who weren't.

I raged at times, usually whenever my mother referred to the idyllic days of my youth. I complained loudly, to my brother, about "what she put us through." I ran away and lived for three years in Vietnam. I pushed thoughts of Judaism from my mind; most Vietnamese had never heard of it, and those who had were impressed by certain tired Jewish clichés. Jews, or so they had been led to believe, were both *thông minh* (smart) and *giàu có* (rich).

So what happened? What brought me to my present state of writerly introspection? How convenient would it be if I could point to some pivotal moment, an inciting incident, tidy lesson learned, or a meaningful epiphany of the sort our West Coast filmmakers so admire? I visited a Holocaust memorial site on vacation in the Czech Republic (it moved me to be sure, but not in this direction); I had children (I love them but that didn't do it either); I lost members of my family (I miss my grandparents but I'm not writing this book for them).

The truth, banal as it might sound, is that I simply wanted to know. Or, more precisely, I *needed* to. Like my mother, I had my own myth to make real. Only mine, instead of entailing the abandonment of a specific and defined heritage, would require its embrace.

But the world and topic of Judaism is too big. I can't embrace it all, can't understand it all, can't *own* it all. Still, I wanted an answer to my question. And I had to start somewhere. I thought about simplifying matters: make the drive out to New Jersey or Long Island one weekend, stop in at some leaf-blown upper-middle-class town thick with synagogues, and if the rabbi happened to be free, grab a seat on the sanctuary, pose my question, and be done with the whole thing in an afternoon, depending on traffic.

Or I could just begin *living* as a Jew. Here in New York I could find role models from virtually every denomination, variation, movement, sect, stream, subset, and schismatic offshoot known to American Jewry, and probably several unknown ones, too. Everything I might need is close to hand. The accoutrements—the food, the Judaica, the *New York Times*—are readily available. I would barely have to move beyond my door. My neighborhood in Brooklyn hosts all manner of congregations large and small, conventional and progressive, Beth Elohim to Altshul. The only challenge would be deciding which one.

If that didn't suit, no cause for concern: I had a few dollars in my pocket, enough for an airline ticket to Israel, round-trip if I were unsure, one way if a bolder urge came upon me. Once in Jerusalem, the rabbinate could no doubt be relied on to provide me an answer, for good or ill.

Simplest yet, why not just start *being* a Jew? My mother never forced me to accept Jesus as the Christ. I was never baptized or confirmed or born again. No exorcism or circumcision would be required for my return. I could learn the prayers, fry latkes in season, and bone up on purveyors of kosher prayer shawls. If the accepted stereotypes are to be believed, I already look the part: sadly under six feet, brown hair fading to bald, proboscis of biblical slope and proportion, torso winterized with fur. No one would contradict me, and if anyone did ask, all I had to do was say, "Yes. Yes, I am."

I chose to do none of these things.

Part II

CRYPTO-JEW

Believe me, there are Jews everywhere.

—Bernard Malamud, "Angel Levine"

I.

My reckoning with the self began at my laptop one lazy evening not long ago, when I came across an odd little children's book. *Abuelita's Secret Matzahs* told the story of a Hispanic boy named Jacobo, who, while visiting his grandmother in Santa Fe, discovered that he was something called an *anusim*, or a "Crypto-Jew," which I learned meant that he was a descendant of the medieval Jews of Spain, who were forcibly converted to Catholicism yet continued, for hundreds of years, to practice Judaism in secret.[1]

I soon began looking into the topic in earnest. My research taught me that only a small population of converted Jews existed before 1391, when anti-Semitic riots in Spain resulted in the conversion under duress of some 200,000 Jews, many of them baptized by clergymen accompanying the mobs. Once this violence abated, Spanish Christians wanted nothing to do with their converted brethren. In fact, the Inquisition was established in Spain in 1481 not to convert the Jews, as I had always thought, but to eradicate what were believed to be large numbers of surreptitiously still-Jewish families among the *conversos*, both *anusim* and *meshumadim* (willing converts). Some of those persecuted fled for locations through-

---

1. *Anusim* is the Hebrew word for "forced." The forced converts were also known by the pejorative *Marranos*, *cristianos-nuevos* (New Christians), *conversos* (converts), and *judaizantes* (Judaizers). The term "Crypto-Jew" dates from 1893 and an article in the British journal *Transactions of the Jewish Historical Society of England*.

out Europe, while others made their way to the New World. Semi-open communities of Crypto-Jews thrived in the Spanish imperial possessions until the late 1500s, when the Inquisition arrived in the colonies. Trials, interrogations, and autos-da-fé ensued, and within a century the Crypto-Jews were no more.

That, at least, is the conventional history. But what if Jacobo's grandmother was to be believed? What if some of her ancestors had evaded the Inquisition in Mexico and infiltrated the conquistador party that later settled the northern wilderness that became New Mexico? Could they possibly have remained in the Southwest ever since, covertly maintaining their religion, avoiding pork in their burritos, substituting tortillas for matzos, co-opting Mexican serapes for Jewish prayer shawls, and somehow hiding in plain sight? Their Judaism certainly would have changed with time—mine had in less than a generation—evolving into something not immediately recognizable as such, even to those practicing it. But could it actually exist?

At first, I had a great deal of difficulty believing it could. My time on the Internet had exposed me to the world's myriad communities of supposed "Lost Jews" (the Hebrews of Cape Verde, Kaifeng, and Timbuktu), but the American *anusim* seemed altogether different. The idea of hidden Judaism in Santa Fe had the feel of a tall tale, of yetis and UFOs and Atlantis. Yet articles on the Crypto-Jews had appeared in practically every major American newspaper; in academic journals; in Jewish publications such as *Shofar*, *Hadassah*, and *The Forward*; and in a slew of books with god-awful titles like *The Marrano Legacy*, *Suddenly Jewish*, and *Sephardic Destiny: A Latino Quest*.

Surreptitious Jews in the American Southwest? A private form of Judaism practiced only in the home? A journey into adulthood that provokes an interest in an eccentric religious past? It was as if they had been designed entirely with me in mind. Here were a people who, if only in a small way, shared my story. And they were doing something about it. Some Crypto-Jews, I learned, had forsaken their Christianity, investigated the family practices and history, and rejoined the Jewish faith. A few had even immigrated to Israel. I began to wonder: If these Jews were brave enough to insist on being reclaimed, what about me? I had to meet a Crypto-Jew for myself.

Unfortunately, finding an actual living, talking, davening Crypto-Jew proved a challenge. Neither the academics who had studied them nor the authors who had attempted their history were willing to introduce me to one, usually citing concerns for their privacy. Then I caught a break. I found an email address for a man named Daniel Yocum, who in 1990 had revealed to the *New York Times* that he was a Crypto-Jew. He agreed to speak with me by phone. Yocum had been raised in Albuquerque's Atrisco Valley, an insular tract of ranch and farmland that had been absorbed by the city only in his lifetime. Raised Catholic, Yocum didn't know he was Jewish growing up, though he told me that "there were always rumors around." The men of his family, he said, used to gather each Friday night in the *morada*, the chapterhouse of a secret society of Catholic flagellants. They would cover the santos—wooden images of the saints—with gunnysacks, light candles, and conduct a modified Sabbath service, reading from a handwritten Book of Psalms. Daniel, who now lived in Colorado, told me that he had learned these practices were Judaic in nature only as an adult. As a child, he thought they were part of the Catholic rituals specific to rural New Mexico. After learning the truth, he said, he had begun to live openly as a Jew. He now attended synagogue regularly, kept kosher, read his Torah portion, and wore a yarmulke. When I asked him if he would help me contact his Crypto-Jewish relatives and friends in New Mexico, he agreed.

II.

Eternal rest in the Santa Clara *campo santo* in Albuquerque is restricted to the descendants of the families of the Atrisco Land Grant, an 82,000-square-acre expanse of mesquite-scented dust bowl, ceded in 1692 to the conquistador Don Fernando Durán y Chavez as reward for his suppression of an Indian uprising. The cemetery sits on a narrow pie wedge of desert scrubland, with perhaps 200 souls resident, in graves obscured by tangles of bunchgrass and windblown trash. A chain-link fence encircles the cemetery on three sides, along with a single cinder-block wall decorated with gangland graffiti and a crudely beautiful mural depicting the Virgin Mary with angel's wings. Behind the fence lurks a decaying subdivision, which in its advanced decrepitude seems ready to collapse onto the cemetery.

Perry Peña, Daniel Yocum's college roommate, had brought me to Santa Clara. Perry was a slightly built Hispanic man in his early forties, dressed in black slacks and a white button-down shirt. He was also wearing a Jewish religious undergarment called a *tallit katan*, with the *tzitzit*, the tassels that edge the cloth, knotted and tucked into his trousers. Perry said this was a Sephardic custom; Ashkenazim wear their tassels outside their pants.

"Let's see if I can't find a little example for you," Perry said.

We walked through the cramped rows of gravestones, past memorials that were little more than a dirt mound, a wooden cross, and a hand-painted icon depicting a New Mexican patron saint.

"Okay, here's one."

Perry pointed to a flat cement slab with a red cross painted on it. No name, no dates. A series of shallow cylinders had been drilled into the cement and filled with pebbles. I noticed that at least half of the graves in Santa Clara were similarly marked.

"Who do you think did this?" I asked.

"You mean the cross?" Perry asked, motioning to the grave.

"Yeah, I guess," I said. "But also that there's a place to put stones."

"That's just a family custom. They don't even think about it. It's just automatic. They built it in for it, as you can see."

Many people in New Mexico had no idea that such "family customs" were Judaic practices. Perry himself had never heard the term "Crypto-Jew" until he was in college. The university paper ran an article about a research project that was exploring hidden Judaism among New Mexico's original settler families. There had been rumors in Perry's family too, so he volunteered for the project and was given a list of questions. Did anyone in his family light candles on Friday night? His grandmother Elvira did. Did they attend church on Saturday instead of Sunday? His grandparents did that. Were there Jewish given names in the family? Abrana, Adonais, Ezekiel, Isaac, Eva, Eliasim, Moises. Perry's recent ancestors, many of them sheep and cattle herders, used to slit the throats of their animals, drain the blood, remove the sciatic nerve, and salt the meat. They never touched pork, rabbit, or shellfish. No one ever used the word "kosher," of course, and in fact, *la dieta*, as it is known, was never discussed directly. Perry's grandfather, for instance, explained his aversion to swine by saying that he once "saw a pig eating a snake and that after that he could no longer look at pork."

Some of the practices documented in New Mexico were either so altered or so obscure that I had no idea they were Jewish. Members of my family buried their dead within a day of passing, and we mourned for a year.

But we certainly didn't cover the mirrors in the homes of the deceased. And married couples aligning their bed on a north-south axis? That was so bizarre I had a rabbi friend of mine look it up: "Whosoever places his bed north and south will have male children, as it says: And whose belly Thou fillest with Thy treasure, who have sons in plenty. . . . His wife also will not miscarry" (Babylonian Talmud, Berakoth 5b). I knew that Orthodox Jewish women changed the bed sheets and "personal" linens on Fridays before the Sabbath. But sweeping dust into the middle of a room? Burning fingernail trimmings and hair clippings (again, to avoid miscarriages)? Religious holidays likewise were observed in transformed fashion. Was the holiday known as *Transito* really Passover, with Queen Isabella as Pharaoh, the Rio Grande as the Red Sea, and hard-baked tortillas as matzos? Were those huts built for *Jacales* really for Sukkot? *Las Fiestas de Los Reis*, when candles were lit every night for eight nights, was recognizable as Hanukkah, but the Festival of Saint Esther? Could that really be Purim?

I was reminded that when the Holy Office arrived in a new town or city during the Inquisition, it would first gather the citizenry for the reading of the Edict of Grace, a document that described, in detail, what Jewish heresy might actually look like. Those who had committed or witnessed such acts were required to confess within a short period of time, in exchange for a lighter penance (hence the "grace"). More stubborn heretics were to be "relaxed," a euphemism for being remanded to secular officials for torture or burning at the stake.

The Edict was intended to root out the covertly Jewish among the *conversos*, and, to an extent, it did. But the descriptions of Jewish practice included in the Edict also served another purpose: for those cut off from rabbinical instruction for generations, it became a rudimentary religious manual, without which many Jewish traditions, and even Crypto-Judaism itself, might have died out entirely. The same might be said for the scholarly study in which Perry had participated.

We continued wandering the cemetery, circling back through the rows of graves, and stopped at a memorial for a baby who had just died. Perry mentioned that the child was distantly related to Daniel. He dropped to his knees to retrieve a stone for the grave, his shoulders slumping almost prayerfully as he did so, and I half expected him to make the sign of the cross.

Perry then pointed to the ground, where a few Easter eggs lay hidden in the weeds, leftovers, presumably, from the previous week's holiday.

"Hunting for Easter eggs in a cemetery," Perry said with a snorting laugh. "That's a little creepy to me. I don't know what anyone else thinks."

III.

Sonya Loya couldn't meet until after her shift making cappuccinos at a café, so it was past ten in the evening when I followed her pickup along the tourist drag in Ruidoso, New Mexico, a dumpy, down-market ski town whose locals had settled on a half-baked Alpine design theme in the hopes of luring some trade away from Taos. Shuttered and dark at this hour, it resembled a remaindered set from the *Swiss Family Robinson* movie.

When we arrived at Sonya's art studio and retail store, Hosanna's Glass Works, she turned on the lights, illuminating the mid-to-pricey glass jewelry and fancy candles she sold to the tourists. She then directed me to a pair of French doors near the back of the shop, through which lay her other business, the Bat-Tzion Hebrew Learning Center.

The shelves in this little cinder-block room were filled with all manner of tchotchkes: menorahs, dreidels, mezuzot, Hanukkah gelt, shofars small and large, prayer books, language primers in Hebrew, English, and Spanish (*¡Hebrew! ¡Tan Simple!*), and general interest titles such as *Twenty-six Reasons Why Jews Don't Believe in Jesus*, which Sonya said was a best-seller.

"I'm out of *tallits*," she said. "Just sold the last one when I was in Israel."

Sonya was in her forties, with rounded features, olive skin, and black eyes that could read enthusiastic or manic depending on your feelings about her. She hosted Torah-study classes here and, simultaneously, via the Internet, on an aging computer set up on a desk behind an old couch. A whiteboard covered with Hebrew alphabet lessons stood in one corner of the room, next to a poster with instructions on "How to Wash Hands Before Eating Bread." Several Ruidosans attended the lessons, she said, linked in with students online in Texas and California. They studied the *parsha*, the weekly Torah portion, with a man named Juan Mejía, a Colombian from a prominent Catholic family in Bogotá, who as a teen had discovered a hidden Jewish background and later was ordained as a rabbi at the Jewish Theological Seminary in New York.

"You have a dog-friendly Judaica store," I said, pointing to the sacks of kibble beneath the whiteboard.

"Listen, we have Shabbat dogs here. People always say, 'Can I bring Belle? She'll be upset if I don't bring her for Shabbat.' Belle, she sees us doing the *berakhah* for the challah," Sonya said, not at all shy with the "ch" sounds, "and she goes and sits right there by the challah."

Sonya had little choice but to accept these unorthodox (for lack of a better word) Sabbath requests, given the difficulties of forming and maintaining a Jewish community in Ruidoso.

"I'm a female. I'm Hispanic. I'm an artist living in a tourist town. I close on Shabbat, the busiest time of the week." Tears came to her eyes. "It's so hard to be a Jew here. It's even harder when you grew up Catholic, because basically people treat you like you have the Black Plague." She caught herself, wiped away a tear, and smiled. "Honey, people here still believe that Jews have horns."

Her biggest problem, however, was not lapdogs or devils but Jesus. Many of the people Sonya brought to the Learning Center had left Catholicism but hadn't committed fully to Judaism. They often belonged to evangelical Christian sects that worked Jewish ritual into their worship, such as the Seventh-day Adventists, the Church of God, or the *Iglesia de*

Dios. Still others were "Messianic Jews," members of a Christian religious movement whose adherents keep the Sabbath and kashrut, celebrate the Pesach, wear yarmulkes, and support Israel but also believe that Jesus, whom they call *Yeshuah*, was the Son of God. Among those who have embraced Judaism (many haven't; they remain Catholic and view their being Jewish as a genealogical oddity), there is a genuine eagerness to learn the context of Jewish practices, but things grow complicated when Sonya explains that they will have to disavow Jesus as the Christ. "Verbalizing that you no longer believe in the Big Lie," as she put it, caused many of them to quit.

Before I left that night, Sonya told me it had become so difficult to find recruits in Ruidoso for her proposed *minyan* that she was considering moving to El Paso, where there was a more established Jewish community, or perhaps even to Israel.

"I love living here," she said. "This is where I grew up. My parents are here. My brother is here. At the same time, I wouldn't be the first one that's abandoned the familiar. Abraham left his family, too."

———

I returned to Sonya's store the next morning. I noticed that she kept the double doors to Bat-Tzion closed, not wanting to disconcert any out-of-town goyim unaware of her religious pursuits. While Sonya helped an elderly couple, I loitered at the cash register, chatting with her assistant, Carl, a former Pentecostal minister whom Sonya had helped convert to Judaism.

"I had several God encounters," Carl told me as he wrestled with a pile of credit-card receipts on the counter. "I didn't know if they were real, but who was I to argue with the word of God? I was a real Bible basher."

Unlike with Daniel and Perry, there wasn't a whisper of Judaism in Sonya's family growing up—no tall tales, no raving mad *tía* whispering deathbed secrets. She was raised Catholic and went to church every Sunday. She had a troubled youth and dropped out of high school at seventeen. She left Ruidoso the following year and fell in with an evangelical Christian man she met while hitchhiking through Arizona. They married, had a daughter, divorced. She was born again somewhere along the way, baptized in a white dress in a back-road Pentecostal church. Even then, though, she always felt "the strangest connection to Jewish people. All my friends called me the 'Jew magnet.'"

She often had "awakenings" in the middle of the night, during which a Voice came to her intoning passages from the Bible. They reminded her of dreams she had had as a child, of cobblestone streets that she said she now knew to be Israel. In 1999 she went with a friend to a "Jewish conference" in the desert outside Santa Fe. It was actually a gathering of Messianic Jews, but for Sonya it was a revelation. A Sabbath service was held during the conference, and when the Messianic rabbis—Hispanic men in yarmulkes and *tallits*—read the prayers aloud in Hebrew, a language she didn't then understand, she found she was somehow able to follow along. She devoted herself to Judaism and, after several years of study, formally converted. She was now a member of a Conservative congregation in El Paso.

Sonya joined me after the old couple left.

"Have you seen my Crypto-ware?" she asked.

We moved to a small display case filled with a selection of rings, necklaces, and earrings. Each one was made with glass that had undergone a special glazing process to lend it certain unique characteristics in different levels of light.

Sonya had come to Judaism with nothing. She wasn't unusual in this respect. As attention paid to Crypto-Judaism increased over the years, a very American thing began to happen: staking a claim to history's most persecuted religion became a mark of pop-cultural distinction. Little distance exists between some Crypto-Jews and the individuals who embrace, say, Native American poetry and dance, veganism, EST, the belief that man has never set foot on the moon, or all of these. Judaism's rituals and cultural dynamics would appear as exotic and meaningful—and therefore attractive—to the insular Catholics of the American Southwest as the swamis, yogis, and mystics who confounded so many right-thinking urban sophisticates during the sixties. Thus, in New Mexico, people "came out" as Jewish; they spoke of reclaiming their "compromised identities"; they read significance into the fact that they "looked Jewish" (translation: big noses) or had an unusual number of Jewish friends; or they saw Judaism through a convex lens of unflattering financial stereotypes, such as the one echoed in this old Crypto-Judaic saying: *Muy judíos . . . muy codo,* "Very Jewish . . . very tight."

Sonya handed me a pair of black earrings decorated with red and green colored glass bands. "Go outside and hold them to the light."

Morning still held in Ruidoso, the sun filtering through the evergreens on the mountains. I felt somewhat silly, but I knew that Sonya was watching me from the store. I raised the earrings and looked at them. At first there was nothing but the colored bands on the black, but when I pivoted the earrings directly into the sun's glow a hazy image of the Star of David emerged. I moved the earrings again and it disappeared.

I went back inside and asked Sonya to box up the earrings for me. They would look nice on my wife for Passover.

IV.

Stanley Hordes moved to Santa Fe in 1981, when he was named state historian of New Mexico. Almost immediately, he began to receive some rather curious visitors: nervous folks who would look both ways before entering his office and then whisper, "My *abuelita* doesn't eat pork"; "She hides in the basement on Friday night and lights candles"; "She sweeps dirt into the center of the room"; "My grandfather let the blood run from the sheep onto the ground"; "Before my *tía* died, she swore I was a Jew."

Hordes at first dismissed these visitors as cranks. "It's not unusual for Catholic women to be lighting candles," he told me when we spoke in a hotel lobby in downtown Albuquerque. "People eat things and don't eat things. Why should I care?"

Still, Hordes had written a dissertation on the topic of Crypto-Judaism in New Spain, and his research on Mexico's Crypto-Jews had indeed unearthed a community of *conversos* that included bakers, tailors, barbers, silversmiths, merchants, miners, doctors, military officers, accountants, a municipal mayor, and even one man who sang in the choir at the Cathedral of Querétaro. One of Cortés's conquistadors turned out to be a Crypto-Jew (Jewish conquistadors!) and was burned at the stake in Mexico City in 1528. Most Crypto-Jews, however, lived relatively safely in New Spain until 1571, when the Holy Office was formally established in the colony, after which periodic campaigns against suspected *judai-*

zantes took place over the next hundred years. It was these persecutions that served as the basis of Hordes's research; the Inquisition kept excellent records of its interrogations, trials, and autos-da-fé. For example, Hordes learned that 80 percent of the men accused as Crypto-Jews had in fact been circumcised, a figure, one Inquisition record noted, that did not count the 11 percent whose penises bore "a mark of undetermined origin, raising the suspicion . . . that some Jewish ritual had resulted in such scarring."

Yet none of Hordes's earlier work helped account for the wayward Jews who now came slinking into his office. He developed a new theory for that. In 1598, as conditions for the Crypto-Jews were deteriorating in New Spain, a settler party of 460 men, women, and children headed north into the frontier wilderness, traversing the barren stretch of desert known as the *jornada del muerto* ("journey of the dead man") into Pueblo Indian territory. At the confluence of the Rio Grande and Rio Chama, they founded a town, San Gabriel del Yunque, which became the first permanent European settlement in what is today known as New Mexico. Hordes could never confirm how many *conversos* there were among the settlers, but he did know that within a couple of generations the Inquisition, now in New Mexico, began prosecuting their descendants for Judaizing.

"The testimony from these trials," Hordes told me, "indicates pretty clearly that not only was Crypto-Judaism being practiced but it was being practiced and nobody cared. Witness after witness after witness comes forward and says, 'Well, yeah, we knew Francisco Gomez was a Jew. We knew that he lived and died as a Jew. We knew that his sons were circumcised. So what?'"

Hordes spent the next twenty-five years playing what he called "the down and dirty game of who begat." He interviewed anyone in New Mexico (including both Perry Peña and Daniel Yocum) who evinced vestiges of Jewish practices, and compared their surnames with the Catholic birth, baptismal, marriage, death, and burial records archived in the state. He cross-checked these records against Inquisition trial and confession documents from Mexico, Spain, and Portugal. And he found links—clear, verifiable, genealogical links—between these modern-day candle-lighters and pork-abstainers and the ancient deceased.

No theory is unassailable, of course. Hordes's research strongly indicated that there were descendants of Jews among New Mexico's founders. No one knows if they were aware of that fact, or if, as Hordes believes, they were practicing Judaism in secret. The trials *suggest* a Jewish presence—but they could easily have been show trials, and the allegations of Judaizing a way for the colonizers to use the Inquisition to settle scores with their enemies.

A researcher from Case Western University named Judith Neulander put forward a forceful counterargument to Hordes's theory. In 1996 Neulander published an article in the journal *Jewish Folklore and Ethnology Review*, entitled "The New Mexican Crypto-Jewish Canon: Choosing to be 'Chosen' in Millennial Tradition." If that wasn't a clear enough indication of where she stood on things, Neulander clarified matters: "The Hebraized New Mexican folkways currently mistaken for crypto-Jewish survivals turn out to be non-medieval, non-cryptic, and non-Jewish," she wrote, subjecting the Crypto-Jews to the indignity of the lowercase. Their claims were "demonstrably unfounded" and "dramatically logic-defying," and their academic proponents (Hordes chief among them) were "pseudo-ethnographers" and "fake-lorists," who had conjured up a "vortex of an imagined cultural canon," with techniques "absent from the practice of ethnographic research, but common to rumor, to legend, and to reconstructions of ethnic past."

Neulander regarded the prevailing scholarship on the Crypto-Jews as a reenactment of the racist, hegemonic literary form known as the "Traveler's Tale." According to the conventions of this genre, the European gentleman explorer discovers a heretofore unknown "race" of "cannibals and wild men" that exists only "in the far flung territories of Euro-Imperial imagination" and those "metropolitan literate communities" hungry for "popular exotica."

Neulander dismissed the evidence Perry Peña found so persuasive. The six-sided stars found in New Mexican cemeteries and churches were a "cross-cultural commonplace," only recently of importance to Jews. They could also be found in the ancient artwork of New Mexico's Pueblo Indians. The ritual slaughter of animals was neither "practiced nor valued" by the medieval *anusim* as a means to demonstrate or maintain their Judaism. By the 1500s, her research showed, the Crypto-Jews had not only ceased to follow the kashrut, but had actually forgotten its existence. The slaughtering of animals in New Mexico did, she conceded, require one to slit the animal's throat and drain its blood, but the New Mexicans did not discard the blood; they collected it, to make regional delicacies such as *guajada* and *morcilla* (blood pudding and blood sausage). Menorahs, which had been recovered in New Mexican homes, were dismissed as a "recognized 'Vessel of the [Christian] Church'"; the mezuzot and dreidels unearthed by researchers dated only to the 1840s, when German Ashkenazim migrated to the state. Names like Moises and Eliasim were an example of "onomastic misappropriation." They only *sounded* Jewish.

Who, then, did Neulander believe the Crypto-Jews were? The remnants of "deeply Hebraized" and "Sabbath-worshipping" Protestant sects that had proselytized in New Mexico in the early 1900s. These groups, which included the Seventh-day Adventists, the Assembly of God, and the *Iglesias de Dios*, used Jewish ritual in their worship, and in fact considered themselves as a point of doctrine to be the "true Jews." As this movement withered in New Mexico, discrimination by the Catholic majority drove them underground, where their practices were privately maintained. With the passage of time, some forgot their origins. Neulander's theory was that New Mexico was home not to Crypto-Jews at all but to *Crypto-Protestants.*

She further contended that the Crypto-Judaic claims were animated by racism, not by religion. In New Mexico, a mestizo or Native American genealogy historically conveyed an inferior social status. A Jewish past, therefore, didn't just make you Jewish—it made you *white.* "The premise for racial identity-switching," Neulander wrote, "is based on the popular notion . . . [that] to claim crypto-Jewish descent in the Southwest, is to claim a less broken line of supposedly white and European 'blood purity' than is generally found in the mixed racial mainstream." New Mexican Crypto-Judaism was not a historical misunderstanding or an anthropological mistake, but "a fairly straight-forward attempt to beat the prejudicial Anglo hegemony by joining it."

I could never bring myself to take Neulander seriously, for a variety of reasons. First, the notion that the New Mexicans had "forgotten" a religious past fewer than one hundred years old struck me as unlikely at best. I had less trouble believing in a history lost over centuries than a handful of generations. The racial argument, which appealed to my liberal instincts (not to mention my weakness for political correctness), changed nothing: The Crypto-Jews could be Crypto-Jews *and* racists. Finally, though, I will admit that I dismissed Neulander because I needed the Crypto-Jews to be real. Understanding them was an important first step in understanding myself.

So it was with intense curiosity that I asked Hordes what it felt like when he first began to believe that these people really were the historical Crypto-Jews. "It was like a lightbulb went on," he said. "I asked myself, 'Could these possibly be the same people? Could there really have been a survival?'"

I was beginning to understand that for him, and more important, for me, these weren't questions at all. They were an affirmation.

V.

At the junction of two dead rivers on the parched mesa outside Los Lunas, New Mexico, a string of foothills covered in desert shrubbery stretches to the horizon. The arroyos where the rivers once flowed run some thirty feet deep, a gash in the lunar landscape of red dirt and volcanic boulders. This stretch of territory, known as *Cerro de Los Escondidos*—Hill of the Hidden Ones—was part of a 1761 land grant awarded to a Spanish settler party that wanted to homestead in the area. It is unclear whether the settlers ever made it here. By the 1800s no trace of them remained. The land then passed into the hands of a family of prosperous Jewish merchants originally from Germany who eventually ceded it to the state of New Mexico.

I had come here with a Catholic priest from Albuquerque named William Sanchez. He was a large man in his mid-fifties, dressed this morning in new-looking hiking boots, a safari shirt, cargo pants, and mirrored sunglasses. A few of Father Sanchez's friends, cheerful older folks done up in varying shades of golf and western clothing, had come along, too. Father Sanchez guided us down a wide, planed dirt track away from the highway until we reached an oak cattle fence bleached gray by the sun and held fast with barbed wire. Beyond it a winding footpath led into the hills. We began to climb, shuffling upward in a slow and careful single file.

As we walked, Vicky, one of Sanchez's friends, plucked a green weed from between some rocks. She mentioned that her mother used to season her eggs with this weed. It tasted like parsley.

"We used to pick up all kinds of weeds as kids," she said.

"As long as you never smoked it," joked her husband, Carlos.

"Oh, we sure did," said Gil, another member of the group, who had told me earlier that day he was a distant relative of an Apache war chief.

After a short while, the footpath plunged into a narrow ravine shaded by sun-blackened boulders. About five yards ahead, a small rectangular stone blocked the way. This stone was the reason we had come here.

Known variously as "Covenant Rock," "the Mystery Stone," or the "Los Lunas Decalogue," the rock was a hundred-ton slab of basalt inscribed with nine lines of text. Theories about the writing's origins abound: It is a poem composed by the ancient Greek sailor Zakyneros; a treasure map of the Acoma Indians; the Ten Commandments, written either by "Hebraic mound builders" originally from Ohio or by ancient Samaritan seafarers who ran aground off the coast of Texas or by Phoenician sailors out of Tarshish; or, as theorized in a 1973 article in *Desert* magazine, the work of an extraterrestrial "intelligence" that had devised a "coded message" whose meaning "we are . . . not yet ready to receive."

Father Sanchez was a proponent of the Phoenician-sailor theory, because the presence of far-ranging biblical-era ocean voyagers squared well with his understanding of his own family history. A devoted amateur genealogist, Sanchez believed that he had successfully traced his ancestry back to before his family's migration from New Spain to New Mexico in 1598; to before they departed Spain in 1492; to earlier even than their flight, in 587 B.C.E., from Jerusalem to southern Spain, following Nebuchadnezzar's sack of the First Temple; all the way to the Negev, where his earliest descendants were *Kohanim*—Israelite high priests of an order founded by Aaron, brother of Moses. That is, Father Sanchez, a Catholic priest, believed he was a Jew.

Genealogy is a slender thread on which to hang one's identity, religious or otherwise. A Jew in the family 400 years ago doesn't really make you Jewish. But Father Sanchez had had his DNA tested for the presence of a Y-chromosome marker called the Cohen Modal Haplotype, which research has shown to be carried by historical descendants of the Israelite priesthood. The test results confirmed that he was, genetically at least, *Kohanim*. Sanchez subsequently encouraged other Crypto-Jews to be tested. Of the 185 people he convinced to submit samples, 100 showed genetic evidence of Sephardic descent, though, to be fair, a peer-reviewed 2006 study in the *Annals of Human Biology* disputed those results. Among the five people Sanchez brought with us that day, everyone but Gil had been tested. Vicky and Carlos were the only ones whose results came back positive for Jewishness.

We sat on the boulders surrounding the Rock, pulled out our water bottles, and mopped our brows. Carlos had brought a harmonica with him, and he played a mournful hymn. The Rock was about five feet square, and was engraved with what I can only describe as a series of exceedingly fake-looking petroglyphs. The earliest confirmed reports of the Rock date to 1933, which meant the markings were no less than seventy-five years old. I had trouble believing they had been there longer than a week.

"Notice the tree," Father Sanchez said, pointing at a withered acacia growing from under the stone. "The Ark of the Covenant was made from this."

The morning was gone by now, and the Rock was engulfed in shadow. It was time to return to Los Lunas for lunch. Father Sanchez led us in a prayer before we left.

"Pray, Father, that you give our ancestors peace," he said. "Bring healing to them and bring healing to our world." He ended with the *Shema*, the Jewish daily prayer: *Shema yisrael adonai eloheinu adonai echad.* Hear, O Israel: the Lord, our God, the Lord is one. Amen.

We made for the cars.

VI.

But is it good for the Jews? I actually asked myself this question, sitting on a bench in the contemplation garden at Congregation B'nai Zion in El Paso. The garden adjoined the modernist pillbox of the temple and was designed to evoke the state of Israel in miniature, complete with a desert oasis filled with blooming flowers and shade trees, a version of the Wailing Wall, and a shallow pool representing the Dead Sea. Eventually I went inside, where I was greeted by B'nai Zion's shepherd, Rabbi Stephen Leon.

"This is a beautiful building," I said as I accepted a seat in Rabbi Leon's spacious, rabbinical-text-cluttered office.

"Yes it is. It really is," Leon replied.

The building was in fact hideous, but after so much time spent unpacking the riddles of the maybe-Jews and the hidden-Jews and the Jews-by-genealogy-or-genetics-or-less, B'nai Zion's high-Scarsdale kitsch was soothing to me in a way I didn't quite understand. And it wasn't just the building—it was the rebbe. Religious authority figures were not held in particular esteem in my family, yet here I was hoping, even expecting, a rabbi to help me understand how I should think and feel about the Crypto-Jews.

Rabbi Leon was a stoutly built man with a stern, self-important mien. He managed to appear dignified despite his blue-and-red New York Giants yarmulke. He had moved to El Paso from New Jersey in

1986, and, much like Stan Hordes, almost immediately began receiving visits from people who wanted to speak to the "Rabbino." A Presbyterian minister came to him in tears because she had learned of her family's Jewish roots and was devastated with guilt because, as a proselytizing clergyperson, she felt that she had betrayed her Hebraic ancestors. She wanted Leon's permission to come to the temple on Yom Kippur to atone for her sin. At home, the cable man noticed Leon's SHALOM, Y'ALL poster and unbuttoned his shirt to reveal a Star of David necklace. These and many other encounters had transformed Rabbi Leon. Providing spiritual shelter to lost Jews became his great passion. He had converted some 200 Crypto-Jews to full Judaism, and he hoped to do more.

"You don't do Returns?" I asked.

"Personally, I view them as returning," Rabbi Leon replied. "But I use the conversion so there won't be a question if they want to make aliyah."

"Aliyah" is the Hebrew term for the Ingathering of the Exiles, the basis of the fundamental right of all Jews to return from the global Diaspora and become Israeli citizens. Israel currently does not recognize the historical claims of American Crypto-Jews, a point of more than just academic interest to Leon.

"I read somewhere that had there not been a Holocaust there would be forty million Jews in the world," he said. "Now we have less than fourteen million. When I got involved with the *anusim*, I said, 'Wait a minute, what if there was never an Inquisition?' What would have happened?"

Rabbi Leon told me he'd read that between 200,000 and 800,000 Jews were exterminated, forced to convert, or expelled from Spain by King Ferdinand and Queen Isabella in 1492.

"Eight hundred thousand seems like an awfully big number," I said.

"It is. It's probably closer to 200,000, but it could be as many as 400,000. Regardless, that was 500 years ago. That wasn't sixty years ago. Those people had a lot of children. Those people were passionate about their religion. What would have happened? Where did they go? In the United States, I know they came here."

He estimated that 10 to 15 percent of the Hispanic community in El Paso-Juarez—about 275,000 people—had Jewish roots and didn't know it.

"Which is okay," he quickly added. "I'm not out to convert the world."

Leon told me about the "*Anusim* Return Center" he planned to found in El Paso. It would serve as a public institution where the Crypto-Jews could learn the history and conventions of the religion (there would be an Inquisition museum akin to those dedicated to the Holocaust), and ready themselves for the ultimate goal—aliyah. Sonya Loya and Juan Mejía, the Crypto-Jewish rabbi in New York, were working with Leon on the project, and he said both planned to move to El Paso to help run it. Funding was still an issue, but not an overly pressing one. ("We have an ear at Soros," he told me.)

"It appears that the fastest growing religion in the world is Islam," Leon said. "We know of the problems going on in the Middle East as a result of that. Imagine if the tiny state of Israel all of a sudden had an influx, a return of the *anusim*." He leaned across his desk toward me.

"All of these Arab nations that are 'afraid' of this tiny state—I don't think you would have war, but it would be a totally different situation. Intermarriage would decline. Assimilation would decline. These people have a passion for the religion. I think it would change the world."

Sonya had told me about the Return Center, but only that it would be a place for the Crypto-Jews to come and find acceptance in the greater Jewish-American community. As far as aliyah was concerned—and Sonya had mentioned it—I understood it to be a symbolic notion, like the toast my family would make each year over the Manischewitz at Passover. *Next year in Jerusalem*—we'd say it all right, but no one was booking tickets for the settlements. Leon had something more definite in mind: the conversion of the Crypto-Jews into a sort of anti-Muslim neutron bomb.

VII.

Thankfully, there may be an alternate future for America's Crypto-Jews, one that remains within this country's geographic and psychological borders, which I suppose is why I found myself standing in front of Joe Morse's double-wide in Meadow Lake, New Mexico.

Joe was waiting for me in his weed-bedraggled front yard. He was in his mid-fifties, a short bowling ball of a man, dressed much like Perry Peña, in black pants, white shirt, and clip-on braces, except he wore his *tzitzit* outside the pants. He pumped my hand in greeting and then checked the sun's progress. Dusk was approaching.

"Come on in," he said. "We still have time to talk before the Shabbat."

Joe's trailer was a study in brown: brown carpet, brown linoleum kitchen floor, brown wall paneling, a tattered brown couch. The earth tones were interrupted by a large blue painting of a waterfall, as well as a Jewish calendar from French's Mortuary and a portrait of Joe—chubby, blank-faced, age thirteen—painted for his bar mitzvah.

We took a seat in the living room. Joe's wife, Gloria, as porcelain-doll tiny as Joe, puttered about in the kitchen preparing the potted chicken for dinner. Trefina, Joe's youngest, sat at the dinner table, quietly reading a Hebrew prayer book.

"Tell me, Ted," Joe said once we had settled in. "What do you know about the Jews?"

Joe grew up in a Boston suburb, the son of a Jewish meat cutter in the

Old Haymarket Square. In his twenties he left the secular Judaism of his family and commenced a process of religious searching that lasted several decades and included stints in such Christian evangelical sects as the Assembly of God, the Seventh-day Adventists, the Calvary Chapel, and the Free Methodists. Despite not one but two born-again experiences, Joe still felt spiritually incomplete, and in the late 1980s he decided to return to Judaism. "With one difference," he said. "The difference is that now I have a Messiah."

Joe joined a Messianic Jewish congregation in Albuquerque that met on Saturdays in a Baptist church. It was there that he first began to meet Crypto-Jews. Perry Peña, at the time also a member of the congregation, became a good friend. (Joe would later bar mitzvah Perry at Covenant Rock.) Perry inspired Joe to research his own family history, where he discovered, in the midst of a Jewish past, a *lost* Jewish past. "I am not Ashkenazi," Joe said. "You are. I'm Hispanic and didn't know it."

His family, which had emigrated to the United States from Ukraine, had, he said, been expelled from Barcelona centuries prior. Joe took this to mean that he was also a Crypto-Jew. "We went from Morais in Spain to Moraz in Ukraine to Morse in the United States. We always tried to fit in."

Both Joe and Perry felt that the Ashkenazi Messianics in their congregation discriminated against the Crypto-Jews. As Joe put it, "They didn't give them an opportunity to really come into their fullness." In 2001, Joe and Perry struck out on their own, founding a Messianic congregation that would minister to Crypto-Jews. They named it *Kahilah Ba'Midbar*, the Congregation of the Wilderness, because at first when they didn't have a place to meet for prayer, they would gather in local parks or by the banks of the Rio Grande.

"I felt like these were a people who needed to explode. We needed to go out, search them out, to bring the Lost House of Israel back. Not fellowshipping in foolishness but through righteousness!" Joe said, his voice rising with sermonic passion. "I fell in love with these people, started hanging out with them. We were kind of a little clique. It felt like an us-against-the-world kinda thing."

Eventually, though, Joe and Perry broke with each other, in part because of Perry's decision to live as a Jew rather than as a Messianic. Joe, however, insisted that he bore Perry no ill will.

"Perry's searching. I'm not searching anymore. I've got what I need. I've got a relationship with the Messiah." Joe patted his royal-blue yarmulke, which was embroidered with the words *yeshua ha'mashiach,* Jesus the Messiah—a phrase one doesn't often encounter in Hebrew.

"The fact is, we have a very Jewish Messiah," he told me. "We don't have the *goyishekopf* Messiah that the Christians are presented. Most of the things taught in the Church are wrong and a lie. First of all, Jesus isn't his name. Think about the term *Jesus.* It's Greek. No one would have used that word for him. Think about him being called home for supper." Joe slipped into a mocking falsetto. "*Jesus, come home for supper.* That never happened. It was *Yeshuah.*"

Joe was vague about how many Crypto-Jews remained in his congregation. But he promised to introduce me to them the following day, at a Saturday service in the home of one of the congregation members. The trailer had grown dark as we talked. The Sabbath had begun. To my surprise, Joe stood up and flipped on the lights. He smiled at me.

"Don't panic," he said. "The lightbulbs are kosher."

———

The next morning, Joe and I drove to Belen, New Mexico, for the service. (Gloria and Trefina came in another car.) As we sped down a narrow country road, Joe pointed to a dusty hill at the top of which I could just barely make out three white crosses. This was Tomé Hill, Joe said. Every

Easter, local Christians make a pilgrimage to the summit to pray to a painted Jesus; some of the more devoted simulate the Crucifixion by tying themselves to one of the crosses.

"Repentance is so easy now," Joe said. "It was a real bloody business out there in the Tabernacle in the Wilderness. They were out there for two years trying to learn to do it right, construct it, build it, and then consecrate it. They were sprinkling blood, draining blood. They were killing animals. It was a factory. I don't know if I could have dealt with that."

We reached the town house where the service was being held. Before I could get out of the car, Joe put his hand on my wrist.

"You're in such trouble," he said.

"You mean today?" I asked, wondering if the congregants might think my book would be hostile to Messianics.

"No, I mean in life," Joe replied. "You're going to go back home, and all of a sudden you'll find yourself thinking about Messiah, and how maybe there's something to it." He paused. "You know what my goal with you is, Ted?"

"What's that?"

"Your soul."

An elderly retiree named Matt owned the town house. He was a hulking, stooped old fellow with military tattoos on his forearms and a yarmulke on his head. He showed me around while Joe readied the living room for the service. Matt had decorated his home with a western flair of near-Lynchian oddness. The paintings on the walls depicted a cowboy feeding his horse an apple at sunset; mustangs drinking from a creek; plus a few glamour portraits of horses Matt had once owned. He still kept two saddles and tack on the floor in his bedroom.

Matt told me he had come to Messianic Judaism late in life, when a friend helped him look into his genealogy and told him he might be Sephardic on his father's side. He enjoyed being a Jew, he said ("I wear my

kipa 24/7"), but as far as a Crypto-Jewish past in New Mexico was concerned, he didn't have one.

"I'm from New Orleans," he said.

Gloria and Trefina arrived shortly thereafter, accompanied by a purple-
haired septuagenarian widow named Wanda. Joe deposited her in a chair
in the living room, where she idly thumbed through a Messianic prayer
book, squinting at the words and humming quietly to herself. Three others joined us. Elaine was a heavily made-up Anglo woman in her forties
who greeted Joe with a complaint about a son who was giving her problems. Joe clucked sympathetically. Also joining us were "Sam," a beefy,
sunburned man who didn't want me to use his real name, and his tow-
headed teenage daughter. They were from Iowa.

The service was conducted at a table in the living room. Joe sat in the
center, his shoulders draped with a *tallit*. He opened with a blessing in
Hebrew, followed by a lively song whose only lyrics were "Shabbat shalom. Shabbat shalom. Shabbat shalom." We punctuated each "Shabbat
shalom" by clapping our hands twice in quick succession.

Joe then recited several passages from the Bible, led us through some
more Hebrew prayers and songs, and expounded at length on Scripture.

"The Christians very often regard what they see here as null and void.
However, to this day the Law of God stands," Joe remarked during an
explication of Leviticus. "We are not saved by the laws pertaining to God,
but they are a manual for us to live by. So despite the fact that we are not
saved by them, we still keep them, including the laws of Kashrut."

Joe motioned to Gloria. She rummaged around in her purse and produced a recipe for salt-crusted shrimp that she had clipped from the back
of a box of Morton's kosher salt. She passed it around and everyone
laughed and tut-tutted.

"I wonder if anyone raised Cain over that," Elaine said.

"They can't," Matt replied as he inspected the recipe. "Because it says
here, 'Good for gourmet cooking.'"

As the joking continued, my mind drifted away to the other Crypto-Jews I had met, particularly Sonya. She kept kosher, was a Conservative Jew, and spoke Hebrew. She could immigrate to Israel, vote Likud, and found the country's last legitimately socialist kibbutz, and it would never be enough. She would never be sufficiently Jewish to eat shrimp. I'm not a historian, an anthropologist, a rabbi, or a referee. For me, a Crypto-Jew who acted as a Jew, lived as a Jew, and wanted to be a Jew, was Jewish. By doing so they had moved beyond the dictates of historical truth or untruth; I watched them go with satisfaction.

The folks listening to Joe hold forth that day were a different matter: not one of them, you see, was a Crypto-Jew. When I first realized this I was annoyed that Joe had wasted my time, but then it struck me that the connection I had felt to the Crypto-Jews—that needful hope in their existence—was shared very strongly by those gathered here. I couldn't condemn them. They were explorers of the same historical—but by this point thoroughly American—deception that had drawn me to the Southwest.

Unfortunately, I knew that I could no longer continue to reside in the historical deception. This was far from a Neulander-style rejection of the claims of the American Crypto-Jews. But their truths—whatever they were or weren't—couldn't be mine. I would need a more tangible and specific definition of the factors that qualified me as a Jew.

When the service ended I told Joe that I was skipping the barbecue lunch. He walked me to my car, threw an arm over my shoulder, and wished me well. He prayed for me and told me that he hoped God would "plague" me until I accepted the Messiah. As I was about to drive away, Matt rushed outside and waved for me to wait. I rolled down my window to see what he wanted. He had a gift, he said, a box of matzos, which he handed me with some ceremony.

"For the road," he said.

Part III

THE ILLUMINATI

I know you've had nose jobs and it was painful. I know your mother makes you feel guilty. I know you've brushed shoulders with Woody Allen and realized he "was just a guy." I know you've stopped fasting and felt liberated. I know you had a botched circumcision and use comedy as a therapeutic outlet. I know you discovered you were Jewish at the Berlin Holocaust museum via a relic; a name in a book; an old photograph; a letter. I know you are a former self-hating Jew who discovered pride in your religion on a mistaken layover in Israel when you finally realized you felt "home." I know you're from a small town in Texas where you were in the only Jewish family and it was hard. I know you eat bacon strips and Hellman's when no one's looking. I know you had a boob reduction; a foreskin implant; your hair chemically straightened to hide your heebishness and then you felt shame and became religious. I know you wrote a book; a play; a short film; an essay; a novella on your mother's painful conversion. I know and I don't fucking care.

—Erin Hershberg, editor, *Heeb*

I.

Union Square Park in Manhattan was the scene of a nighttime festival. Mobs of bicycle and skater punks had crowded into the park's main plaza, pulling tricks on the short steps leading to the street. Chess hustlers had set up their boards on card tables next to the subway entrance, ready for all comers: speed chess, take your time, try your luck. Artists hawked their paintings, posters, and novelty carvings at a row of tables adjacent to the chessmen. Beside them, a cluster of vendors sold T-shirts for classic rock bands; another offered nutcrackers and lighters that doubled as sex toys; a separate group of tables was dedicated to political engagements, encumbrances, and causes. Two men bedecked in flowing Middle Eastern robes and spiked armbands—Bedouin tribesman meets Megadeth—loudly delivered a speech on the Lost Tribes of Israel. A full brass band worked through a peppy jazz set, hitting perhaps half the notes, competing with several guitar heroes and a harmonica novice. A troupe of break-dancing tumblers busked a crowd for applause and donations. Young couples huddled on the lawn and benches, ignoring the drug dealers and homeless.

I was in fact here for a festival, but not the one provided by this effusion of local color. Sukkot, the Jewish "Festival of Booths," was nigh, and Union Square was set to host the winners of Sukkah City, an architectural design contest organized by a Jewish nonprofit called Reboot. Entrants to the contest had been assigned a single, ambitious task: to redesign the religious structure particular to Sukkot, the huts or booths that symbolize the shelters the biblical Israelites lived in during the forty years they spent wandering the Negev.

For seven days during Sukkot, observant Jews pray, eat their meals, and sometimes sleep, in these huts. Sukkah construction is a complex business, requiring substantial biblical and rabbinical guidance. Because of this, many Jews who keep the holiday purchase their sukkahs prefabricated, these days often from online firms like Sukkah Outlet or the Sukkah Center. A rudimentary specimen made with thin steel poles and plastic sheeting runs about $350, and can be collapsed easily and stored for the following year. A thorough exploration of the Talmudic design codes governing the sukkah would require a degree from the Jewish Theological Seminary, but here are a few of the main points, courtesy of the information provided by Reboot to the contestants:

- The sukkah must have walls that remain unshaken by a standard continuous wind.
- The sukkah must have a roof made of *schach*: the leaves and/or branches of a tree.
- The sukkah must enclose a minimum area equal to 7 × 7 square handbreadths.
- The sukkah must have three walls, but the third doesn't need to be complete.

Twelve of the design teams that had submitted to Sukkah City had been invited by Reboot to erect their creations in the park. A ceremony was scheduled for the following day, with Mayor Michael Bloomberg, among other city luminaries, expected to attend. Reboot was also going to publish a coffee-table book, *Sukkah City: Radically Temporary Architecture for the Next Three Thousand Years*. Directly following the holiday, the sukkahs would be auctioned off by Housing Works, a nonprofit that supports the homeless and people living with HIV/AIDS.

I had come to Union Square to learn more about Reboot, which had been described to me variously as an insider's club for "Jewish hipsters"; "an attempt to make Judaism cool"; "snobby"; "elitist"; and this one, from a prominent Jewish nonprofit director, that really caught my attention— "the Jewish Illuminati." Reboot's mission statement describes itself as an "innovation network" designed for young Jews to "question, explore, and re-examine Jewish identity, community, and meaning on their own terms."

Reboot was cofounded in 2003 by Rachel Levin from the Righteous Persons Foundation, Steven Spielberg's Jewish-focused nonprofit, and Roger Bennett, a senior vice president of the Andrea and Charles Bronfman Philanthropies. It produces and supports a range of Jewish programming, but it is perhaps best known for its "Reboot Summit." Held annually in Park City, Utah—when the Sundance people aren't around— the summit is like a Clinton Renaissance Weekend for the Jewishly inclined. "An eclectic and creative mix of people from the literature, entertainment, media, technology, politics, social action and academic realms," each vetted by previous summit attendees, spend a weekend among their coreligionists, swapping Jewish ideas, ironic, earnest, oblique, and otherwise. There are no stated goals for the sessions, no incoming agenda, and no outgoing report. Reboot hopes only that after the summit the participants return home and choose to publish a Jewish magazine, shoot a Jewish movie, write a Jewish book—something or anything with any level of Jewish content—sometimes with funding from Reboot, often without.

Reboot is a Jewish delivery system, one aimed at influential, connected, young people who have left the synagogues and are not likely to return, but who still want to engage with Jewish identity in ways that they are free to define. I can imagine why people might find this notion discomforting, but it spoke to me. The traditional locales of Judaism—in fact, the traditional locales of any religion—strike me as unappealing, and frankly, a synagogue seems no more likely to be the home of my Jewish self than a madrassa. What I mean is this: If I am a Jew, I am most likely a Reboot kind of Jew.

I had contacted Roger Bennett—the Jewish Illuminati aren't as difficult to reach as one might imagine—and asked if I could attend the summit and write about it. He told me that I was welcome to come to Park City, provided I could find a Rebooter to vouch for my bona fides, but the summit itself was strictly off the record. If I was still interested in writing about Reboot, he suggested I come to Sukkah City.

When I found Roger in the park that night he was having at it with two nicely appointed smartphones, adroitly tapping one-handed messages on each. He was in his early forties, with thinning light brown hair, tired eyes, a crooked mouth, and a way of holding himself—half stoop, half sprinter's crouch—that suggested both middle-aged aches and pains and Type-A tirelessness. He was dressed in a flannel shirt and blue jeans, puffy down vest, Docksider shoes, and a Kangol cap.

"Wicked, Ted. Glad you made it," he said, once the messaging had subsided enough for him to notice me. "Magic. Absolutely magic!" Grandson of a Liverpudlian kosher butcher, Roger, when calm, had the tamped-down British accent of someone who has made a close study of American conversational patterns and rejected everything but the ironic bits. When he punctuated things he liked, he radiated an Austin Powers–like exuberance.

The sukkahs had been stored in a warehouse in Brooklyn and then loaded earlier in the evening, partially built, onto trucks for transfer into Manhattan and assembly in the park. The first one had already arrived, and a team of deeply nervous-looking architects and assistants, armed with screwdrivers, hammers, and laser levels, were swarming over its component parts, connecting joints and ratcheting down anything that moved. We stopped to watch the activity.

All of the sukkahs in the contest had silly art world names. This one was "it will bend but . . ." a cute bit of lowercase gallery labeling that seemed prescient under the circumstances. Designed by the architecture firm THEVERYMANY™, "it will bend" was billed as "an experiment within a certain form of fragility/unstability"—and indeed it was. Fashioned from sheets of walnut veneer screwed together with blue and black metal rivets, the sukkah was equal parts shelter tree, flailing octopus, and Danish Modern bookshelf. It was also threatening to collapse under its own weight.

"Not promising," I said to Roger.

"Not too," he replied.

A slight young man in his late twenties, whom I thought I recognized, joined us. He had curly hair, dark eyes, and was dressed in jeans, a well-ironed oxford shirt, and professorially hip black-rimmed glasses. Roger introduced me to Joshua Foer, his partner on Sukkah City.

Joshua is a reporter and writer whose book on memorization, *Moonwalking with Einstein*, was published some months after Sukkah City, to wide acclaim. At the time we were introduced, however, he was better known as the youngest of the Foer brothers: Franklin, the eldest, is the former editor of the *New Republic* and the author of *How Soccer Explains the World*; and Jonathan Safran is a novelist and essayist (*Everything Is Illuminated*, *Eating Animals*), who in 2010 was named to the *New Yorker's* list of the twenty best American writers under forty. Most likely I recognized Joshua from book-jacket photos of his brothers. It also occurred to me that if Joshua and his family aren't Jewish Illuminati, then there are no Jewish Illuminati.

Joshua later told me that the event was inspired by a recent move to New Haven, Connecticut, with his wife; for the first time in his life as an adult, he had an apartment with a deck. The Foers are a relatively observant family, and most years they put up a prefab sukkah in the backyard. Now, with the extra room, Joshua decided to try his hand at building his own hut. As he set himself to the task he grew fascinated by the religious dictates overseeing the construction, especially the interplay between rabbinical philosophy and architectural design.

"Here were these rabbis," he told me, "sitting around two thousand years ago, asking questions like, 'What is a wall? What makes a ceiling achieve the effect of ceiling-ness?' These are questions about the metaphysics of architecture. And they were being asked from this totally bizarre perspective. I thought there was actually incredible room within these constraints to do something beautiful and amazing and different and interesting. I thought to myself: What if we got the best architects in the world to try to take on the sukkah?"

He brought his idea to Roger, who happened to be friends with one of his brothers ("Kinda everyone knows Roger"). Roger turned Joshua's offhand biblical brainstorm into $160,000 in funding from Reboot and other private Jewish family foundations, 624 entries from architects and designers in 43 countries, and partnerships with the American Institute of Architects, *Dwell* and *Architect* magazines, and the New York City Department of Parks & Recreation.

I tried not to feel inferior. My little ideas rarely prove so grand.

———

By 11 P.M., several more trucks bearing sukkahs had arrived, along with the heavy equipment needed to off-load and set them in place: two pallet movers, a flatbed truck, a small forklift, and a panoply of ropes, pulleys, grapples, and large hand tools. Electrical cords snaked around the plaza, powering a bank of work lights. The equipment transformed the atmosphere in the park from festival to construction site.

The one police officer I had seen meandering about the park earlier in the evening had disappeared, but the union laborers minding the heavy gear did a good job of keeping any undesirables behind a line of yellow security tape. The barrier attracted a gaggle of rubberneckers who passed the time haranguing the teams of self-important architecture geeks puttering about with their huts.

I tagged along with Roger and Joshua as they made the rounds. "Bio Puff," courtesy of a Brooklyn firm named Bittertang, resembled in its state of half-completion a giant deflated air mattress, staked down with bamboo staves and topped with eucalyptus leaves and Spanish moss.

Reboot had enlisted rabbis to help draw up the contest guidelines and to ensure that each entry was kosher. I was curious if it had been difficult to find religious clergy with an interest in high-concept architectural design. Both Roger and Joshua assured me it hadn't.

"I met this rabbi in New Haven," Joshua explained. "He said to me, 'What is a Jew? Someone who becomes an architect once a year.'"

Roger wandered off, returning a few minutes later with a petite Asian-American woman dressed for cocktails.

"Josh, this is Angelica Berrie," Roger said. The Russell Berrie Foundation had contributed much of the money for Sukkah City, and Angelica was the Philippines-born, converted-Jewish widow of the departed Russell.

Angelica expressed her admiration for Bio Puff. She liked it so much, in fact, that she said she wanted to take it home with her, to her Jewish Community Center in North Bergen, New Jersey, so that all of her friends could see it.

"We could invite Geraldo Rivera," she said. "He's Jewish."

———

Just past midnight a team of what looked to me like anarchist carpenters (black jeans, spiked belts, levels) began assembling the most striking sukkah of the evening. "Repetition meets Difference" consisted of three rings of knotted wooden spikes, the spikes tied in geometric configurations inspired by the KNOT studies of Konrad Wachsmann, a German-Jewish architect and engineer. The rings were going to be braided together, one on top of another, in a series of offset spirals designed to resemble a hut, but which also seemed to suggest the barbed wire of a concentration camp, a crown of thorns, and a postmodern porcupine.

The spirals were sharp and fragile and intimidating, and they had to be lifted into place and ratcheted down by hand. One of the architects asked for help with the lifting and ratcheting and was soon joined by volunteers from several other sukkah teams. Roger and Joshua jumped in as well. This, I should point out, was an act of bravery. The spikes appeared to be genuinely lethal, and the design seemed to embody less the impenetrable ideal of "Repetition meets Difference" and more the implicit threat of the sukkah's subtitle: "Stability meets Volatileness." I kept my distance and busily scribbled notes.

The head anarchist, an intense fellow with a clipped foreign accent that I couldn't quite place, barked out instructions. When the bottom ring was laid on the ground he ordered everyone to slowly lift the second. Once it reached eye-gouging level, two assistants slipped inside an opening in the rings and began an attempt to bolt them to each other. A few moments of grunting with socket wrenches passed until it became clear that the rings weren't sufficiently aligned.

"Now we rotate clockwise!"

They rotated clockwise.

The assistants struggled with their tools, pushing and pulling at the knotted spike rings and trying to make them fit.

"Everybody step BACK!"

They stepped back.

The volunteers were beginning to tire. One guy lost his grip for a moment and the upper ring dipped, nearly impaling someone.

"You! Reporter guy! Yes, you!"—it took a moment to realize that I was reporter guy—"Get in here."

I got in there.

———

One in the morning came and went. The spiked sukkah was, after much dangerous labor, completed. "The Sukkah of the Signs," a hut constructed from cardboard signs purchased from homeless people ("Helping people helps your soul," read one; "Need cash for alcohol research," read another) was assembled without incident.

Roger and I stood and admired it, and I complimented him on the success of the contest. The sukkahs were beautiful objects, and their self-conscious modernism didn't interfere with the sense that a ritual was in play. I said I was impressed and even a little moved.

But that didn't mean I understood Sukkah City. It was a Jewish design contest, but the contestants weren't necessarily Jewish—some were, many weren't—and they were under no obligation to advance Jewish identity. Was the idea that young, hip, irreligious Jews—people with secular backgrounds like mine—would see the designs and be inspired to build their own sukkahs? If so, I was skeptical, and not just because "cultural creatives" generally lack the requisite carpentry skills.

Sukkot is not a widely observed holiday. The students at my high school in Manhattan, for example, were almost entirely Jewish, but I don't recall a single person whose family had a sukkah. Hanukkah and Passover, yes; Rosh Hashanah and Yom Kippur, perhaps. But Sukkot? I could see people being interested in the sukkahs from any number of perspectives—religious, artistic, philosophical—but actually going out and building or buying one? I doubted even the Rebooters thought that was going to happen. So what was Sukkah City about? Was it truly an attempt to "re-imagine and renew" the sukkah, as Reboot claimed? Or was it merely an art exhibition, yet another contribution to the city's endless supply of thoughtful cool?

"It's like this," Roger said. "When I was kid in Liverpool, we had this old, out-of-the-box sukkah that my father kept in the garage. Filthy thing. We'd put it out each year, decorate it with plastic flowers. That's all. It was Judaism-by-rote." He could see I didn't entirely see where he was going. "Meaningful identities have to have something to offer the individual," he said. "Judaism hasn't done that. It hasn't adjusted because it's always felt it had a monopoly."

Roger suggested that I read "A Great Awakening," an article by Jonathan D. Sarna, a professor of American Jewish history at Brandeis University, which detailed an earlier effort to revive a neglected Jewish ritual. In 1879, the Young Men's Hebrew Association of New York (YMHA) staged an event that they advertised as the "Grand Revival of the Jewish National Holiday of Chanucka." Hanukkah, however it is spelled, wasn't then the Jewish-American version of Christmas, but a rather obscure Jewish fighting myth, not particularly associated with Hebrew nationhood, and having not overly much to do, at least in this country, with gift giving or fried potato cakes. The YMHA changed that. I came across a notice for the YMHA gathering at the Academy of Music in New York: "The greatest Jewish event chronicled in the Post-Biblical History"— Hanukkah—would be observed with "living representations of the stirring scenes and glowing events of the Maccabean war and triumph," a chorus of "Hebrew melodies" performed by 100 children from the Hebrew Orphan Asylum, and a "grand ball" to follow "the tableaux."

"If you lift up a festival," Roger said, "and represent it with self-confidence, people will come to it."

———

A chill set in. I took out my hip flask, had a sip, offered it to Roger. Across from us, a guy from the *Wall Street Journal* was snapping photos of Volkan Alkanoglu, a Turkish-German architect from Los Angeles. Volkan's sukkah, "Star Cocoon," was among the simpler ones: an oversize bamboo-and-rattan reclining chair that looked like a cross between a giant Moses basket and a killer clam.

"What's in it?" Roger asked, gesturing at the flask.

"Irish whiskey."

"Bushmills?"

"Powers."

He took the flask and helped himself. "God love you."

———

Fatigue eventually caught up with everyone. Work on the sukkahs flagged. By two, though, things perked up noticeably, motivated perhaps by the arrival of the largest and most physically impressive sukkah: "LOG."

Another team of union workers had materialized and quickly built a ten-foot scaffolding with a platform. When they were finished they unloaded "LOG's" wall components from a glass rack truck: four eight-foot panes of tempered and laminated glass. It took six men with suction cups on their hands to deposit the panes edgewise into two receiving stanchions. The stanchions, made from plasma-cut steel, were configured in a semi-open array that minimally met Joshua's (and his rabbi's) metaphysical requirement of "wallness." When that was complete—it took well over an hour—a forklift fitted with sturdy leather straps began moving the eighteen-foot, one-ton log into place above the glass panes. The creators of this sukkah, the New York architectural firm Abrahams-May, described "LOG" as a "zone of programmatic intensity, within a very simplistic and poetic structure." Part of me wanted to ridicule it—we are, after all, talking about a column of very-phallic timber suspended above a set of tinted windows—but the silence that came over the plaza once it was assembled was impressive.

A roar from the opposite corner of the plaza spoiled the quiet. About twenty young men in black suits, curled forelocks sticking out from underneath their wide-brimmed hats, were marching into the park, shouting "We want *Meshiach* now!" Two boys in the vanguard carried a large yellow banner with a blue crown at its center, and beneath that, the word "Messiah" written in Hebrew. They were Hasidic Jews from the Chabad Lubavitch sect, which meant that the messiah they were demanding was probably not Jesus, like my friends in New Mexico, but the seventh Lubavitcher Rebbe, Menachem Mendel Schneerson. Their fervor for his arrival was apparently undaunted by the fact that Schneerson had died sixteen years before.

A few of the Lubavitchers stopped marching long enough to examine "The Sukkah of the Signs." They seemed puzzled by it and I walked over and asked one of the boys if he understood what he was looking at. He paused before answering, taking time to scrutinize me with the same care as he had examined the sukkah.

"It's a sukkah," he said, in Yiddish-accented English. We faced each other for a moment, neither one sure what else to say.

"Are you Jewish?" he asked.

The Lubavitchers ended up loitering outside the security cordon, just opposite a group of twenty or so African-American kids who had arrived earlier in the night, and who had been providing a running commentary on the "LOG" construction efforts. A few of them had asked the workers and designers to explain the structures, but most hadn't. They weren't indifferent—even though the build was slow, they stayed to watch the whole thing—but they seemed to accept the sukkahs as nothing too far out of the ordinary, one more oddity you encounter if you stay out late in New York City.

One of these kids had a radio going, and soon a dance circle was under way. The Lubavitcher boys gathered around to watch, laughing and pointing at some of the more formidable maneuvers. This made me nervous. New York's Lubavitcher community resides primarily in Crown Heights, a predominantly African-American and Caribbean neighborhood in Brooklyn. Relations between the two groups have historically been tense, with periodic outbreaks of violence, including the deadly riots that shook the neighborhood for three days in the summer of 1991. The riots were a long time ago and the two communities seem to have resolved many of their differences. Yet it remains, I think, no small thing for an ultra-Orthodox Jew to laugh at a black kid in New York City.

Things only seemed more perilous when the Lubavitchers started their own dance routine, busting exuberant moves that I recognized from the wedding scene in *Fiddler on the Roof*. Their clapping and cheering caught the attention of the African-American kids, who stopped their dancing to watch the Lubavitchers, the laughter and pointing now reversing course. The movements of the Jewish boys were not without a certain spasticity, and soon one of the African-American kids moved into the Lubavitcher circle and began mocking them. The Lubavitchers ignored him, but I could feel the muscles in my neck begin to tighten. I began to imagine the headlines in the morning papers: UGLY RACIAL INCIDENT MARS JEWISH EVENT.

Then, unexpectedly, the Lubavitcher dance morphed into a display of impressive leaping and tumbling maneuvers. The boys formed a line and took turns leapfrogging one another, some of the fitter kids vaulting themselves high into the air. One heavy and thickly muscled boy separated from the throng, squatted down, and meshed his hands together to create a brace; he nodded toward another boy, this one short and built like a cannonball, who, fighting back a smile, took several powerful strides and leaped feet first into the cradle formed by the boy's hands. The bigger boy then jerked up and backward, sending the smaller boy skyward. In complete control of his body, the airborne boy pulled himself into a tuck and executed a graceful backflip, landing squarely and easily some ten feet away. The African-American kids exploded in surprise and appreciation, and the Lubavitchers smiled in return, quietly proud.

The Lubavitchers collected their hats and their flag, and with enviable timing disappeared into the night. The African-American kids departed not long after, leaving Reboot once again in sole possession of the park.

"Did that just happen?" I asked Roger. He only shrugged.

II.

I caught up with Roger a couple of weeks later, for lunch in a Korean restaurant in Midtown, and over kimchi and *bibimbap* he told me a story. It was the early 1990s, and he had been in the United States only a short while when he took a trip out to California to visit a girlfriend. After he had been there a few days, his girlfriend's father, a doctor, mentioned that he would be hosting a gathering of the Maimonides Society, a Jewish philanthropic organization for medical professionals. He told Roger not to miss it.

The meeting got started at sunset with whiskeys and a short kibitz for forty middle-aged docs crammed into the living room of a house in Tarzana. Roger stood in the back, watched everyone, listened to the clink of ice cubes in cut-glass tumblers. There was a film—a three-and-a-half minute documentary on the plight of impoverished Jews in some perilous corner of the globe—and the second it was over a bald guy from the UJA Federation, dressed in an electric blue suit, jumped up, grabbed a pen from behind his ear and a little notebook from his back pocket, and shouted: "It's *miiiiiittzvah* time! Bernie, you start!"

"I give $75,000!" said Bernie. One doc shouted "$50,000"; another gave $30,000; cries of "Double *chai*, double *chai*!" echoed throughout the room.[1] One guy said it had been a tough year: he gave $20,000.

---

1. Hebrew numerological theory, or *Gematria*, assigns a value to each letter in the alphabet. *Chai*, which means "life," consists of two letters—*chet* and *yud*—which equal eight and ten, respectively. Charitable donations and gifts are typically made in multiples of eighteen. Double *chai*, then, is thirty-six, or in this case, $36,000.

The shouting ended after a few moments. The bald man's notebook disappeared back into his pocket, he smoothed the lapels of his electric blue suit, returned the pen to his ear.

"Basket's yours, Bernie."

Bernie accepted his small token of appreciation from the Jewish people: a cellophane-wrapped fruit sampler. Thirty minutes later the room was completely empty. Bernie left without the basket.

Such was Roger Bennett's introduction to organized Jewish life in America.

———

In 1991, the Council of Jewish Federations released the National Jewish Population Survey (NJPS), the first comprehensive census of American Jewry in twenty years. The NJPS data painted an extremely disquieting picture: The Jewish population of the United States was aging; Jewish adults married late, and, with alarming frequency, tended to marry non-Jews; they had few children whom they provided with little religious instruction or sense of Jewish identity; they weren't members of synagogues, they didn't observe traditional ritual practice, and they didn't like giving money to Jewish charities. In short, their connections to the historical conventions of Jewish life and community were tenuous at best; at worst, they had been wholly severed.

Jews—or at least those Jews aware of and concerned with Jewish censuses—panicked. *Fifty-two percent of Jews married since 1985 were married to non-Jews! Only 41 percent belonged to a synagogue! 625,000 Jews were practicing another religion! Jewish women between the ages of eighteen and forty-four gave birth, on average, to .85 children—how is that even biologically possible?*

The reaction in the Jewish and mainstream media bordered on the hysterical. The findings of the NJPS were described as "gloomy," "dismal," "shocking," "disturbingly bleak," "notorious," and—inevitably—a "Holocaust"; the census "sent shock waves around the world"; "permanently altered the tone of Jewish communal discussion," "inflamed communal debate," and caused "deep anxiety," "anomie," and a "radical inner shift." It was so "unpleasant" that "some people working in the Jewish community" asked themselves, "What's the use?" The data was "devastating"; the demographic changes were "not only unparalleled but catastrophic"; people were anxious, depressed, and "scared out of their wits." America's Jews were being "wrenched apart by [their] own centrifugal force." There was "doom and gloom"; there was a "continuity crisis"; a "threat to continuity"; it was the "continuity, stupid." "The astonishing chain of Jewish continuity" had been rent asunder and Jews were "assimilating with the speed of the Ten Lost Tribes." There were panicked calls for an "inoculation against assimilation"; the "temptations of assimilation" must be countered. If "the erosion of Jewish numbers" weren't halted, Jews were "destined for the future of an endangered species."

Some were in favor of reaching out: "We have to do everything to encourage [assimilated Jews] to come back to Judaism," said one rabbi. An article in the *Forward* counseled "retaining as many Jews as possible from all measures of involvement." Jonathan Sarna, the historian, suggested shifting the definition of Jewish identity from "descent to consent." Edgar Bronfman advocated emulating the patriarch Abraham, whose "tent, according to rabbinic tradition, was open on all sides to welcome travelers coming from all directions." Panels were convened, task forces created, studies conducted, all with the goal that the "disengaged" be persuaded to reengage, the "unaffiliated" convinced to affiliate once again.

Others preferred a strategic retrenchment. An article in *Commentary*, self-importantly entitled "How to Save American Jews," claimed that "so-called 'outreach' effort[s] aimed at interfaith couples" have a "tendency to denude Jewishness of its particularity," and that attempts to recapture lapsed Jews "subvert[ed] the tribal nature of Jewish identity, and [are] anyway unlikely to work." "If the purpose [is] to ensure Jewish continuity for the next generation," the article continued, "it would seem clear that the place to begin is with the sectors of the community that are already engaged to a greater or lesser extent. . . . These are the core of the future community; surely they should be nurtured accordingly."

For the most part, organized Jewish America opted for outreach, shifting focus from Zionist issues (although these certainly didn't disappear) and support for Soviet Jews (less pressing with the collapse of Communism), and toward a full-scale assault on the numbers. Interestingly, the more effective agents of this change were not old-line institutions like the Foundation. Instead, family-run charities, including, among others, Roger Bennett's employer, the Andrea and Charles Bronfman Philanthropies, took the lead.

Bronfman created perhaps the best known of these outreach programs: Birthright Israel. Birthright offers a free ten-day tour of Israel to Jews (or those with at least one Jewish parent) between the ages of eighteen and twenty-six, who do not actively practice another religion besides Judaism.

Since 2000, when the first Birthright cohort traveled to Israel, over 250,000 young people have availed themselves of this hard-sweat timeshare tour of the Promised Land. The motivations of the participants may vary, but Bronfman's intentions are clear: to give the kids such a meaningful Jewish experience, be it swaying in religious delirium at the Wailing Wall, sitting astride a camel in a Bedouin camp, or floating in the Dead Sea, that upon return they begin paying dues to their local synagogue, giving to Jewish charity, uncritically supporting Israel's actions in the Gaza Strip, and, of course, marrying Jewish (and making Jewish babies). Whether this works is an open question, and one that cannot easily be answered. Birthright has existed for a decade. Two hundred fifty thousand Jews is a lot of Jews, but it will take time to determine with any accuracy Birthright's impact on intermarriage and how "Jewishly" the new generation of Jewish-American children are being raised.

Besides which, much of the NJPS data has since been challenged, because of methodological problems with the survey. The 52-percent figure for intermarriage, for example, is now believed to be a still-serious-but-considerably-lower 43 percent. The follow-up NJPS, which was released in 2001 and was supposed to correct the errors of the previous census, also came back with disturbing numbers, most notably that the total population of Jews in the United States had declined over the previous ten years. This number was also subsequently questioned, and the U.S. Jewish population is now believed to be stable, if not growing. And efforts by the second NJPS to rectify the technical errors of the first seemed only to create a new set of problems. The introduction to the second NJPS report included a discussion of its "analytical limitations," in which the researchers noted that they had "frequently changed" the wording of questions used in the previous census. This resulted in "more precise questions" but also "reduced comparability between the surveys."

The Federation chose not to conduct another census, but "U.S. Jewry: 2010," a study conducted by researchers at Brandeis University, showed that two decades of work to engage, affiliate, and ensure Jewish continuity had achieved little fundamental change: many Jews continue to intermarry, and many Jews still run screaming from the synagogues. What's more, they seem to be increasingly untethered from a basic aspect of all religious identification: denomination. A full 60 percent of American Jews identify themselves not as Orthodox, Reform, or Conservative but as the more nebulous "just Jewish."

None of this troubled Roger Bennett. In fact, he didn't care about the numbers at all.

"If Judaism disappears it will be because it has stopped being meaningful for its target audience," he said as we sipped our post-meal teas. "The whole premise of Reboot is that you can't command people to be Jewish or to do Jewish stuff or to trick them into doing Jewish stuff. You can make sure that being Jewish is relevant and meaningful and speaks to its time and place. You can control that. You can't command people to return to their ghetto."

III.

I took Roger at his word when he said that he didn't care about the numbers. Frankly, nothing about Sukkah City suggested an interest in luring Jewish kids back into the synagogues or beneath the chuppahs. But there was money involved in Reboot's programs—over $1.5 million in grants and contributions in 2009 alone—and surely those funds had to be justified in some manner.

To get a better sense of this I paid a visit to Roger's boss, Jeffrey Solomon, the president of the Andrea and Charles Bronfman Philanthropies, at Bronfman headquarters in midtown Manhattan. I was early for my appointment, and the receptionist asked me to have a seat in a nicely appointed waiting area. I passed the time perusing the selection of Bronfman's glossy promotional pamphlets and copies of different Jewish newspapers and magazines. After a few moments, the receptionist escorted me to Solomon's office down a long hallway decorated with artwork of a caliber sufficient, even to my untrained eye, to shame the curators of many small-city art museums.

There was something about the office—the cheery light, the clean elegance—that communicated confidence in the position of Jews in this country. It was a workplace with a narrative: *Jews succeed; they are secure; they are so far removed from the threat of ill fortune that its potential no longer registers.* Such a Jewish tale can be told in many American contexts—a bank, a Hollywood studio, a corporation, a doctor's office. The sense of self here reminded me of a quietly humming corporate campus, one dedicated to defining, shaping, and controlling Jewish identity, both in this generation and the next.

Solomon, who is coauthor with Charles Bronfman of *The Art of Giving: Where the Soul Meets a Business Plan*, was waiting for me. He, too, seemed of a piece with the official narrative: a handsome man in his sixties with a neat orange beard, dressed in crisp trousers, a tailored oxford, tie of commensurate power, and suspenders decorated with British flags on one side and the Stars and Stripes on the other. A plaque on a table behind his desk, directly opposite a bewildering collection of small glass owls, read: TROUBLE IS OPPORTUNITY.

Here, no doubt, was a man who cared about the numbers.

He asked me to tell him a little bit about myself, which I did, and when I had finished, he smiled.

"You know, and this is anecdotal—I'll give you statistics in a minute—but the number of people who've had . . ." he paused, searching for the right word, "*versions* of your life experience, who wind up going on Birthright, and drinking the Kool-Aid, is beyond belief."[1]

"That's interesting," I replied. "I've never heard of anyone with a similar life experience to mine."

Solomon conceded the point, and the conversation passed on to Reboot.

"With Birthright, from day one, we said that research and evaluation was going to be part of the core budget," Solomon said. "There's a team up at Brandeis that has been studying every one of the 250,000 kids who have gone on Birthright. So we can tell you that if you are the child of intermarried parents, you are one hundred percent more likely to marry a Jew if you went on Birthright than if you applied to go and were put on a waiting list and never went. Which is as perfect a control group as one

---

1. I was twenty-seven in 2000, too old by one year to have sampled Birthright's Kool-Aid.

could ask for in social science research. And we can demonstrate exactly how much you learned during the trip, how you feel differently, and what of your behaviors have changed, because we've got ten years of research. So that's sort of the ideal scenario in terms of true program evaluation. We can make policy decisions based on that kind of thing."

Reboot, however, didn't lend itself to this form of number crunching, Solomon said. Its structure was based on the "Law of the Few" concept from Malcolm Gladwell's *The Tipping Point*: Gather together the right Jewish "thought leaders" and they will create models for a religious life compelling enough to attract even the truly irreligious, the ones Solomon said were "so far from their Jewish identity that they won't even apply for a free trip to Israel."

But that didn't mean that Reboot's activities have gone unevaluated. In 2007, Bronfman commissioned a report analyzing four projects either inspired by the Reboot summit or that received funding from Reboot: Ikar, a progressive congregation in Los Angeles that "stands at the inter-section of spirituality and social justice"; JDub Records, a nonprofit music label, famous, at least in part, for having discovered the Jewish reggae artist Matisyahu; Storahtelling, which organizes creative Torah-inspired performances; and The Salon, a gathering for "young, culturally savvy" Jews in Toronto. They could just have easily included any number of other groups, not all of which can be linked to Reboot, but which are, in some sense, a response to the 1991 demographic shock: Hazon, a non-profit that links environmentalism, sustainable food, and Judaism (think CSA vegetable pickups in synagogues); Yiddishkayt, a project "calling on contemporary artists to reengage with classic Yiddish artifacts"; and ir-reverent publications such as *Plotz* and *Heeb*, among many others.

The authors of the report, Steven M. Cohen and Ari Y. Kelman, ad-opted a rather fizzy style, claiming that the projects were part of "a new cultural efflorescence spanning prayer groups, music, journalism, social justice, politics, Jewish learning, scholarship, information technology, and more." But what is of actual interest is the way they identify the shared characteristics of these groups. Judaism, they argue, operates in a "competitive marketplace for what is essentially people's leisure time." Organized Jewish endeavors, if they are to succeed, must be "quite careful about delivering high-quality experiences and tending to the reputation for doing so, a function referred to by marketers as 'branding.'" In short, these new groups are trying—and in the study's opinion, succeeding—to sell Judaism to people who don't have to be Jewish but want to be, and are doing so with techniques that have nothing to do with traditional Jewish American norms or avenues of approach. Take *Heeb*, for example. In 2010 *Heeb* ceased publication of its print edition. An online version still exists, but much of *Heeb*'s work now involves a boutique-advertising agency that "specializes in the creation of multimedia branding campaigns" for companies marketing to young Jews.

While there may be something jarring about proffering a mode of spirituality with the same tactics used to sell cars, there is, from what I can tell, little doubt among the Jewish professionals—Solomon, Roger, and the like—of its necessity.

"Something like sixty-plus percent of American Jews belong to a congregation at some point," Solomon told me. "But only *thirty-nine percent* belong at any one time." He called this phenomenon "bar and bat mitzvah blackmail."

"You know how it is," he said. "People think, 'If my kid has to be bar mitzvahed in your synagogue, and he or she has to belong for four years, then I guess I have to belong for four years.'" Once it's over, though, the ritual complete and the child showered in Cross pens and college money, they are gone without ever looking back.

"The best bar mitzvah gift is that it can stop. The whole family can stop going to synagogue." He smiled. "There is something wrong with that model."

IV.

One of the most interesting things Jeffrey Solomon said to me had nothing to do with numbers. I wanted to know if groups like Reboot, events like Sukkah City, or publications like *Heeb* could be criticized fairly for not being "authentically Jewish." Here is a typical example of this mode of attack, made in 2009 by D. G. Myers, in *Commentary*:

> Hipster Jews claim that they want to reinvent Jewish identity—to reboot Jewish culture, in an expression that is popular with them. But because they are largely strangers to Jewish tradition, their movement is merely the latest manifestation of the desire, familiar to students of Jewish history, to rewrite Judaism in line with the current fashions.

Solomon begged to differ. "I don't think there's any such thing as inauthentic Judaism," he said. "Look at the history. There's always been different ways of viewing Judaism." He asked me if I knew of the story of Shammai and Hillel, the Talmudic-Manichean debate over strict observance and individual spirituality. Hillel favored lax rules and urged that practically all converts be accepted into the faith, including, famously, one man who demanded that the Torah be taught to him "while standing on one foot." Shammai rejected this, stating that such converts weren't really interested in being Jewish.

"Shammai's thinking was that if you're not going to be serious about your Judaism, then go fuck yourself. But we believe that Hillel had it right: there's enough good stuff in Judaism that if you engage people where they're at and then they begin to explore it on their own, they're going to find enough to continue to be engaged. One of the problems of Jewish life today is that most of the organizations are functioning like Rabbi Shammai, when the world is crying out for Rabbi Hillel."

We also discussed how an observant Jew might perceive Reboot. Solomon said he didn't care if the Orthodox considered Reboot kosher or *goyishe*.

"I didn't wake up this morning thanking God that I wasn't a woman," he said. (Among the *Birchot Hashachar*, or morning blessings, recited by many Orthodox men: *Blessed are You, Lord our God, Sovereign of the Universe, who has not made me a woman.*)

"It's not who I am. I don't swing a chicken over my head before Yom Kippur." (Another element of ultra-Orthodox practice: Before the Jewish holiday of atonement, you get a chicken, pass it over your head three times while reciting a prayer, and in so doing, transfer a year's worth of sin to the bird, which is then slaughtered. This has apparently fallen out of favor among some Orthodox Jews, whose rabbis have deemed it acceptable to swing money above your head instead.)

"You know, if you want do that—as long as you're not hurting anybody, I couldn't care less. But don't tell me what to do."

This sentiment reflects the tensions caused by a juxtaposition of modern and traditional notions of Jewish identity. "Traditionally, a Jew was a Jew by virtue of a dual relationship: a vertical relationship with God, the concrete image of which is the law handed down to Moses, and a horizontal relationship with the Jewish people, which takes shape in history," Myers noted in *Commentary*. "The shift from external authority to individual control over Jewish identity is the hallmark of the hipster movement."

Rebecca Walker, daughter of the novelist Alice Walker and Mel Leventhal, a civil rights lawyer, articulated a Rebooter counter-opinion, in an interview for the "Kids Issue" of *Heeb* (which included items on Bob Saget, Aziz Ansari, and "JMILFs"): "I used to roll out a complete discussion about being culturally rather than spiritually Jewish . . . but these days, I just don't care to expend a lot of energy proving I belong somewhere. If you get it, cool. If not, go police someone else's identity."

Or, as Solomon put it: "It's all about choosing for yourself. I had a rabbi once, and he always used to say to me: 'Jeffrey, I'm not going to Jew for you. You have to Jew for yourself.'"

Such an open tent! Abraham would surely have been pleased. I didn't ask Solomon what limits there were, if any, to the dimensions of his next-generation sukkah. It sounded big enough for me, but it didn't really matter. Pick a point of extension receding from the spiritual source—the Bible, the Burning Bush, the bris, wherever—and the answer should remain the same: *Jew for yourself.*

I put this theory to the test at the Brooklyn Bowl, a music hall and sixteen-lane bowling alley in the Williamsburg neighborhood of Brooklyn, which was hosting the "teaser party" for the New York Burlesque Festival. Included among the performers scheduled to doff their outerwear (and most, but not all, of their underwear) that evening were the Schlep Sisters, two kosher striptease artists.

Brooklyn Bowl is a cavernous space, darkly lit and strenuously cool, with a bouncer checking IDs at the door. A stylishly eccentric crowd had come out, and particularly striking were the women: clusters of pale, smartly tattooed art chicks in classic stripper garb; bone-thin girls in dungeon-mistress getups; and quite a few ladies in zoot suits modified to accentuate their body art.

Each act, male or female, did a one- or two-minute turn about the stage, undressing to g-strings and, for the women, pasties. There were shimmied breasts and shaken rumps, Sapphire Jones stripping in a yellow apron and cleaning gloves, Harvest Moon in a space-lady outfit, and Go-Go Harder Faster Stronger, a "Boy-lesque sensation," who started out in a schoolgirl's outfit and ended up in a g-string.

The Schlep Sisters performed last and were introduced by Albert Cadabra, a small and muscular bald guy with flaming red sideburns, who bore a disturbing resemblance to Carrot Top.

"Everyone knows there are boys and girls in burlesque," he said, bounding onto the stage. "But are there *Jews?*" The crowded yelled that there were. "Are you kidding? We got the two Jewiest girls in New York City!"

The Schlep Sisters stripped in blond wigs, frilly pink frocks, black high heels, and ruby red parasols. If I had one word to describe them physically it would be "zaftig." Creamy skin, abundant bellies, curvilinear thighs; the women twirled about the stage, discarding their outer garments to reveal pink polka-dotted bloomers and bras and, under that, pasties that matched the color of their umbrellas. Part of the act involved strategically opening and closing the parasols, concealing and revealing in ways that were silly, sexy, and arty all at once. Songs by the Barry Sisters, 1940s Yiddish pop's answer to the Andrew Sisters, provided musical accompaniment, with the Schlep Sisters gyrating suggestively to jazzed-up versions of "Hava Nagila," "Chiribim Chiribom," and a Yiddish rendition of "Raindrops Keep Fallin' on My Head."

Darlinda Just Darlinda and Minnie Tonka (the Schlep Sisters refused to tell me their real names) met at Burning Man and have been performing together since 2003. Neither is currently observant, but Darlinda, who grew up in California, went with her family to synagogue each weekend, and was bat mitzvahed as a teen. Minnie is the cofounder of Kosher ChiXXX, producer of the Menorah Horah burlesque show, and number 32 on the "Burlesque Top 50" list of "Burlesque Industry Figures." She also holds a master's degree in Jewish education from the Jewish Theological Seminary in New York, and has worked for the University of Minnesota's Hillel Center, the Jewish community center at Manhattan's 14th Street Y, and Birthright.

Cadabra joined the Sisters onstage when the music ended, shouting, "I love Jews," as the Sisters made a show of rubbing against him in mock-porn-star style. This went on one beat longer than I considered necessary. "Judaism is just another historical kink," Cadabra said. "It doesn't have to be tragic or ominous."

The crowd registered its appreciation of the word "kink." The Schlep Sisters took a bow, Cadabra encouraged everyone to tip their waitresses, and I headed for the door.

My ride home that evening took me through the southern part of Williamsburg, which contains a sizable enclave of Hasidic Jews. The streets, despite the late hour, were crowded with men in black frock coats, white leggings, and black hats, and women, many of them pushing strollers, in long modest skirts and head coverings. It was a disorienting experience after the Brooklyn Bowl, one that could have made me think of the potential inherent in Abraham's expansive tent. But it didn't. Instead I thought of goods and services being sold on an open market of spiritual ideals, of branding techniques and marketing campaigns in irreconcilable conflict.

V.

I have been married twice and have two children, one with each spouse. Neither my first wife nor my present wife is Jewish. One was raised Catholic, the other Buddhist. What religion my children are or will be remains to be seen. My divorce settlement requires my son to be raised without religion, but that may change as he grows older and is able to choose for himself. My daughter's faith depends, to an extent, on what happens with my son, as I would like them to practice the same religion, or none at all, if we can't reach a consensus. I offer these personal details to explain a problem I encountered in trying to understand secular Jewish outreach: most of its efforts are directed at singles.

Married Jews with school-aged children, if the 2001 NJPS is to be believed, are four times more likely to belong to a synagogue than unmarried Jews, and they are eight times more likely to pay dues to a Jewish Community Center or contribute to a Federation campaign. Cohen and Feldman, in "The Continuity of Discontinuity," noted a common assumption within the Jewish establishment, which "questioned the import of the discontent with prevailing options for Jewish engagement, suggesting that the alienation . . . would evaporate when the younger adults would marry and bear children. On more than one occasion we heard: 'Leave 'em alone and they'll come home.'" Reboot and the like, with money and encouragement from private family foundations, instead fill the void.

Sensibly enough, the void gets filled with the kinds of projects and programming that appeal to the young and unmarried: entertainment and recreation. If the goal is to employ modern-day techniques in a youth-driven campaign for Judaism—if you want to re-brand the religion—then a Matisyahu concert or one of Hazon's "Jewish Environmental Bike Rides" speaks more directly to the aspirations of the target audience than, say, a brain-bending lecture on illuminated Torah manuscripts at the local Jewish museum.

A week or so after Sukkah City, I attended "Judaism and Sacred Space," a panel discussion inspired by Sukkah City, at the Center for Jewish History in Manhattan. I hesitate to criticize this type of programming—I'm old enough to enjoy a panel of scholars chatting in a "highly interactive mode"— but the fact remains that it drew approximately 100 people, whereas Sukkah City brought more than a hundred thousand to Union Square. Which, then, is more *effectively* Jewish? A debate with Lawrence H. Schiffman, Ethel and Irvin A. Edelman Professor of Hebrew and Judaic Studies at NYU (author, as it happens, of the book *Who Was a Jew?*), squaring off against Jacob J. Schacter, Yeshiva University Professor of Jewish History and Jewish Thought? Or a hipster melee in Union Square that revolves around a crucial Jewish object, however newfangled, which itself encapsulates the better part of Jewish thought and studies? A question of age and inclination, but not as easily answered as one might initially suppose.

Before the panel discussion, I eavesdropped on Professor Schiffman as he complained to one of the event organizers about the size of the lecture hall. "There's room here for four hundred people," he said. "Four hundred people! It's *raining!*" A weather-beaten old man in stained khakis and a rumpled Knicks yarmulke sat down next to me, gave me a boozy once-over, shifted into another chair, and then went almost immediately to sleep, snoring loudly throughout the entire discussion. I told Roger Bennett about this fellow. His comment: "I think I know that guy."

That guy is why Jewish outreach focuses on single people: kids stay

awake for the lecture. Or for the date. I see no need to explain the mechanics of contemporary dating and mating rituals, other than to say that
something exists for everyone, and definitely for Jews. A cursory Google
search, for example, will yield an almost limitless range of electronic Jewish dating options, including, along with the most famous site, JDate.com,
SingleJew.com, JSoulMate.com, JWed.com, JewishMingle.com, Jewcier
.com, and, my favorite, Yenta911.com.

I don't mean to suggest a connection between organized Jewish outreach groups and the dating sites. Their goals may, at times, overlap—
some rabbis pay the JDate membership fees of their congregants—but
their motivations likely differ.

Gay Talese frequented massage parlors as "research" for his book on
the sexual revolution, *Thy Neighbor's Wife*. My wife offered me considerably less leeway for my endeavors. I did go to *Heeb*'s annual Christmas Eve
party, Heebonism, at a bar on the Lower East Side, with my wife's blessing, and with a measure of writerly protection: I brought my cousin Greg.
Jeffrey Solomon's social scientists would, I imagine, consider Greg an
ideal data point: twenty-seven years old; raised in suburban New Jersey;
lavishly bar mitzvahed; a Birthright alumnus; no synagogue membership
at present; inclined, at least in theory, to date and eventually marry a Nice
Jewish Girl. At Heebonism, Greg—the target demographic—would be
my eyes, ears, and proxy-libido.

Heeb began throwing its Christmas Eve party in 2004, as a corrective
for the holiday season malaise suffered by many U.S. Jews. Barbara Rushkoff, founder and publisher of the zine *Plotz*, writes in her book *Jewish
Holiday Fun . . . For You!* about her feelings each year during the Yuletide
festivities:

> I frequently met bona fide grown-ups who had no idea what Jews do
> on Christmas. I was cautiously asked about my whereabouts on De-

cember 25th, as if that was the day I set aside to do human sacrifice. . . . I would explain that sometimes I did laundry or met with friends, but most times you could find me laying face down on my bed wishing that they'd stop running the creepy movie *A Christmas Carol*. That usually shut them up.

My father always held a movie marathon on Christmas Eve and Christmas Day. He would spend twenty-four hours or more watching art films and avoiding the holiday cheer, noting for anyone willing to listen that Santa Claus was, in fact, a pagan. I never joined him, daunted perhaps by the memory of my mother's elaborate tree decorations and gingerbread architectural masterpieces. My father, by the way, no longer holds the marathon. His third wife is Catholic.

In 2009, the Travel Channel filmed a short spot on Heebonism for a special on "Extreme Wild Parties." It presented the gathering as an ironic bacchanal, replete with smarmy, attractive young Jews making self-aware merry. Joshua Neuman, then-publisher of *Heeb*, called Heebonism "the sickest, twistedest, raunchiest party on Christmas Eve," and a "Who's who of Jew."

The reality proved less risqué. Heebonism 2010 in New York was held at Fontana's, a nondescript bar in a neighborhood that was once dangerous and now serves mostly as a playground for young college graduates and artists with rent-controlled apartments. The bouncer at the door, a chubby Jewish boy who seemed to be praying that no one would give him trouble, flirted with the woman in front of me in line. When it became clear she wasn't interested, the bouncer turned to me and said, loudly, and in mocking tones, "Watch out for that one—she's an anti-Semite." Then he took my fifteen dollars, stamped my hand, and waved me inside.

Other than footage of a flickering Yule log projected onto a movie screen in the back, little effort had been expended on decorations. The evening's advertised entertainment had yet to begin, but they promised the musical stylings of DJs Terry Diabolik and Cowboy Mark, among others; and following that, the "Kinky Jews," a group dedicated to "edgy, open-minded, and otherwise unconventional Jews (and those who love us!)," would organize a game of Strip Dreidel in the private room upstairs.

I was early, and only a handful of Jewish revelers were mingling, in subdued fashion. A few wore dollar-store Santa hats. One sad-faced young man was carrying a mistletoe sprig but couldn't yet find anyone to menace with it. Two others were dressed in vintage suits and bowties, whether out of irony or nerdiness I couldn't tell. A table filled with Asian-American women appeared, at first, to be at the wrong party, but then I remembered the Travel Channel video of the 2009 event. After watching it several times, who should appear briefly on screen but my Asian-American wife, who happened to be enjoying herself with a group of friends in the days before we met. I headed to the bar and bought a drink.

I stood awkwardly at the bar, until Steve, another stag guest, introduced himself and asked my opinion of the "quality of the chicks" so far that night. In short order, I learned the key facts about Steve: six feet, eight inches tall; stocky; suspiciously tan; wearing baggy jeans, brown corduroy sports jacket, and a T-shirt depicting Chewbacca in a yarmulke, with "Jewbacca" printed underneath. He had been raised in a Conservative Jewish family, was no longer religious, kept kosher at home, and was an unemployed marketer from Morristown, New Jersey. He also told me that he had "fucked chicks from nine states," had an interest in "Jewish babes," and preferred events like Heebonism to prowling the Jewish dating sites.

"I gave up on JDate," he said. "I have too much game."

Cousin Greg arrived a few minutes later and the three of us sat down at a Galaga tabletop video-game machine and ordered another round. We talked local sports allegiances for a while, until Steve abruptly stood up and announced his intention to "get laid." He struck up a conversation with an unimpressed-looking blonde a few tables away. Moments later he came back. I asked him how things had gone.

"Catch and release," he said.

—

The night progressed, the room grew crowded, the DJs did their best. Nothing transpired that I would consider truly hedonistic. A handful of women—and men—had come dressed in garb that might rate as risqué, given the cold weather; a few couples paired off to neck; that was about it. At one point, Greg—tall, handsome, athletic by the standards of the room, gainfully employed as a corporate consultant—decided to help Steve and rustled up a couple of women. Sasha and Lana, deadpan Russian girls from Brooklyn, seemed willing to be spoken to, despite Steve's inability to make eye contact, and the fact that I was taking notes. Things veered unexpectedly out of control after Greg excused himself to go to the bathroom. Steve produced a dreidel from his pocket and suggested that we jump the gun on the spinning festivities. Lana allowed herself a bored titter, as if she had heard this exact line several times already that night. Sasha stared at Steve with what I interpreted as derisive pity.

"Why do you come to these things?" she asked him.

Steve paused before answering.

"Because Jewish women are such cunts," he said.

—

Greg left Steve on his own after that, and found himself two Jewish Pilates instructors, Yael and Lauren, with whom to flirt. Yael, a lapsed Orthodox Jew from Riverdale in the Bronx, seemed not a little unnerved by the bar scene, despite all efforts to appear otherwise, and didn't say much.

Lauren was the gregarious one—she had invited Greg to her table—and told me she supplemented her income as a fitness instructor by blogging ("I'm a writer, just like you!"). She also said she knew I must really be somebody because my notebook was "very classy"; then she grabbed it away and began to conduct her own interview.

"So why are you here tonight?" she asked, using a mock-newscaster voice and jabbing a virtual microphone into my face.

"You'd be better off asking Greg. I'm here but not really here."

"He's got kids," Greg said.

"That's a lame answer but I'm going to let you off the hook," she said. She pretended to write "lame answer" in my notebook. Then, with a sly smile, to Greg: "What's your story?"

"Looking to meet a nice Jewish girl, get married, and move to the suburbs," he said. (Greg, it should be pointed out, went home with both Yael's and Lauren's phone numbers.)

Among the people I met and spoke with that evening, only Steve would admit to attending Jewish singles' events with any regularity. Greg, Lauren, and Yael each said that they preferred to date—and expected to marry—someone Jewish. But it took an excessive amount of prying to get them to say it. No one at Heebonism had any reservations about wanting to be with a Jew. That's why they were here. But stating it explicitly revealed that this wasn't just going to happen—they wanted it, and wanting it was too much. Wanting it wasn't cool. And uncool meant Steve.

"The object of the outreach game," according to Douglas Rushkoff, author of the 2003 book *Nothing Sacred: The Truth About Judaism*, is

> to get disaffected Jews to marry and then make more Jews. It doesn't matter what the target market thinks Judaism actually is, only that they identify themselves with the word. Once they feel like Jews,

they'll see the importance of . . . preserving the faith for future gen‑
erations. Or so the logic, and the demographic research, goes.

Rushkoff is no doubt an expert on the subject of the "outreach game."
He is not only a Reboot Summit alumnus but he served as host for the
inaugural session, and claims to have come up with the name Reboot. I
also think that while he is, to an extent, correct, he is also being unfair.
Heebonism and Sukkah City may be a poor end point for anyone's un‑
derstanding of spirituality, but they are more than mere efforts to inspire
endogamous procreation. They are a start.

Still, I thought of Rushkoff's comment at every Reboot event I at‑
tended; with every page of *Heeb* that I read; with each visit to hyper‑
ironic blogs like *Stuff Jews Hate, Stuff Shmeckles Hate,* and *Stuff Nazis
Hate*; when I read about the protestors in Williamsburg who spray
painted WE'RE SELF-HATING JEWISH HIPSTERS on streets where bicycle
lanes had been removed at the behest of Hasidic Jews; and on the Na‑
tional Day of Unplugging, Reboot's streamlined version of the Hebrew
day of rest, as I slipped my phone into its "Sabbath Manifesto Sleeping
Bag" ($7.99 from Sabbathmanifesto.org) and endeavored to relax like a
Jew.

"Sure, I want a mensch," Yael had said, eyeing Greg. "But I'm not
going to go crazy looking for one."

Clearly, the brand and I still had a long way to go.

Part IV

THE MASTERS OF RETURN

Do you believe that you really understand the object which you are thus condemning? Have you acquired with your own eyes, and by dint of honest, earnest investigation, an actual understanding of a matter which, inasmuch as it is the holiest and most important consideration of our life, should at least not be cast aside thoughtlessly and unreflectingly?

—Samson Raphael Hirsch, *The Nineteen Letters of Ben Uziel*

I.

Although I am not an atheist, at least not exactly—drop me in the proverbial foxhole and I will pray with commensurate fervency—I have no particular affinity for God. No doubt this is a consequence of the religious subterfuge of my childhood. Under those circumstances, from whom would I have drawn my spirituality—my absent father or my self-abnegating mother? My spiritual state does not stem from some strenuous bout of introspection or a systematic consideration of faith. I underwent no reckoning with belief, no survey of the contradictions inherent in the Judeo-Christian God, no conclusive cycle of doubt, crisis, and repudiation. Maimonides, in the introduction to *The Guide for the Perplexed*, writes that the object of his treatise is to "enlighten a religious man," a student of his struggling to reconcile God with a scientific and philosophical understanding of the world. This man, Maimonides informs us, "finds it difficult to accept as correct the teaching based on the literal interpretation of the Law." His doubts "give rise to fear and anxiety, constant grief and great perplexity." I can empathize with the feelings of this tortured young seeker. But I would be lying if I said that I shared his concerns.

How, then, can my religious indifference be squared with an exploration of Jewish identity? I can, of course, insist that Jews do not believe in God. Or not that they do not believe, but rather that they do not *have* to believe, that Judaism is a religion of ethnicity and code, one in which faith plays only a minor role.

Americans lack a shared vocabulary for God. The diversity of our backgrounds and beliefs; intermarriage between classes and cultures; the marginalization of tradition by popular culture and, in turn, the increasing prevalence of secular thinking: all of these render the articulation of God, or at least a universal god, absurd. The American God is one of fragmentation, of small holy pieces cleaved to by partisans of each shard. But to conceive of God this way makes Him awfully easy to dispense with. A subjective God is a weak one. If your God is only your God to you and my God is only my God to me, then God is all things and nothing. He is beside the point.

I have, therefore, always understood that my question has no answer without the Jewish God. Mine is ultimately an inquiry after clarity, a quality that religion offers and demands. Again I rely on Maimonides, this time from his most famous work, the *Commentary on the Mishnah*, with its Thirteen Foundations of Jewish Belief. First among these is the requirement "to believe in the existence of the Creator, Blessed be He":

> There exists a Being that is complete in all ways and He is the cause of all else that exists. He is what sustains their existence and the existence of all that sustains them. It is inconceivable that He would not exist, for if He would not exist then all else would cease to exist as well, nothing would remain.

This seems, by Maimonides's linguistically contorted standards, a rather straightforward evocation of an Almighty. By the Third Foundation, however, the picture has grown more complex:

> The One whom we have mentioned is not a body and His powers are not physical. The concepts of physical bodies such as movement, rest, or existence in a particular place cannot be applied to Him.

Such things cannot be part of His nature nor can they happen to Him.... In all places where the Holy Scriptures speak of Him in physical terms, as walking, standing, sitting, speaking and anything similar, it is always metaphorical.

Maimonides teaches us that God cannot be known—"There is no relation of distance between corporeal and incorporeal beings." Yet he also insists that we *must* know Him—"Man's love of God is identical with His knowledge of Him." Maddeningly, Maimonides further seems to contend that seeking *not* to know God offers the best chance of understanding His nature—"Each time you ascertain by proof that a certain thing, believed to exist in the Creator, must be negatived, you have undoubtedly come one step nearer to the knowledge of God."

The arguments advanced today in favor of secular Judaism do not often include Maimonides's negative theology. Neither do they dispense with God entirely; rather, they attempt to co-opt His absence. Douglas Rushkoff, in his book on contemporary Jewish identity, *Nothing Sacred*, maintains that the core principles of Judaism, "iconoclasm, abstract monotheism, and social justice," depend on an undetectable Supreme Being. "The natural result of settling for an abstract and unknowable deity," he writes, "is to then focus, instead, on human beings and life itself as the supremely sacred vessels of existence. There's no one around to pray to, so one learns to enact sanctity through ethical behavior."

This reassuring depiction of non-belief cannot be adapted to my purposes. For Rushkoff, perhaps, an incorporeal—or nonexistent—God yields a higher order of ethical behavior. My sacred vessel of existence, however, often needs a firm push in the right direction. There could be no avoiding it: To understand if I am a Jew requires that I learn how faith works among the faithful.

Does that mean I found it in me to believe? I'm afraid not. In a chapter in *The Guide* devoted to the "Attributes of God," Maimonides writes, "By 'faith' we do not understand merely that which is uttered with the lips, but also that which is apprehended by the soul." I am unlikely to meet this bar. To grow close to God, positively or negatively, requires, in my case, the assistance of people with conviction greater than my own. If in the end I fail to find them, or if the pieties they mouthed didn't quite meet Maimonides's high standards, no matter. The effort to tread, however lightly, in a trail cut by devotion, will in the end have been worth it.

II.

My first tentative steps along that holy path led to the Avenue R Café, in the village of Monsey, New York. The Avenue R sits in a small strip mall adjacent to Monsey's main drag, about an hour's drive from New York City, in a part of Rockland County that not long ago was farmland and is home today to an exurban agglomeration of subdivisions, shopping malls, and Orthodox Jews.

There has been a Jewish presence in Rockland County since the early 1900s: summer visitors, mostly, eager for a respite from the close quarters of Brooklyn and the Lower East Side. Seasonal hotels, shops, restaurants, and groceries sprang up to meet their needs, but permanent settlers didn't appear in force until the 1940s, when the leader of an Orthodox synagogue in Williamsburg, Brooklyn, established two yeshivas in the county—one in Monsey, the other in the nearby village of Spring Valley. These institutions drew a mini-Diaspora, not only of Orthodox Jews, but of all three primary denominations. The strong Orthodox character of Rockland County's Jewry dates to the mid-1950s and the founding of New Square, a hamlet established by an insular sect of Hasidic Jews, on the site of what was once a dairy farm. Over the next decade, other Hasidic and Orthodox communities took root. Some, like New Square, functioned as bounded fiefdoms for specific Jewish micro-minorities— the New Square settlers are *Skverist* Jews, a Hasid group that traces its lineage to the Ukrainian city Skvyra; nearby Kiryas Joel is home almost exclusively to Hasids of the Satmar sect, who descend from Hungarian and Romanian forebears. Other areas, in particular Monsey, are more "diverse," with a mixed populace of Orthodox, Hasidic, and Modern Orthodox Jews.

I didn't have this information at hand when I walked into the Avenue R, but neither was I completely uninformed: I had played around with the county's census data, and read Jerome Mintz's 1998 book, *Hasidic People: A Place in the New World*, which contains a well-drawn history of the ultra-Orthodox decampment from New York City to Rockland County. I had even consulted the sages at Wikipedia. But the only direct information I had about Monsey came from some of my earlier journalism, when I had unsuccessfully tried to contact several rabbis living there. That small statistical sample had become, in my mind, a global picture of the area's observant Jews: a locale of atavistic isolates, living in a self-constructed and self-maintained *judería*, one in which time has been trapped in a historical-religious-cultural amber. Judith Neulander, an expert on the Jewish Traveler's Tale in New Mexico, would have recognized what I was doing. Who was I but a "metropolitan literate," hungering selfishly after "popular exotica," insinuating myself among the Jewish tribes? Unfortunately my most recent attempts at insinuation had again failed. After a series of frustrating unreturned phone messages and emails, I had decided to try to commune with the faithful without an introduction.

The red-cheeked blonde taking orders at the counter at the Avenue R gave me a brief visual inspection when I walked in. Avoiding eye contact, she handed me an English-language menu. The chalkboard next to her, which I believe contained the day's specials, was written in Hebrew. Behind her, a skinny kid with his forelocks poking from beneath a hairnet pushed eggs and pancakes around a flattop. The girl told him my order and he muttered something back to her, in Yiddish, which the girl then relayed to me: he wanted to know if I wanted my burrito spicy or mild. I opted for spicy, the girl made a note of it on her ordering pad, and I took a seat and waited for my food.

I was the only adult male in the Avenue R dressed in something other than black and white. The married women favored wigs or head covers and long skirts; the unmarried ones long skirts, no wigs. The aisles of the café were jammed with strollers and other baby conveyances, evidence of the prodigious reproductive output of the Orthodox, whose families, on average, number six or more children; the little ones were lulled to sleep by the music playing on the loudspeakers: versions of 1980s power ballads with klezmeresque instrumental touches. After a few moments, the girl at the counter motioned for me to come fetch my coffee, and as I stirred in my milk and sugar, I eavesdropped on a group of young lunching ladies. They were chattering away in a pidgin that veered dizzily from Hebrew to Yiddish and to English and back again. A plump young girl in a burgundy wig and a simultaneously tight-fitting and all-covering dress joined them. She parked her many shopping bags beside her, took a long draw from a latte, and then turned to her friends with eager eyes.

"And so I missed much?" she asked.

"*Oy gevalt*, sweetie," one of her friends replied, punctuating with a dismissive wave. "You didn't miss nothing. We're just talking *sidduchim*."[1]

David Baum, in *The Non-Orthodox Jew's Guide to Orthodox Jews*, writes that secular Jews find the Orthodox "no different than the Amish except that the Amish aren't as irritating." He's right, at least in my case, although I wouldn't limit the associations to the Amish. My mental bigotry cross-indexed the Orthodox with evangelical boobs speaking in tongues; Left Behind crackpots predicting biblical cataclysm; white supremacists training for a showdown with the federal government; gold

---

1. I looked up this word later. It means "matchmaking."

bugs, conspiracy theorists, cultists, and cranks. Even to sit in the same room with them, sipping the same overpriced coffee that I might waste money on in Brooklyn, eating the same bland burrito, listening to the same inane jabbering, infuriated me. Why? Because *they were making me look bad.*

Whatever sort of Jew I might be, I am far from Orthodox. Yet I still felt that their external identity, the face that they showed to the world, reflected on me, and adversely at that. Worse still, I believed, admittedly without really knowing, that they didn't care what I thought, that my opinion didn't count. These Jews thought they were the only ones doing it right; they were the proper Jews and everyone else fell short of their archaic standards. *I* was making *them* look bad: my impiety, and the impiety of the rest of secular Jewish society, tarnished them. Here were the people I wanted to understand. These were the Jews who would tell me something about my true self. And I couldn't stop the flow of slanderous thoughts.

I had brought along my copy of Maimonides that day, to use as a sort of prop, in the hopes that it would help me fit in. This, I admit, was a wildly stupid idea. What did I expect? That some Talmudic scholar would notice me reading it and be so overcome with fraternal emotion that he would invite me home, to chat about my Jewish past while his wife plied me with European sweets and introduced me to the family's comely daughters?

No one, of course, took any notice of me. I was a guy in a café, flipping through the pages of a book that, if any one of them had read it, was one they probably knew only in Hebrew. I finished up and hurried to my car.

Remnants of Monsey's agrarian past, now badly faded, could be seen from the road. Rolling hills and green trees and even a few fields still under cultivation abutted a blast zone of disposable architecture, clogged roads, and big-box retail. Superimposed onto these familiar postmodern juxtapositions was the Monsey shtetl, with its kosher butchers and bakers, knife sharpeners and locksmiths, religious schools and day cares, and its streets peopled with religious purists parading about in the native finery. I needed an illustrated dictionary to make sense of the clothes: the suits, frock coats, and caftans, in silk, satin, and cotton; flat hats, round hats, felt hats, fur hats, fedoras, homburgs, and head covers too obscure or irregular for my millinery knowledge; yarmulkes black, brown, and various; long skirts, longer skirts, wigs, and head wraps; beards and forelocks; stockings, breeches, fringes, shawls, and shoes.

At one intersection I noticed a young man thumbing a ride. He was a fleshy, big-boned boy, no more than twenty, with a sparse beard and *payis* in need of a good scrubbing. He was, of course, clad in black, in a bulky frock coat, white shirt, and black pants that he had tucked into his knee-high black hose. His hat was a kind of squat bowler with a wide brim and a silk ribbon knotted on the band. I slowed down and nudged closer to the roadside. I wasn't sure, really, if I intended to pick him up, but before I could make that decision he saw me, dropped his thumb, and turned away.

I sped on, past the Monsey Lingerie Shop, and Weingarten Shoe Repair, and the Sukkah Center of Monsey, until I reached Shopper's Haven, a retail complex with a large kosher grocery. I stopped here, thinking I might bring my son home a box of cookies. I parked outside and headed for the entrance, pausing to read the sign posted at the sliding glass doors: WELCOME TO THE SHOPPER'S HAVEN. SLEEVELESS CLOTHES, SHORTS, & BARE FEET: STRICTLY PROHIBITED.

Shopper's Haven housed about twenty stores spread out over its three floors. I puttered about in several seemingly redundant Judaica outlets; inspected the bottles at a kosher wine shop; and wandered into two bookstores, each stocked with an array of Hebrew prayer books, Torah-story coloring books, primary school texts with lessons on Moses and

other biblical figures, and a selection of "For Dummies" titles dedicated
to the rudiments of everything from computer programming to super-
foods (presumably kosher). At the food court downstairs, I bought a
knish and wolfed it down before entering the Toys 4 U, where I picked up
a plastic construction set and a jigsaw puzzle for my son.

I took home from the grocery a small Orthodox starter kit: there was
my package of King Star Foods halva-flavored wafers; a bag of Israeli-
made corn chips dusted with cinnamon sugar; a patent-pending "*Shabbos
and havdalah travel set*," complete with a tin of ground cloves, four tea
candles, a single braided candle, a box of matches, and an aluminum tray
to catch the wax drippings. I also grabbed a jar of Prima brand gourmet-
blend havdalah spice, a box of Kitchen Collection extra-heavy challah
bags, and a kosher beef sausage from the butcher department. I toyed
with the idea of bringing home a bottle of schmaltz (rendered chicken
fat) but decided against it. I left Monsey and returned home to Brooklyn
having reached the limits of my appetite for cultural tourism. I vowed not
to return until I felt more like a local.

III.

I decided to hazard a second attempt among the pious, this one closer to home. My travels in the Jewish Internet had led me to Shabbat .com, a website that connected secular Jews with an interest in observance (Ortho-curious?) with Orthodox families willing to open their homes to them. The website resembled a sort of down-market Jewish Facebook, with a similar profile setup, except the banner ads touted community-specific businesses like Britpro.com ("Traditional circumcision by Rabbi Boruch Mozes, certified mohel"). Other features included a "My Jewish Friends" mapping application, which afforded users a cartographic representation of their Hebraic interactions, and a *sidduch* referral service.

My plan was to find a family on Shabbat.com willing to invite me to a Friday night meal, and then proceed back to Rockland County with greater confidence. First, though, I had to create a profile. I uploaded a photo, entered my location and profession, and wrote a short bio that described me as "a newly observant Jewish man" seeking to "live a more fully Jewish life."

This was true in a technical—or perhaps Talmudic—sense. Most Orthodox would not consider me *ba'al teshuvah*, the Hebrew term for newly observant Jews,[1] but I would argue otherwise, because I had in fact taken steps toward a level of observance that was new to me. I had, for

---

1. There is a literal translation of the term that I prefer: "Master of Return."

example, occasionally followed the guidelines detailed in Reboot's Sabbath Manifesto. The Manifesto's exhortations to "Avoid technology," "Get outside," "Drink wine," and so forth, happened to coincide with what I tend already to enjoy doing on my weekends, but performing them consciously as Jewish was new and, therefore, arguably, observant.

My profile posted on a Thursday, and by the following morning I had an invitation to share the Sabbath with Yaakov and Feige Goldstein in the Kensington neighborhood of Brooklyn. According to their profile, the Goldsteins were a "very lively" bunch, their home often filled with Sabbath guests, "Whom we enjoy having very much. Please join us! We would love to meet you!" They seemed a kindly pair, judging from their photo, in which they smiled vaguely for the camera in the way of people unaccustomed to being photographed. They were about the same age as my parents, and I found myself imagining my folks in their roles: my dad, coaxed out of his clean-shaven, business-casual Dockers and golf shirts and into a boxy black suit, Borsalino fedora, and tie, his face masked by an unruly gray beard. My mother, her eyes cast demurely downward, in a shapeless blue dress, her head shaved, and wearing a red wig, flummoxed my imagination.

Friday afternoon arrived with me in my bedroom, shaved and showered, and unsure what to wear. Were my black slacks and white shirt a form of respect—*look, I'm dressing just like you!*—or the same kind of silliness as toting my Maimonides to Monsey? I decided that I was being respectful, if for no other reason than that I was unwilling to iron anything else. I spent a full twenty minutes rummaging about in my closet looking for my only yarmulke, a royal blue number salvaged from my cousin Douglas's bar mitzvah seven years earlier. I headed out once I found it, armed with a bouquet of cheap flowers and a bottle of kosher wine.

The Goldsteins lived in an ethnic micro-enclave in Brooklyn populated by *Yeshivishe* Jews. Yeshivism is a form of ultra-Orthodox or "Haredi" Judaism, one whose adherents organize their communities around a yeshiva—an Orthodox Jewish school or seminary. "Haredi" is Hebrew for "The Trembling Ones." "Haredi," along with "ultra-Orthodox," serves as a catchall term for a wide spectrum of strict Orthodox observance, dress, and communal organization. Hasidic ultra-Orthodoxy, for example, differs from Yeshivism in that Hasidic communities revolve around the "court" of a hereditary rebbe rather than a school. The Yeshivist orbit here extended only a few square blocks, and was anchored at its center by Yeshiva Torah Vodaath. A few blocks in any direction, and the Orthodox Jews largely disappeared, replaced by Muslims of every ethnicity and level of piety; émigré Russians and Ukrainians; West Indians, Indians, Pakistanis, and African Americans; and, increasingly, rent and real estate refugees from Manhattan and the pricier sections of Brooklyn, not a few of them Jews of the sort found at Sukkah City and Heebonism. Interaction between groups is minimal.

The Goldsteins' three-story apartment building was flanked on both sides by single-family homes and low-slung tenements, all battered and in disrepair. The sidewalks on their street were cracked, and large ruts marred the asphalt roadway. Weeds choked the few small front yards, and when the wind picked up, refuse whipped down the block—runoff from the overburdened municipal trash cans on the corners.

Yeshivishe communities tend to be poor. The men, devoted to intensive Torah and Talmud study, often don't work, or they work part-time. Theirs is a unique penury, one born not of incapacity but from a specific set of values: the intellectual contemplation of God and His works leaves little time or allowances for the pursuit of money. Their Judaism assumes and requires poverty.

I rang the bell for the Goldsteins' apartment, and after a moment someone buzzed me in. As I entered I noticed a keypad above the standard key lock to the building. The symbols on the keypad were in He-brew. I had done some reading on the Orthodox Sabbath before coming to the Goldsteins' house. I didn't want to embarrass myself by violating the rules, and so I knew about the keypad: the residents use it during the Sabbath, when observant Jews must avoid all forms of work, including carrying their keys.

Yaakov Goldstein was waiting for me at the door to his apartment (they had a keypad entry, too, along with a mezuzah) in black pants and a white undershirt, and he was holding a dish towel. He offered me a shy and formal hello—"Hello and welcome, Mr. Ross"—and ushered me in-side. Like the street, the apartment was modest and untidy, a railroad with a cramped living and dining room to one side, and a kitchen to the other. Hadassah, the Goldsteins' teenaged daughter, was in the kitchen, mopping the floor. She was a slender young girl with dark hair and olive skin, her brown eyes set close together; she, too, greeted me as "Mr. Ross." The clutter appeared to be of appropriately Jewish provenance: Bibles and Hebrew textbooks; delivery menus from local kosher restaurants; posters and paintings of Jerusalem and the Negev; framed photos of the other Goldstein children; and a collection of silver Judaica—a menorah, Sab-bath wine cups, and a candelabra—kept at a high shine.

I found Mrs. Goldstein twitchy and self-conscious, her bird-like movements accentuated by the off-kilter placement of her wig. Her eyes darted quickly toward me as we said hello. She seemed friendly enough, smiling anxiously and asking if I had any trouble finding the apartment. She was wearing a long denim skirt and a black blouse, and she had a thick packet of identification and business cards dangling from a lanyard roped around her neck.

"So, I don't know your plans," Yaakov said, wiping his hands with the dish towel, "But I need to wash up before *Shabbos*, and then I'm going to shul. You're welcome to come back, if you like"—this seemed what he wanted me to do, but I didn't have anywhere to go—"or you can come with me."

"I'm happy to do whatever it is you normally do," I said.

Yaakov shrugged, motioned me toward the living room couch, and retreated to his bedroom for a shower. Mrs. Goldstein busied herself with the final Sabbath preparations. She shut down the family computer, but only after entering the details of her day's meals into a Weight Watchers spreadsheet. She set the timers on the light switches to turn off at some point that night, and then on again in the morning, without her having to touch them. She covered the white lace tablecloth on the dining table with a clear plastic sheet, ran a damp cloth over the dustier recesses of the room, and then pointed to the stack of books on the couch that I had been flipping through.

"I took out some books in case you wanted to read while I clean up," Mrs. Goldstein said. There were mostly guides for the newly observant that I suppose the family offered to the seculars who came by each week, along with a copy of *All for the Boss*, a biography of the American "Torah pioneer" Rabbi Yaakov Yosef Herman, whose "age-old religion," the introduction stated, "taught him that the world has one Boss, the Almighty who created it. For the sake of that Boss's Torah and mitzvos he was ready to act. And act he did." (I looked up the book later.)

Mrs. Goldstein kept apologizing for the mess: "We're rat-packers." Once she was satisfied with her efforts, she took a chair at the table next to me and asked how I felt about public speaking.

"Public speaking?"

"Yes. Delivering speeches and things like that."

Mrs. Goldstein, it seemed, had a strong interest in self-improvement. Along with the dieting—she was sipping at a diet kosher cola as we spoke—she took occasional classes at a nearby junior college, did a little volunteer work, and, to overcome her innate shyness, had joined Toastmasters International, an oratory club for glossophobes. I told her that I was generally comfortable with strangers, but Mrs. Goldstein was undeterred; she had me commit the Toastmasters Web address to memory.

Yaakov returned a few moments later with his hair and beard still damp. Mrs. Goldstein helped him put on his suit coat, and then she checked the clock—Sabbath commenced at 5:49 P.M. that week: we had only a few minutes to go. She rushed around the room until she found a coffee can with an Israeli flag wrapped around it like a label. She explained that it was traditional to make a donation on behalf of a Jewish charity before the onset of Sabbath; perhaps I would like to contribute. I plunked a few coins into the can, emptying my pockets, which was good, as once the Sabbath started it was forbidden to carry, and to use, money. Then Hadassah and Mrs. Goldstein lit the Sabbath candles, extended their hands over the flames, and with their eyes closed, mouthed a few short prayers. By the time they opened their eyes the Sabbath had begun. Yaakov and I set out for shul.

Yaakov, as it turned out, worked as a scribe, mostly preparing *Getts*, or Jewish divorce decrees. He had been raised in East New York and Canarsie, two working-class Brooklyn neighborhoods that weren't particularly Jewish. Mrs. Goldstein grew up in Astoria, Queens. Both of them, he said, had been raised in nonobservant households; they had only "gotten serious" about Judaism as young adults. Yaakov and Feige were *ba'al teshuvah*.

The shul was located in the school cafeteria at the yeshiva. The venetian blinds had been drawn closed, and harsh fluorescent lighting illuminated the space. Hebrew prayer books and Bibles were strewn about the long metal lunch tables, some of which had been covered in cloth, others not. A makeshift altar stood at the front of the room—a book bench, I think—with a finely crafted Torah scroll placed atop it. A wizened old man, thin to the point of emaciation, with his head and shoulders wrapped carefully in a prayer shawl, davened in a creaky twang, leaning

on the altar for support. Accompanying him was the cacophonous hub-
bub of the assembly, men and boys praying at different speeds and volumes. Their bodies moved with each prostration to God, some swaying
with boredom, others jerking in fervent release. Every few moments the
inchoate streams of Hebrew murmuring would overlap and the men
would bark "*Amein*" at the same time. I couldn't make sense of the pace
or the order of the prayers. Different men seemed to be leading at different times. For long stretches some would say nothing and stare off into
space or make a half-hearted attempt to discipline one of the squirmier
boys. Then they would jump up unexpectedly, swaying and gesticulating
at some signal I couldn't discern.

Yaakov and I sat at an empty table in the back corner of the cafeteria.
An older man in a wrinkled gray suit and black yarmulke pressed a Hebrew prayer book into my hands and mutely indicated the proper page.
Yaakov began to pray, rather sedately in comparison to some others; one
young man, alone at a table next to us, worked through his prayers with
an almost lustful vehemence, swaying sensuously and occasionally buck-
ing his hips in a most un-penitential way.

This was not a service as I understood it: no sermon, singing, or break
in the prayers. It lasted a little over an hour, during which time the exoti-
cism of the surroundings eventually faded. Unable to follow what was
going on, I grew bored, and then sleepy, and I had to fight to stay awake.
The room was stifling, and I removed the thin jacket I had worn that night
and placed it beside me on the cafeteria bench. This, for some reason, drew
a few looks. Until this point no one had paid any attention to me.

The prayers ended and everyone stood and shook hands with the men
next to him, offering each one a polite "Good *Shabbos*." Yaakov signaled to me
that it was time to go, and I grabbed my jacket and trailed him out of the
door, again drawing a few looks. Outside, Yaakov asked me what I thought.
I told him that I had done some reading on the Sabbath before coming to

his home, so I felt I had an idea of what to expect. I pointed to my pockets, which were empty, as an example. "See? No keys, no wallet, no mobile phone. I left it all at home. Not supposed to carry on the Sabbath, right?" But I hadn't read anything that described the chaos and shapelessness of the prayer service. Yaakov explained that Orthodox men are obligated to say a set number of prayers throughout the course of the day, plus a few extra for the Sabbath. Many had completed a portion of their prayers earlier in the day; others had had to start from the beginning. This accounted for the lack of structure. Then he smiled at me and pointed to my coat.

"I thought about saying something, but I didn't want you to feel bad," he said. It took a moment to realize what he meant. My coat: I was carrying it. This was why the men kept looking at me. The Orthodox understanding of Sabbath rest, like the concepts governing sukkah construction, is complex. Determining with accuracy the theological definitions of labor requires a nuanced grasp of Torah and Talmud and years of indoctrination with how these concepts apply in real-world settings. I had neither. But I knew that all forms of carrying were forbidden: whether keys, wallet, mobile phone, or jacket. Carrying is among the most fundamental, and in some ways, simplest, Sabbath notions.

It's hard to be the ignorant one among a group of highly informed people. Everyone in that crowded cafeteria, on this uncared-for side street, in this proscribed world, knew things I didn't: how to act, how to dress, what to eat, what was appropriate, and what wasn't. I felt resentful toward the exclusion. This is, I suppose, a normal reaction to being an outsider among a conformist group. But part of what I felt was envy. It was a Friday evening, like every Friday evening here, and the entire assembly in that cafeteria could enjoy the certitude of knowing where they would be, how each moment would transpire, and the intention of their every act. Although my nights were filled with the diversions of family, friends, and even solitude, often enough I felt the emptiness of secular life, the insufficiency of materialistic routines, the failure to advance a reason for my presence. These people knew their Boss and so they never had to ask why or what for.

I enjoyed the dinner Hadassah prepared for us at the Goldsteins', although the food came as close to inedible as one may venture to eat without risking bodily harm. A potential excuse for this culinary failure leads again to the subject of work and what it means in the Jewish sense. At its most basic, the Sabbath obliges observant Jews to avoid "creative" work; creative here referring not to art or aesthetics but to labor that yields something new at its conclusion. For the Sabbath period—sunset Friday to sunset Saturday—cleaning, writing, pushing a stroller, carrying a pot, tearing paper (including paper towels and toilet paper), conducting business transactions, and spending money, among many other activities, are forbidden. The Talmud identifies thirty-nine broad categories of proscribed Sabbath labor. Cooking violates two: kindling and extinguishing a fire. Both are creative, by Jewish definitions: you must turn on the oven to roast the brisket; you must then switch it off once the meat has been overcooked.

Kindling is interesting because it transgresses not only a discrete category, but also veers into prohibitions against acts of creative *transformation*: the application of heat to raw food alters its basic substance, thereby creating a new, if not always appetizing, item. But while understanding the point at which a fire has been lit is straightforward, definitions of "cooked" are less so. At which point has food been transformed by heat? From the moment the flame licks the pot? When the steak reaches medium-rare? Say Hadassah had put a nice lean brisket on at 4 P.M. that afternoon. We ate at approximately 8 P.M. This means the meat spent four hours soaking in a hot pool of canned beef broth before the Sabbath began. Had the brisket been fully transformed by sunset? That is, was it completely cooked before the cessation of labor? Strangely, it didn't have to be. Most observant Jews allow food to be half-cooked prior to the start of the Sabbath. What's more, once the fire is lit, it can remain on through-out the Sabbath. Many Orthodox Jews will, on Friday afternoon, put on a roast in a crockpot and let it bubble away until the Saturday afternoon meal. The fire has not been kindled or extinguished during the period of rest; so long as the food is half-done prior to sunset Friday, it is kosher.

The evening passed easily, despite the food. The Goldsteins fielded my questions about Sabbath practice, reviewing some of the details of cooking, ritual hand-washing, the ban on lights (creation of electricity; kindling of fire; extinguishing of fire), and the order of prayers. They traded amusing tales of Hadassah's Birthright trip, which had several awkward themes: secular Jewish girls are wicked and sinful; Jerusalem is the repository of our hopes and dreams; riding a camel in a Bedouin vil-lage is great fun even if Bedouins hate Jews and are not really Israeli citi-zens in any meaningful way. Mrs. Goldstein encouraged me to tell them something about my background, and I recounted the story of my child-hood in Mississippi. Commendably, no one seemed scandalized.

The only difficulty came when I made ready to leave. The Goldsteins had assumed that I would be staying with them through the Sabbath. A place had been made for me, nestled in among the rest of the family. They seemed a little insulted that I wanted to go. Besides, how would I get home without violating the Sabbath? No subway, no car, too far to walk.

I should have stayed. I needed a way in and here it was, presented ready-made. But I couldn't. My mind kept returning to the coat, the cook-ing, the keys, the light switches, and how much I would need to learn before I could rest easy during the Orthodox Sabbath. I had a disquieting thought. Here, in this place, I had my first glimpse of an answer to my original ques-tion: I was *not* a Jew. Not by these standards, not now, and perhaps not ever. I thanked them, said something about enjoying long walks—my apartment was more than four miles away—and left, sneaking around the corner to my car. I drove home, blasting the radio and checking my voicemail.

IV.

I was bar mitzvahed a few months later on a Saturday morning, in Monsey, at the home of Benzion Klatzko, Orthodox rabbi, Jewish outreach professional, and founder of Shabbat.com. I had spent the night at Klatzko's house, a guest at one of his weekly *Shabbatons*.[1] I woke early and stumbled to the bathroom, a bit bleary from the previous evening's *Shabbos* entertainments. These had extended into the far reaches of the night, and had included a sumptuous multicourse meal—three kinds of kugel, and unlike Hadassah's, none of them gray—a lengthy bout of Talmudic disputation, and a confusing religious quiz game loosely based on *Family Feud*. There had even been cocktails, prepared, oddly enough, by the younger of Klatzko's eleven children.

Without thinking, I reached for the light when I went into the bathroom and, meeting some sort of resistance, I fumbled with the switch until I felt it give and the lights turned *off*. Confused, I turned to look at what I had done: The light had been turned on and the switch covered with masking tape, providing light in the bathroom during the Sabbath, when the switch couldn't—or in my case, shouldn't—be used. Not only had I just violated the Sabbath, but I had also consigned the good Jews

---

1. *Shabbaton* is the Hebrew word for "sabbatical," though it also refers to a Jewish youth retreat, with the purpose of reflecting closely on the values of the Sabbath. In practice, it tends to be a sleepover for Jews.

in Klatzko's house to peeing in the dark, windowless bathroom until sunset.

I relieved myself, brushed my teeth, washed up a little, and then reached down and tore free a few sheets of toilet paper to blow my nose, thus committing another Sabbath violation. Number twenty-four of the thirty-nine proscribed acts: No tearing. This was a great frustration for me. I had decided that while among the Orthodox I would do my best to keep their rules. It was one thing to violate an obscure or complex prohibition that I didn't understand—there were rules on how far one might walk over the course of a day, what circumstances one might use a leash for one's dog, and more. But using the lights and tearing sheets of paper I knew were forbidden. Worse yet, a full box of tissues, perfectly suited to my nasal needs, had been placed atop the toilet, but I tore a piece of toilet paper instead.

How was I going to tread in the path of anyone's devotion if I couldn't use the bathroom without sinning? I admit that I panicked a little, and I gave some thought to sneaking out of the house, jumping in my car, and driving home to Brooklyn. After a moment, though, I reconsidered, and resolved to be more mindful of my actions. Then I headed out of the bathroom and without thinking reached up and turned the lights on again. I hurried away to the kitchen, wolfed down a couple of chocolate rugelach and a cup of instant coffee (brewing: creative act), and tried not to do anything sinful.

Rabbi Klatzko joined me in the kitchen soon after, looking rested and chipper. He was a short and portly man in his early forties, who held himself with the validated self-confidence of someone with a large and well-appointed home, a brood of mannerly children, and the resources to fund the whole operation.

Klatzko had hosted about forty people at his home for this Sabbath, a modest number, he assured me, by the standards of his typical "blowout

Shabbosim." Most of the guests were not long out of college, and ranged in background from an Orthodox born-and-raised graphic designer and yeshiva student from Far Rockaway to a *ba'al teshuvah* substitute teacher named Roy, who prayed as if he were freestyle rapping, wore a tweed fedora instead of a yarmulke, and had recently taken a non-Jewish and possibly mail-order Brazilian bride. The graphic designer and I chatted about my book project, and he told me to look him up if I needed help getting out the word. I interacted less with the young women who were there: single girls from observant families in Brooklyn and Monsey, on the make for a good match.

Klatzko grew up in Cleveland, the son of a surgeon from a secular family who had transitioned to Orthodox as an adult. Klatzko's wife, Shani, hailed from a prosperous *frum* (observant) household in Brooklyn. *Kiruv*, or Jewish outreach, came naturally to them. Shani's family was renowned for its generosity, their house filled each week with what Klatzko called "decorous vagabonds and schleppers," looking for a free Sabbath meal. People would simply walk in, help themselves to a bowl of soup or stew, take some donated clothing, and either stay for a spell or leave. Klatzko was proud of his wife's lineage. "Her family," he said, "displayed a level of kindness that is totally unheard of outside of legend." His family helped people in similar fashion, although, he admitted, not on the same scale; because his father was wealthy, they catered to a "higher class of schleppers and vagabonds."

Klatzko graduated from an Orthodox seminary in 1993 and was a pulpit rabbi in Perth Amboy, New Jersey, until the late 1990s, when he devoted himself full-time to outreach. He was inspired by the unexpected death of his younger brother, Gavriel, a rabbi living in South Africa who was noted for his ability to connect with *ba'al teshuvah*. ("He's the stuff of legend today.") Klatzko moved to California, where he began organizing outreach programs for college students through an organization called the Jewish Awareness Movement, or JAM. At the same time, Klatzko made an "impressive splash" in the movie industry, and earned the nickname "The Hollywood Rabbi." In 2005, he left California and moved to Monsey, to work as a national organizer for a private foundation funded by a reclusive and wealthy investor. Shabbat.com, Klatzko told me, was a hobby. "It's important to know what motivates me," he said, "because, you know, we have lost tremendous amounts of money on this so far."

"Sleep well?" he asked, and I assured him that I had, although it wasn't true.

I was perhaps the oldest of the *Shabbaton* guests, except for one *ba'al teshuvah* man in his sixties, whom I will call Ben. As elder statesmen we were given a small bedroom upstairs, instead of suffering with the young bulls in the finished basement the Klatzkos had converted into a dormitory. Ben had kept me awake the previous evening, chatting in our room, which was awkward, because it meant hearing in detail the narrative of his mastery of return, and what he considered to be the high prospects of my Judaic reclamation, with him dressed only in a dingy undershirt and baggy boxers.

Ben must have come to his observance at Woodstock, as his statements on the virtues of Orthodox living were delivered in bursts of Yiddish-inflected New Age jargon. He wanted to "rap" with me about Torah; *Shabbos*, he said, was "heavy stuff, man." This isn't as strange as it sounds. Orthodox Judaism, like the rest of American culture, underwent a transformation during the 1960s and 1970s. The American Orthodoxy of the first half of the twentieth century differs greatly from that of today. It was, both in terms of practice and rabbinical leadership, an ethnic holdover from Europe and, to a significant extent, devoid of spiritual content. Charles Liebman, the political scientist and social critic, in his 1965 essay "Orthodoxy in American Jewish Life," characterized many Orthodox as "residual," "marginal," and "non-observant." They were, he wrote, a "dying generation," who maintained their practice "more out of cultural and social inertia than out of religious choice." A by-product of this laxity—many were observant only in public; they might not keep kosher at home, for example—was the assumption that Orthodoxy might disappear. And in a way, it did. The children and grandchildren of the residual-marginal Orthodox abandoned observance in great numbers and were subsumed into other denominations, other religions, or opted for secular lives. Certainly not all Orthodox were of this kind: the proliferation of religious day schools, which began in the 1940s and helped produce a new generation of religious Jews, attests to that. But until the upheavals of the 1960s and 1970s, the dominant belief, as stated by Yaakov Israel in "Hasidism in the Age of Aquarius," a 2003 article published in *Religion and American Culture*, was that "The tide ran only in one direction—away from tradition."

A combination of cultural forces converged on Orthodoxy during the sixties. First, the children of the Jews who had immigrated to this country in the earlier parts of the century felt, far more so than their parents, fully American. The impulse to assimilate and forgo the traditional forms of worship, very much a factor in the secularization of their parents, weakened. This process, along with the decade's renaissance of spiritualism, fostered an environment in which, as Ariel writes, nonobservant Jews became open "to join[ing] a way of life that their grandparents had left behind."

This new wave of *ba'al teshuvah* brought their own ideas and impulses to the tradition, modernizing parts of Orthodox practice and altering their congregations to suit their needs. There was the *havurah* movement, with its independent, non-rabbinical, non-institutional Orthodoxy; the House of Love and Prayer, in San Francisco, and its "Hasidic hippies"; the adoption of vegetarian and macrobiotic cuisine by groups of Orthodox;

the updating of liturgical music, particularly by Rabbi Shlomo Carlebach;[1] and in general, a renewed focus, both from conventional ultra-Orthodox and their more progressive peers, on spirituality and strict adherence to the laws. The outreach infrastructure that Klatzko migrated to after his brother's death was created in this period. Ariel describes how Orthodox Jews built an extensive network of outreach, one that, in an echo of the Bronfman-funded study of progressive outreach groups, "reflect both the growing concern over Jewish survival and the trust that Orthodox Judaism can market itself successfully and capture the hearts of young persons."

Klatzko did a quick head count once most of the male guests had emerged from the basement and helped themselves to breakfast. "Looks like we have a minyan. Let's get started."

We hurried into the dining room for the davening. The women remained in the kitchen and finished breakfast, watching, a little sourly, or so it seemed to me, as the men met their religious obligations.

Dining *hall* would be a more apt description of this room. It could easily have accommodated 100 Jewish souls at its long table. Klatzko told me he had done a major renovation a few years earlier, after a fire had gutted most of the house. The result, at least in the dining room, was a cross between a country club restaurant, corporate conference room, and

---

1. Carlebach, "the father of Jewish soul music," was an early Orthodox outreach rabbi. Originally a Lubavitcher Hasid, Carlebach broke with the sect's teachings over gender issues. He allowed men and women to pray together without a partition, and was famous for his willingness not only to touch women, but to hug them—a controversial stance among the Orthodox, where even inter-gender hand-shaking is a scandal. Complicating matters is a 1998 article in *Lilith,* a Jewish feminist magazine, entitled "A Paradoxical Legacy: Rabbi Shlomo Carlebach's Shadow Side." Published four years after his death, the article levied allegations of sexual harassment and abuse by Carlebach, including this from a woman who claimed he molested her as a teenager: "He rubbed his hands up my body and under my clothes. . . . I presume he had an orgasm. He called me *mammele.*"

an art gallery. Klatzko owned an expansive collection of Jewish paintings, and he had covered the walls with oil works of shtetl ragamuffins, biblical scenes, Zionist iconography, every conceivable iteration of Judaic senti-mental art, all tastefully illuminated. Contributing to the cultural ambi-ance were the upbeat religious tunes—including some from Carlebach, Klatzko told me—piped into the room from hidden speakers.

The praying began. One of the young men, an almost comically pious Orthodox kid from Monsey who told me to "rock on" with my faith so that I could "take it to another level," handed me a prayer book with En-glish translations. This was a nice gesture but as the davening was entirely in Hebrew, not particularly useful. As in Kensington, Klatzko and the boys would mumble in rapid-fire Hebrew for a while, and then, seemingly without warning, shout "Amein" in unison. Occasionally, everyone would click their feet tight together and shuffle a few steps forward, and then retreat backward. Sometimes we were seated. Then we would get up. Mo-ments later we would sit back down again. At one point everyone held his hand in front of his face as he prayed, shielding himself from what, I did not know.

I found myself longing for the formality of the Christian church. I wanted something familiar: a religious figure at the front of the room, leading us through prayer, delivering a hectoring sermon on morality, and, perhaps, in conclusion, passing a hat. Here, though, was a mystery, a spir-itual blank.

Judaism, and particularly Orthodox Judaism, has few centralized structures: no pope, no all-encompassing hierarchy, no institutional flow-charts. Rabbis have great authority, both within their communities and beyond, but there is no "Jewish church." In fact, even the word "denomina-tion" is somewhat inaccurate, as the distinctions between the forms of the religion aren't rigidly codified: one man's Orthodoxy is another's Conser-vatism, and vice versa.

Orthodox Jews have obligations to meet: to keep kosher, to pray, to observe the Sabbath and religious holidays, and so forth. But each Jew is allowed, and expected, to ascertain in what ways and to what extent he or she will accede to these requirements. Rabbis can and do offer opinions and rulings, but they do not issue binding policy in the way that their Christian counterparts do.

An example would be "Sabbath elevators." A Sabbath elevator is a conventional elevator, but one that has been set to stop automatically at each floor during the Sabbath. (Pressing the elevator buttons initiates—*creates*—a jolt of electricity powering the elevator, and is, therefore, a Sabbath violation.) I have seen them in practically every large U.S. hospital that serves a Jewish population. In 2009, however, a rabbi and respected Talmudic scholar named Yosef Shalom Elyashiv issued a decree publicly denouncing Sabbath elevators. The rebbe reasoned that even though no buttons were pushed in these elevators—and thus, no Jew directly caused the elevator to create electricity—the extra weight of the passenger required an upsurge in power to ascend and descend, thus violating the Sabbath. Elyashiv is considered a *posek ha-dor*, or "generation's decider," of religious questions. Yet the Sabbath elevators still run, and each Jew may accept or reject the *posek*'s wisdom. Roman Catholicism does not work this way.

Klatzko interrupted my reverie with a question.

"You ever have a bar mitzvah?" I admitted that I hadn't. "You want one?"

Klatzko brought me to the front of the room and had me help unfurl a Torah scroll, placing it on a reader's table. He intoned a few prayers in Hebrew and instructed me to repeat them phonetically. The "rock on" kid from Monsey recited several others on my behalf. Ben helped me don a prayer shawl.

Klatzko wanted to know if I had a Hebrew name. When I said I didn't, he asked if, perhaps, I had one I liked. I told him that I had found much inspiration of late in my reading of Maimonides. He seemed pleased.

"Moshe it is," he said. "What's your father's Hebrew name?"

My father had been bar mitzvahed but I didn't know his Hebrew name. Klatzko assured me that this, too, was no problem. I would henceforth be Moshe ben-Avraham, or Moses, Son of Abraham, an accurate enough moniker, as, ultimately, all Jews are considered sons of the Patriarch. Klatzko blessed me, in Hebrew, using my new name, and then with some ceremony, we rolled up the Torah and stowed it away in a cabinet opposite the liquor caddy.

Klatzko smiled at me. Ben made a great show of shaking my hand, the women tittered approvingly from the kitchen, and the stronger boys wrestled me into a chair and threw me high up into the air, yelling out my good fortune. The children joined us and had a high time pelting me with sucking candies, a symbolic stoning, Klatzko explained, to remind me of the punishments for those who contravene their responsibilities as a Jewish adult.

V.

I did not *have* a bar mitzvah. Neither did Klatzko *do* my bar mitzvah, give me one, perform it, lead it, facilitate it, achieve it, or accomplish it. No spiritual transition transpired in that dining hall, at least not one involving me. I did not accede from one state—Jewish Child—to another—Jewish Man—and if I did, it had nothing to do with the prayers. I had *become* bar mitzvah, or an adult bound by the precepts and dictates of the Jewish religion, long ago, and quite without ritual, on February 4, 1986, the date of my thirteenth birthday.

A bar (or bat) mitzvah, as it is understood today, with prayer and pomp and a bitchin' party, is a fiction. At the onset of the fourteenth year of life a Jew is automatically adjudged competent, and expected to act accordingly. I have no recollection of the celebration held by my family when I turned thirteen. Yet it was then, and not that morning in Monsey, that I entered into my religious majority.

Klatzko, of course, knew this. What, then, was he up to? Did he think that this religious contrivance would inspire me to adopt an Orthodox life? Was he trying to "reach me," communicating in terms I would understand and not find intimidating? For someone like me, a bar mitzvah might prove a familiar and even comforting experience. Slaughtering a chicken on Yom Kippur and waving it about my head, would, in all likelihood, be less so.

Rabbi Sarna, the chaplain at NYU, knew Klatzko professionally, and we spoke about him, as an individual, and as an example of the rabbis and organizations who do his sort of work. Klatzko and his confreres, Sarna told me, are in the business of creating "pathways" for people to become Orthodox. Those pathways rely on outreach rabbis to engage with and encourage religiously curious young people, whether college students on their campuses or professionals in large cities. The engagement occurs mainly at social events, including lectures, movie series, and open *Shabbosim*. Once a connection has been forged, the rabbis urge the newly interested—not newly observant, as no pressure toward observance is brought to bear—to travel to Israel on an organized junket, such as Birthright, or with organizations whose programs are tailored to a more overtly Orthodox agenda. In Israel, arrangements are made to visit an Orthodox yeshiva, and the rabbis suggest an extended period of Torah and Talmud study. If the rabbis succeed this far, the chances of the subject embracing an Orthodox lifestyle are high.

"It's a pretty clear plan and strategy," Sarna said.

I should say that Rabbi Sarna, who is a member of the relatively speaking progressive Modern Orthodox strain of Orthodoxy, never suggested there was anything wrong with this model, although saying that a program of spiritual assistance has a "plan and strategy" implied some disapproval. From my perspective, though, it seemed no different in method or motive from those of Bronfman, Reboot, or any of the other, more progressive, outreach groups: ultimately, numbers matter.

I was reminded of Sarna's analysis some weeks later, when I attended another *Shabbaton*, this one in Manhattan, at an Orthodox synagogue on the Upper West Side. Avraham Cohen, an American rabbi who runs an Orthodox yeshiva in Jerusalem for pre-Orthodox young people, was hosting the event, through his organization, Talmudic Destinies.[1] I made my way to the synagogue more than an hour before sunset and Rabbi

---

1. Avraham Cohen and Talmudic Destinies are not real names. Cohen asked not to be identified because his outreach work would undermine his standing in the fully Orthodox community.

Avraham hadn't arrived yet. I wasn't the first, however; a handful of young
men had also come early. I introduced myself and was hospitably wel-
comed and then put to work: I helped set a table for about fifty, laying out
paper tablecloths, plastic plates, and plastic wine, water, and shot glasses.
I went into the kitchen and tinkered with the pilot lights on the two commercial ovens until one of the boys produced a lighter and started the
flames. Hotel pans filled with brisket, salmon, and kugel went in the
ovens to warm. Jars of humus, tapenade, Israeli salad, salsa, and other
dips were transferred onto platters and distributed along the length of the
table, along with loaves of knotted challah. Bags of *hamintaschen* (jelly-
filled cookies) and other sweets were held in reserve in the kitchen.

A small room adjacent to the dining hall would be used for prayer.
We opened folding chairs and set them in rows, distributed prayer books,
and then used a card table to divide the seating into two sections, one
each for men and women: no Carlebachian mixing here.

No one said much to me as we worked, but they were friendly
enough. They had the look of former fraternity boys working at their first
post-collegiate jobs: confident, well groomed, slick suited, indifferent.
Most knew each other from a trip to Israel that included a stint at Rabbi
Avraham's yeshiva. One kid, a redhead in the first flower of a desk jockey's
potbelly, worked as a stockbroker. He was new to the job and the city, and
insisted that his "junior two" apartment was located in "South Harlem."
He chatted with another boy who had interned at the same brokerage.
They swapped stories about cold-calling potential clients and pretending
to be the broker they worked under.

"They had *no* idea!" said the redhead.

I talked with a college student from Manhattan's Yeshiva University,
a slight, pale kid with a nervous demeanor, who was studying accounting
along with his religious subjects. He had recently become engaged to a
proper young girl, a match arranged for him by his family. He didn't say

much about his fiancée, but he did have the satisfied air of an introvert whose social standing had been improved by his betrothal.

The conversation stopped when Rabbi Avraham arrived. He was a towering man, well over six feet tall, and dressed in a Hasidic black frock coat, fur hat, and black stockings. He had a red face, thick and vividly red lips, a bushy triangle of brown beard grown to his chest, shining black eyes, and a restless, wheezing energy: a hybrid of Zero Mostel and Dom DeLuise. The boys rushed to him, insisting on taking his packages, offering their deferential greetings. He hailed each one, made eye contact, and crushed a few in a sweaty embrace. I introduced myself, reminding him of our mutual friend who had asked him to invite me to the *Shabbaton*. (This was another outreach rabbi who also refused to be identified in the book.) He stared at me in a way that a less cynical person might describe as "looking into my soul." I found it intensely uncomfortable, even more so when he burst into a beaming red smile that creased the many folds of his round and inflamed face. He grasped one of my arms in his giant hands, kneading my biceps like dough in a pasta machine.

"Mr. Ross, Mr. Ross, Mr. Ross," he said, his gravelly voice redolent of Yiddish and Hebrew—*Mr. Rawus, Mr. Rawus, Mr. Rawus.* "Am I happy to see you!" he shouted. "Don't worry, don't worry, we'll find a time for a schmooze, you and me."

I apologized for not having met him sooner. Our mutual acquaintance had tried to put us together before, but I had fallen sick at the last moment and missed the appointment.

"I'm sorry you didn't make it," Rabbi Avraham said. "But did I pressure? I never pressure! No pressure!"

He turned away and began issuing orders, telling the boys where to stow the provisions he had brought with him: an ample supply of beer, bottles of bourbon and vodka, a handle of scotch, and a selection of sweet and dry kosher wines, soda, juice, and seltzer, and several bundles of bodega floral arrangements. He handed me the flowers and a box of small plastic vases, with instructions to cut the stems and "make them nice" on the table for the female guests, also alumni from his yeshiva, who had begun to trickle in. Then he rushed away to ensure that everything was completed before sunset.

Rabbi Avraham led the davening in a full-throated Hebrew bellow that turned his face such a deep purple that I feared he might collapse. The singing, too, was of an uplifting and dynamic cast, rhythmically complex, and delivered at concert-hall volumes. I watched my friend the accountant as he prayed and sang with his eyes clamped closed, drumming away on his prayer book, humming, and even doing a passable version of a beat box.

As the service progressed, ties came loose, sweat dripped, the rabbi danced and clasped his fists and howled his prayers. At one point he summoned the boys to him, and I was pulled along with the tide. We held hands in a tight circle, swaying and singing. Then everyone began to jump, leaping in an aggressive kind of spiritual ecstasy. No one rose any higher than the rabbi, though, who was like a giant beast of prayer.

Dinner began with the rabbi's blessing over the challah, and an invitation for those so inclined to ritually wash their hands at a sink in the corner of the dining hall. Then the drinking commenced, and we drained our plastic shot-sized cups and refilled them and drained them again. Each person clamored for the rabbi's attention, shouting, "l'chaim rabbi, l'chaim" and raising a glass in his honor. Rabbi Avraham returned each l'chaim with his own.

After the fish course, the rabbi called me up to sit with him at the head of the table. He quizzed me about my past and I told him about Mississippi and my mother and he smiled. He launched into a rambling disquisition about "vessels and lights," and how "light was individualized" and "dark was homogenized," and how there "are two ways of going about spirituality: amputation and transformation." I tried to ask questions, but he brushed them all aside and continued in a hoarse monotone whisper.

"We're going to begin discussing how we get close," he said, his breath hot and boozy in my ear. "Many organizations have agendas. God has no agenda. Each person has his own personal agenda. If you have an agenda, then you're *schtupping* it down their throats."

I told him I wasn't interested in having anything *schtupped* down my throat.

"You need to awaken something in them," he said, gesturing to the rest of the gathering. "Everyone knows what the outreach agenda is: to make people observant. But there is another level of spirituality: infinite and finite. Each person needs to find their specific light." He paused, drained a shot of vodka, and gestured to one of the girls for more. "We've all gone through different emotional experiences. It usually dictates how we live our lives. At the depths of our soul who are we really and how do we live?"

I was rushed from the rabbi's presence soon after by other young supplicants, each wanting sweet sagacities whispered in his or her ear. I sat back down next to the accountant, who by now was so deeply drunk that he could barely speak. His beat-box routine continued, though, and he sang, too, punctuating each remark from the rabbi to the table with a refrain of "*oho, oho, ya, ya, ya*," which I recognized from one of the davening songs, but which also appeared to be some kind of inside joke for the people who had studied at the yeshiva in Jerusalem.

Rabbi Avraham told a story about the Holy Drunk of Krakow. Perhaps I had had too much to drink myself, but I couldn't make sense of it, other than it had something to do with the biblical obligation toward drunkenness for the upcoming Purim holiday. The rabbi cited the wisdom of the Talmud: "A person is obligated to become inebriated on Purim until he doesn't know the difference between 'cursed is Haman' and 'blessed is Mordechai.'" He moved on to the story of Little Yidderle, poor boy, who was conscripted into the Russian army one winter's night. Much to the dismay of his mother, the Cossacks refused Little Yidderle the solace of his religious garments and books. "Never forget the privilege of being a *YEED*," the rabbi said, pronouncing the slur with great reverence. "What does a good *YEED* do?" Little Yidderle's *mammele* tracked her son through the frozen wasteland. When she found him, finally, miraculously, she smuggled him his phylacteries and a Torah in a bread sack.

Then we danced: a conga line of men, holding each other's hands and charging about the room. After a few turns the line degraded into a bounding and crashing mosh pit and the women departed for the prayer room and their own festival of movement. One of the young men horse-collared me from my chair and dragged me into the melee. Some of the more athletic boys performed an athletic stepping routine much like the one I'd seen in Union Square. One of them did a flying and kicking back-flip and accidentally knocked off my yarmulke. Stunned and winded I tried to creep back to my chair, but Rabbi Avraham grabbed me around the nape of my neck with one paw, and smiled. "Don't even fucking *think* about sneaking out of here," he said.

The dance ended with the room reduced to a rubble of empty bottles, greasy plates, torn flowers, and upturned chairs. The rabbi, exhausted, collapsed into his chair and began to speak about how we must all come to Judaism freely, openly, on our own terms, with "no judgments, wherever you are."

People began to depart when the alcohol ran out. I made my way to the rabbi and thanked him for having me. He was slumped over in his chair, his eyes shut and his chin resting in the cradle of one of his hands. My voice seemed to revive him, though, and he sprang from his chair, grabbed me by the elbow, and rushed me into a corner of the room.

"You see things quickly and deeply," he said. "That is your gift. But you have *no idea* what this all means. You are at the beginning, the very beginning of a journey. You have to open your heart to see where it will go."

He released me and I hurried away.

VI.

I didn't keep in touch with the Goldsteins. For a short while after we
met, Mrs. Goldstein sent me a series of emails through the Shabbat
.com site. She wanted to put me in touch with several rabbi friends of her
acquaintance who had volunteered to counsel me on the transition to
observance. She also recommended a number of websites that "captured
the essence" of her family's *Yeshivishe* Judaism. To foster my relations with
other Orthodox families, she inscribed a note in my Shabbat.com "guest-
book." I was, she wrote, "pleasant," "courteous," and a "pleasure to have." But
she never invited me to her home again, and I never asked to return.

It came as something of a surprise, then, to receive an envelope in the
mail a few months later inviting me to Hadassah's wedding. "With gratitude to Hashem Yisborach," read the invitation, "Rabbi and Mrs. Yaakov
Goldstein" and "Rabbi and Mrs. Moshe Levinson"—the parents of the
groom, presumably—would be "honoured" by my presence at the nup-
tials of Hadassah and Sholom.

The wedding took place at Kings Terrace, a four-story banquet hall
on a crowded commercial thoroughfare in Borough Park, Brooklyn. The
retail surrounding Kings Terrace included a 99¢ Store; a real estate business specializing in foreclosures; Pulseworks (laser hair removal special-
ists); Wig Showcase II; and Café Renaissance, a kosher restaurant with a
Hebrew-and-English sign stating that it serves pizza, pasta, and sushi.

Kabbalas Panim, the pre-wedding reception and veiling ceremony, was scheduled for six-thirty and would be for "mixed company." The wedding ceremony—chuppah, according to the invitation—as well as the dinner-and-dancing reception—*simchas chosonv v'kallah*—would be gender segregated.

The reception was held on the third floor, in a room the size of a high school gym. Three buffet stations had been arranged throughout, one offering fruit and salad served in bowls made from melons carved into the shapes of flowers and animals; another with chafing dishes of brisket and other braised meats; and a third with a curious mélange of mysterious brown meat, water chestnuts, bean sprouts, and zucchini—Cantonese Chicken, one of the waiters told me.

Behind the line of buffet tables was an elevated platform decorated with flowers and a white crepe backdrop. Hadassah and Mrs. Goldstein were seated there, receiving female guests, Hadassah in a white silk and lace dress and a train, and Mrs. Goldstein in a dark blue dress and a different wig from the one I had seen her in before. Yaakov stood nearby, chatting with a cluster of old men.

The guests were a relatively diverse group. Along with the black-hatted seniors—Yaakov's peers—were a good number of Hasidic men in frocks and fur hats. Both were outnumbered, though, by the *Yeshivishe* youths, students at various Brooklyn yeshivot, including, I learned, the one the groom attended. I also noticed a small number of "rebellious-looking" characters, dressed in ostensibly secular fashions—their sport coats and ties varied from the stringent black of the yeshiva boys—but who still wore *tallit* and yarmulkes, including one guy with his lips and septum pierced in two places. These were friends of the groom as well, less-religious kids from the Jewish suburb of Detroit where he was raised, who had traveled to New York for the wedding.

The women presented a more unified front: proper ladies in dark dresses, some velvet, others raw silk, with appropriate head coverings for those who needed them. There was also a fair number of children, the boys careening about in black polyester suits, and the girls in kiddie-beauty-pageant gowns.

I was curious to know if any other secular Shabbat.com guests had been invited. I scanned the room for men who might not be wearing a yarmulke, but there weren't any, although I was unsure about one older man. He looked to be in his early sixties, and had come dressed in jeans, a button-down, and a black straw porkpie. He looked familiar to me but I couldn't place him.

Suddenly there was a loud commotion at the entrance to the room. I turned to see a flying wing of *Yeshivishe* boys pushing their way into the room, bleating in an excited fashion that could have been praying, singing, or just shouting. In the vanguard an older man walked arm and arm with a tall, very skinny, nervous-looking boy, who was silently mumbling his prayers as he marched to the platform where Hadassah awaited: the groom and his father.

By the time the *Yeshivishe* mob reached the platform the rush of tension and anticipation radiating from Hadassah and her mother (as well as the mother of the groom who had her own seat on the platform) was palpable. Hadassah kept her head down and worked at her own litany of prayers.

The guests all crowded in behind the boys to get a look. A *Yeshivishe* videographer and his assistant with a boom mike forced their way to the front. I watched, on tiptoes, as Sholom, praying with increased fury and fear, scaled the platform, stood over Hadassah, and covered her in a full white veil. And by full I mean not the mesh, see-through kind, but a thick covering of white silk that left her completely blind. Then Sholom's parents approached Hadassah and uttered prayers over the cloaked form of the bride, followed by Yaakov and Mrs. Goldstein. When they finished, cries of joy and applause rose from the crowd. Hadassah was slowly led from the room, leaning heavily on her mother, and followed by a retinue of women, girls, and curious little boys.

A call went out to descend the stairs to the second floor and gather in the room where the ceremony would take place. I took a seat on the men's side next to a pudgy kid in his early twenties who, with great reluctance, admitted that his name was Gershon. Gershon had rightly sized me up as someone with a great number of questions that he had little interest in answering. I did learn from him that one particular Hasidic young man, a fat and sturdy boy who resembled a Jewish SpongeBob SquarePants, was the *shadchan*—matchmaker—responsible for linking bride and groom, via Shabbat.com.

Sholom entered the room ahead of Hadassah and took his seat under the chuppah, nervously awaiting his nuptial fate. Hadassah came moments later, still veiled and being led by her mother. The pace of Sholom's praying—ceaseless, it seemed—picked up at the sight of Hadassah. His body began to sway spastically like, well, a young man seeing the woman he would be religiously and socially permitted to have sex with that night.

When Hadassah reached him there were more prayers, and then, with assistance, she was led around the groom seven times.

"What's with that?" I whispered to Gershon.

"Kabbalah," he replied, tersely unwilling to look at me.

"Kabbalah?"

"For good luck."

"Really?"

"It's traditional."

Then came more prayers, and blessings, and then the bride and groom took a sip from a glass passed to them by Yaakov. (Me: "What are they drinking?" Gershon: "Wine.") Next came the reading of the *ketubah* (marriage contract) by a procession of elderly rabbis. The name of each rabbi would be announced and he would dodder or limp or stride, depending on his health, to the chuppah to read his part. The *Yeshivishe* boys rose in obeisance to whichever rebbe they favored.

"Who's this?" I asked Gershon, after perhaps the tenth old man hobbled his way forward.

"Rebbe."

"Yeah?"

"From Detroit."

"He have a name?"

"Shh."

I gave up and just watched and within minutes Sholom stood and smashed the cup with his foot and Hadassah pulled the veil up over her head and everyone began yelling like rednecks at a rodeo hoedown.

The reception room had been made ready for dinner during the ceremony. There were perhaps twenty tables arrayed on each side of a series of seven-foot-tall white cloth panels that served to partition the room, one side for men, the other for women. Perpendicular to the partition, half in men's territory and half in ladies', was a long table for the wedding party. Each table came stocked with carafes of seltzer and iced tea, platters of pickles and coleslaw, small loaves of challah, and bottles of sweet wine. Plenty of floor space remained for the dancing, and when I looked up to the balcony overhanging the reception hall I could see an Orthodox wedding musician setting up his synthesizer and microphone.

I found my name card on a table in the corner of the hall. A man about my age had already seated himself. He didn't strike me as particularly Orthodox-looking: a mop of reddish hair, no beard but a well-tended goatee, and wearing a purple yarmulke. He proved to be a cousin of Mrs. Goldstein, by marriage; he was a professional opera singer—a tenor—and he had never met the religious side of his wife's family. He had the look about him of a tourist kicking himself for having left his camera at the hotel. We sat next to each other in silence for a few minutes, chewing purposefully on our challah until the other guests arrived. There was one young man dressed in the traditional black and white, but whose sharp-edged line of beard seemed more reminiscent of Justin Timberlake than Maimonides. He was, I learned, a plumber and volunteer fireman from Monsey, and another of Mrs. Goldstein's distant cousins. Next to him was another cousin, another secular like the opera singer, from Queens who announced almost the instant that he sat down that he was vegan, adding, apparently as some sort of a joke, that he would only be willing to dance later in the evening if they "make sure no one gets chicken grease on me. All these Jews with their hands covered in chicken grease!"

Two Orthodox men joined us. Neither introduced himself. Every few minutes one of the men, the younger of the two, would solemnly blurt out the word "okay," as if he had decided something. Then he'd help himself to the sweet wine. The other man only spoke once, to tell a joke.

"How do you wine and dine a Jewish woman?" he asked. "She whines, you dine."

Last to arrive was the man in the porkpie. He removed his hat for a moment after sitting down, revealing a balding pate but no yarmulke. He told me he had grown up in Queens, too, but now lived in the Bay Area, working as an electrical engineer. He had three children and a wife he had left at home; he made a point of mentioning that his wife, and by extension his children, weren't Jewish. He asked me whether I was a friend of the bride's family or the groom's. I replied that I was more of an acquaintance of the bride's family.

"And you?" I asked.

"I'm Caroline's brother," he said.

"Caroline?"

"Yeah, Caroline."

He gestured with his thumb toward the wedding party's table. That's when it clicked. He had reminded me of Mrs. Goldstein. She was his sister. Feige Goldstein was Caroline.

I don't know why this shocked me. Mrs. Goldstein had told me about her secular upbringing the night we met. But I had assumed when she said this that she meant secular in the way that many present-day Orthodox do: that her family had been part of the marginal Orthodox, as defined by Charles Liebman. Yaakov, in fact, had come from such a household. His mother had kept kosher and observed the Sabbath, but his father had worked late on Fridays and listened to the radio on Saturday—and belonged to an Orthodox shul. Mrs. Goldstein—Caroline—had grown up in a conventional Jewish-American secular household, in Queens, not far from where my mother was raised.

Then the dancing began, and as at the Talmudic Destinies *Shabbaton*, I was swept into the vortex of sweaty Orthodox men holding hands, this time circling the groom, who had abandoned himself utterly to the moment. He danced within our circle and was a blur of moving body parts. His father had joined him and they moved together with their arms linked, spinning in a wild circle, kicking their legs in the air, stomping the floor. Then the circle broke and the boys grabbed Sholom and heaved him into a chair and paraded him around the room. There was a mad energy afoot, and new circles formed and collapsed, and different men—fat, elderly, ungainly—had their turn in the center, each one competing for the most stunning display of exuberance and bravado. One barrel-chested hulk emerged from the throng, ripped off his black suit coat, and began to shake with a violent and muscular rhythm. Overcome with a raging joy, he rushed to the partition, hoisted aloft one of the panels, which must have weighed close to fifty pounds, and pranced around the room with it carefully balanced on his chin.

I decided to take the opportunity of the fractured partition to sneak a look at the women's side. They were dancing, too, more slowly, and with none of the frenzied athleticism of the men. That said, two women had dressed themselves up as clowns: rainbow wigs and red-button noses and pancake makeup; another had transformed into an American Indian, with a plastic headdress and moccasin boots. The men began to organize themselves to replace the panel, mending the wall just as the native woman raised her warrior's axe and let loose with a battle cry. Then the partition was complete and I couldn't see any more.

I had heard of wedding shtick—the toys, costumes, games, and sundry props employed at Orthodox weddings as a pleasant, if juvenile, part of the celebration. There can be balloons and bouncing balls and glow sticks and Jews rushing around on rollerblades, blowing whistles, banging tambourines, and waving sparklers. I have passed an hour or two on the Internet watching Orthodox wedding-goers perform Irish Riverdance shtick; men-line-dancing-to-disco shtick; fire juggling shtick; folk singing shtick; male stripper routine shtick (fully dressed)—a shtick for every taste, some professional, others homespun, all, to my eyes, surreal. But nothing compared to seeing it in person.

I noticed Mrs. Goldstein's brother standing beside me, staring, as I was, at the partition. He looked shell-shocked. The *Yeshivishe* boys had been ducking out periodically and returning with bottles of Jameson and Jim Beam; one kid, noticing me eyeing his bottle, asked me if I wanted "a little schnapps, maybe?" Mrs. Goldstein's brother turned to the wedding table and I turned with him. He watched his sister in the distance for a while and didn't say anything. She must have noticed because she looked at him and smiled and waved briefly. He didn't return the gesture and her smile faded. She adjusted her wig and went back to her guests.

I left shortly after the first break in the dancing. I didn't get a chance to say goodbye to Yaakov or Hadassah or Mrs. Goldstein. The Orthodox had formed a perimeter around them all. There was no way for me to reach them.

Part V

JEWISH MOTHER

For her sake I too would become a Jew. Why not? I already speak like a Jew. And I am as ugly as a Jew. Besides, who hates the Jews more than the Jew?

–Henry Miller, *Tropic of Cancer*

I.

We never spoke about Judaism or the past: I never did, my mother never did, nor did my brother; not as a child, not when I moved back to New York as a teenager, not as an adult. As a boy it was a simple matter of wanting to keep my worlds separate: I didn't want the Jews to know I was a Christian (of a sort) and the Christians to know I was a Jew (of a sort), and the only way they ever would was if I said something, so I didn't. I never consciously avoided the subject, but I liked maintaining separate domains. It allowed me to pretend that nothing in either place moved, progressed, or evolved without my permission.

This changed only slightly as I grew older. Some Mississippians learned of my double life, but only those few who visited me outside of the South. Typically, though, they had moved away from Mississippi as well, which in my mind exempted them from the information blockade.

The careful reader might ask, "But what about this book? And your earlier journalism about Judaism? Do you mean to say you did all this writing about your childhood without ever once talking about it with your mother? And without anyone in Mississippi reading any of your stories?"

My mother did read my work and we did talk about it. She thought my writing was very nice and that I was a very talented boy. We did not, however, discuss the substance of what I wrote. As for friends and family, well, I guess they never came across my work, which may suggest less about the range of their literary pursuits and more about the obscurity of the publications in which I've been published. Either way, the topic never came up.

My mother remarried when I was fourteen, to a Catholic man, and before the wedding they both converted to Episcopalianism. There was no discussion of my brother and I converting and no expectation that we would participate in this new religion—with one exception. My mother had a thing for Midnight Mass. Each year she would try to get me to attend it with her, and each year I would refuse. "But it's so beautiful!" she said, refusing to understand why I didn't share her enthusiasm for the Yuletide pageantry. I never did go, but she had her revenge, blasting Gregorian chant albums on our home stereo system throughout the Christmas holidays.

My stepfather, for his part, knew from very early on that my mother was Jewish. His rather conservative family didn't, and they still don't; nor do my mother's employees, her colleagues at the hospitals, or her friends. My stepfather never cared about our religion—or his, for that matter. Converting was my mother's idea.

I warned my mother well in advance of publication whenever my writing turned to Jewish topics, out of a certain respect for her feelings. I wasn't asking for permission, mind you, but I didn't want her to be blind-sided if any one of her friends came across my work. I also didn't go out of my way to publicize what I was doing, and I assumed that my mother kept the subject to herself. How could she not? Talking about it with others would mean admitting to the old lies. Aside from the impact it could have on her professionally, what would it imply about her friends and family? We had hidden our Judaism because my mother was convinced—justifiably or not—of their bigotry. I figured our secret was safe with her.

Then I learned otherwise. In the summer of 2010, I flew to Mississippi for a week's vacation with my son. The last night before we returned home my mother held a barbecue for about twenty close friends and family, during which I found myself by the pool, eating ribs and drinking beer, and, to my surprise, accepting congratulations for my book deal.

"Quite an achievement there, Ted," said one friend. I struggled not to choke on my baked beans. His wife agreed, as did the rest of the folks, each murmuring their best wishes.

I turned to stare at my mother. She returned my look with a vague smile that did nothing to communicate the direction in which I should take the conversation.

"Now, maybe you can tell me what it's about," the friend said.

Again, I never imagined that my mother had shared news of my project. If she had, though, wouldn't she have had to tell them what it was about? How could you tell a person about a book without telling them *about* the book? Apparently my mother had managed that very trick. A long moment passed as I tried to organize my thoughts. I decided to hedge.

"Well, I guess you can say it will be about eccentric Jews"—more glaring at my mother—"and, you know, communities of odd Jews, writing about them, that sort of thing, their practices. I don't know, 'Identity'?"

"But you're not a Jew, are you?" asked the wife.

"Well, actually, I am."[1]

"But your mother isn't?"

I paused, my cognitive wheels spinning out of control.

"Is that what she told you?"

"Yes, when we read your earlier articles"—another surprise—"we asked her and she said no."

I managed to cough up a very limited answer, something about my father being Jewish but not my mother, which, given her conversion, was technically true but misleading, and the conversation moved on. I hadn't asked my mother why she had opened up to these people. But I decided that if she could talk to them, then she could do the same for me.

---

1. Regardless of the title of this book, I am Jewish in Mississippi. Anything else would be a betrayal.

II.

—*You decided you were not going to be Jewish when we got to Mississippi.*

—*Yes.*

—*Do you remember how you decided what you were going to tell us?*

—*No.*

—*Did you give it any thought? What you might say to us about this?*

—*I was just going to make it a rule.*

—*You realize, Ma, that sort of seems irrational, right?*

—*I just don't remember.*

—*Well, I'm asking you to try to remember.*

—*I don't remember. I don't remember.*

—*You don't remember it at all? That this was the new rule? Think.*

—*Yeah, I do remember when we got to Mississippi that I told you and your brother that.*

—*What did you tell us?*

—*I said don't tell anybody you're Jewish.*

—*But you have no real recollection of the conversation itself? Because that is like a huge moment in my life and you don't remember it at all.*

—*I don't think there was one conversation.*

—*Really? How did it work?*

—*Uh . . . I just, I think when you started school I said, 'Listen, just don't tell anyone you're Jewish.'*

—And how did we react?

—You didn't say anything when I said that. It didn't come up as a big conversation.

—We didn't react.

—Right.

—Is that basically it?

—Yeah.

It was a gray, fall day just after Thanksgiving, and my mother and I, flush with tryptophan and boredom, were in my car, driving along the pockmarked failure of the Grand Central Parkway in Queens. The occasional raindrop crashed against the windshield, and perhaps a few wisps of early snow, and there was enough wind that I could see small, whitecapped waves on Flushing Bay pushing the water toward LaGuardia Airport. Typically, I wouldn't have noticed the details of a road I had driven practically my entire life, but the fact that I had lured my mother into the car for a *talk* cast even small details into stark relief. We were like strangers introduced by a mutual acquaintance: You focus on the surroundings to avoid noticing the awkward pauses.

—If you have a tumor, you cut it out.

—Judaism was a tumor?

—Well, it can kill ya.

Is it so remarkable that we never spoke about the old days? I don't know. Discarding the past is a venerable American cultural tradition, on a par with corrupt electoral politics and the Super Bowl. I cannot be the only person who has found it easier to keep my memories at a healthy remove, although I do think that writing of these matters actually contributed to the distance. Press hard enough on the past, probe its details, verify its stories, facts, and lies, and your life becomes an object of study. This has its benefits: Emotional detachment allows one to substitute analysis for understanding. Again, I suspect I'm not alone in feeling this way.

—*You know that Tom Lehrer song, right?*[1]
—*I do.*
—*Well, what'd he say?*
—*He said everybody hates the Jews.*
—*Exactly. And it's true.*

We exited the parkway in the Jamaica section of Queens, the neighborhood where my mother was raised. I lived here too, as a small boy, after my mother left my father and moved back in with her parents. I was six when we moved again, first to Long Island for a couple of years, and then to Mississippi.

We turned onto Hillside Avenue, a forlorn commercial corridor of Caribbean roti shops, junk shops, dollar shops, laundries, used car lots, an incongruous strip of Chinese-Ghanaian restaurants, furniture stores selling African trinkets and Jamaican-themed wall coverings, shuttered banks and real estate brokerages, and at nearly every corner, greenmarkets run by Asian women and frequented by Muslim women in modest headdresses, African women in blazingly colorful headdresses, and Orthodox Jewish women in expensive wigs.

My mother didn't seem to notice any of this. Her mind was taken with everything she once knew here. Memories lingered at each intersec-

---

1. The refrain from Tom Lehrer's 1965 song, "National Brotherhood Week": *Oh, the Protestants hate the Catholics,/ And the Catholics hate the Protestants,/ And the Hindus hate the Muslims,/ And everybody hates the Jews.*

tion, of a playmate whose name escaped her, a clothing store where she and her mother shopped for dresses. I was particularly surprised at how well she knew her way around. Diane Ross struggles to locate the bathroom in her house; but in Jamaica, she barked out terse and accurate directions. I found this amusing and said so, and she did her best to look insulted.

> —*When did you decide that you were not going to tell people you were Jewish?*
> —*I knew that anywhere I moved I probably wasn't going to tell them.*

We stopped in at a dollar store to buy batteries for my tape recorder. The owner was a solemn South Asian fellow who had filled his shelves with global treats and spices and enough home-repair equipment to renovate a small city. My mother seemed to be enjoying herself, despite being forced to submit to my cross-examination. She chatted up the owner, made a joke about something that exceeded his limited supply of English, and laughed on his behalf.

> —*You could have said we were atheists.*
> —*A woman from New York? And a doctor? First question is going to be 'Are you Jewish?' So I said I was Unitarian.*
> —*Where the hell did you come up with that?*
> —*They don't really believe in Christ. So it's the next best thing to being atheist.*

We turned off Hillside to see the apartment my mother lived in until she was five. It was a second-floor walkup on a narrow block, across from a Greek Orthodox church and a prison-like elementary school with its doors chained shut for the holiday. An Asian toddler done up in Yankees gear tottered down the street holding his father's hand. A Middle Eastern woman—head covered, hobbled by grocery bags and her long robes—passed them without a glance. Two South Asian girls in skinny jeans and Day-Glo sneakers darted between the pedestrians on pink bicycles, ringing their bells. Latter-day melting-pot kitsch, to be sure, but it helped me imagine my mother here as a little girl, in the neighborhood's 1950s Americana heyday. The methods and expectations for absorbing newcomers into American society have changed dramatically over the years, and insisting on connections between generations of immigrants is its own form of kitsch. These folks might not want, as my mother clearly did, to be absorbed—nor, given persistent racial biases, might they be accepted even if they desired to be. My mother is white and they are not. And even that statement isn't as simple as it might first appear.

Karen Brodkin's 1998 book, *How Jews Became White Folks*, characterizes contemporary Jewish-American history as one of "racial change," in which "prevailing classifications at a particular time have sometimes assigned [Jews] to the white race, and at other times have created an off-white race for Jews to inhabit." Brodkin, like my mother, grew up in 1950s outer-borough New York, and she shared her sense of alienation from the mainstream culture:

> My goal in life [was] to have a pageboy hairstyle and to own a camel-hair coat, like the pictures in *Seventeen* magazine. I thought of storybook and magazine people as "the blond people," a species for whom life naturally came easily, who inherited happiness as a birthright, and I wanted my family to be "normal," . . . the mythical "normal" America.

This elusive "normal" America seemed to haunt not just Brodkin and my mother, but many American Jews of their generation. In part I think it is a symptom of the relatively fragile role of U.S. Jews in post–World

War II society. The memories of war, and the Holocaust, were fresh, but there were also more immediate, domestic sources of anxiety:

> The trial and execution of the Rosenbergs [for selling atomic bomb secrets] heightened our sense of difference. It was a terrifying thing. . . . My parents talked about these things with their friends, but I do not think they discussed them with our non-Jewish neighbors. I believe this was out of a fear that to do so might evoke an anti-Semitism they suspected our white neighbors harbored but which they didn't want to know about.

Combine these influences from my mother's background and perhaps her choices become less than totally irrational. She wanted to be seen as a nice American girl from Queens, with all the ethnic and social privileges that implied; yet she knew, with the conviction that youth brings to assessing certain truths, that she wasn't seen as any such thing.

—*Did Grandpa ever talk about the Holocaust?*
—*No. Except to say that he got his mother and brother out and that they did not want to leave and he knew what was coming. And that the rest of his family was killed in the camps.*
—*But there was nothing like, 'This is the lesson of Judaism,' one way or another. You know, like 'It's bad to be a Jew,' or 'It's good to be a Jew because everybody tries to kill us and we survive.'*
—*No. I only grew up knowing that Jews were smarter than everybody else. And we were better. That was an a priori assumption.*
—*That's why people remain Jewish even if it's only cultural. Because part of the religion is that you're better than everyone else.*
—*Yeah, well.*
—*You wanted to cast that off?*

—*Yes.*

—*You wanted to give up being the smartest guy in the room!*

—*I don't have to say I'm Jewish to be smart.*

Jamaica High School, my mother's alma mater, is a statuesque red brick pile, built in a Greek classical style, with limestone columns, a bell tower, and an ornamental clock in the pediment. Perched atop a steep hill, the school's towering shade trees and decorative shrubbery slope downward to a pocket park complete with a duck pond. We parked at the curved lane cutting the park from the school and got out to walk, my mother snapping photos on her phone as we went. The sky darkened and I pulled on a warm cap and my mother flipped up the collar on her fur coat. The wind rose and the ducks on the pond squawked southward, honking in complaint.

The school's elegance is evocative of a nearly forgotten era of confidence in the city's educational capacities, one that had academic ambitions on an Ivy League scale. Such was the seemingly idyllic nature of the spot that when a police officer approached to ask about my car, it wasn't to give me a ticket, but to ask me to move so that I *wouldn't* be ticketed.

—*I read The Rise and Fall of the Third Reich.*

—*When was that, Ma?*

—*When I was twelve years old. That was it. I did not want to be a lamp shade. I did not want my kids to be lamp shades. I knew I could not prevent it for me, but at least I could prevent it for my grandchildren.*

—*But you were living in an environment where being Jewish wasn't risky at all.*

—*It was post–World War II. I felt that it was risky. I felt that it could happen again. It happened with Torquemada, it happened in France— every Western society has killed the Jews.*

—*But that sort of obsession with it, that belief that it will happen again, you understand that that's totally fucking Jewish, right? That is exactly what Jews think.*[1]

—*Okay, so I decided to go in a different direction with it.*

In 2007, Jamaica High appeared on New York State's list of "persistently dangerous" schools; in 2010, it was added to the roster of "Persistently Lowest-Achieving and/or Schools Under Registration Review." It has a suspension rate three times higher than the rest of the city and a 77 percent truancy rate. There is a dedicated "truancy center" located in the school's basement, and two teachers work full-time tracking truant students and their parents. "The problem," said the parent coordinator at the school, "is that parents of truant kids are also truant." In February 2011, the Board of Education voted to close the school altogether.

—*You never had a damn religion anyhow.*

—*Sure we did, Ma. We had a religious identity.*

—*No, you had a cultural identity.*

—*A cultural identity based in religion.*

—*You were American.*

—*Yeah. Jewish American.*

—*No. American. Fuck that Jewish American shit.*

My grandfather immigrated to the United States from Germany in 1936.[2] A family story, almost certainly apocryphal, helps explain the tim-

---

1. Of course, the Jews have an old joke about this: "The history of Judaism can be summed up in nine words: They tried to kill us. We won. Let's eat."

2. Descendants of Jews forced from Germany by the Nazis are today entitled to return as citizens. On a lark, I filed an application for citizenship with the German consulate in New York, only to discover that the official to whom I was instructed to send my paperwork was named "Ms. Maus."

ing of his departure. He had a job working as a manager in a brewery in Berlin owned by a distant family relation. In each office in the brewery there was a framed portrait of the family patriarch. My grandfather, who spoke no Yiddish, had a Christian girlfriend, was a member of the Ethical Culture Society, and ate his bratwurst without consideration or remorse, arrived at work one day to find that the portrait in his office had been replaced with one of Hitler. Some time passed and my grandfather discovered another alteration to his office: He too had been replaced. A Nazi was seated at his desk.

    —Did you ever fuck up? Did you ever say to people, 'Hey, when I was a kid and we were at Passover . . .'
    —No.
    —You never let on? Nobody ever caught you?
    —No.
    —Were you concerned about that? Did you think about it?
    —No.
    —Why not?
    —What was I supposed to be concerned about?
    —That you might say something that would allow people to realize that you were Jewish.
    —No. Because I didn't think I had grown up particularly Jewish.
    —You didn't think you'd grown up particularly Jewish? You were the child of a Jew who left Germany because of the Nazis. You went to Sunday school at the synagogue and to Barnard! What are you talking about?

I experienced practically no anti-Semitism in Mississippi. Christ Episcopal even had its own "out" Jewish pupil, a shy, chestnut-eyed fifth grader named Hilary who, if memory serves, went to the library while we were in Mass. No one singled her out for ridicule or censure that I can recall. While this might make the decision to hide our Jewishness seem pointless, to my mother it remained necessary. Avoiding the disapprobation of peers seemingly more tolerant than she had anticipated wasn't good enough. She needed to belong in a way that required no approval and brooked no condescension.

I was, however, witness to one unpleasant incident in Mississippi, when I was a teenager. It was around Christmas, and I had gone to a party at the home of a girl named Nikki. Nikki was a fairly common specimen of Mississippi young lady: round with fried food, capable with a softball bat, liberal with eyeliner, foundation, and hairspray. Her parents owned a vinyl-sided ranch in one of the exurban subdivisions cut from the pine tracts north of the Mississippi Sound, and they had been foolish enough to leave their little slice of heaven unguarded for the evening. Seizing the opportunity, Nikki had sent out word, and her friends had rounded up sufficient beer and marijuana to inebriate the better part of the state.

The house had roughed-up wall-to-wall carpeting; a recently renovated kitchen with cabinets jammed with junk food my mother never let me have; a television shrine with that moment's cutting-edge viewing technology; family photos arrayed in one of those frames with little cutouts for the photos; a crucifix; and the "Footprints" homily carved into a wooden placard hung above the fridge.

I had come to see a girlfriend of mine, Melanie, a cute girl with close-cropped hair, whom I saw whenever I came to Mississippi (I had moved back to New York to live with my father by this point). She was there with Mary, a scowling and strange girl with dyed blond hair and angry eyes, whom I was always trying and failing to get alone. There were others with us that night, perhaps my brother even, although I don't remember him being there. There was also Brad Levine, the only other Jewish kid I knew. Brad's appearance was conventionally Jewish: curly brown hair, a prodigious honker, hair on the back of his hands. His father liked to throw a word or two of Yiddish into his dirty jokes. Yet Brad was a Southerner, too—heavy drawl, liked to fish, drive drunk, and call black people niggers (not to their face)—in short, a mass of contradictions in pegged Girbaud jeans and Tretorn sneakers.

The evening's entertainment took place mostly in the kitchen, at a breakfast table littered with half-empty Doritos bags, ashtrays, packets of rolling papers, and tins of French onion dip. Empty beer cans collected in heaps on the floor as we played Quarters and Three Man—a weird dice game whose rules escape me—and smoked joints. At some point I managed to convince Melanie to accompany me into one of the bedrooms. We passed some time there together and didn't come out until we heard a commotion in the kitchen. I rushed back to find Mary and Brad yelling at each other. Brad, I should mention, was from a section of the local "cool crowd" that had no room for Mary, who, although attractive and sneaky-smart, was something of an outcast. I don't recall what they were fighting about, but Brad was calling her a "skillet"—the local term for a slut. Brad's invective came in a rapid-fire staccato—"You fucked so-and-so . . . fucking skillet . . . blew the other guy . . . probably fucked the whole . . . skillet . . . probably take it in the . . . skillet . . ."

Mary couldn't muster much of a rejoinder and I could see her distress building. Her face reddened and her eyes widened with outraged hurt. She looked ready to cry and I think I muttered something to Brad about knocking it off, but if he heard me—Nikki punctuated each "skillet" with a hyena-like guffaw—it had no impact.

Then, finally, in a whisper Mary stumbled onto something that worked.

"Jew," she said. And then louder: "You're just a *Jew*."

Brad stopped speaking, Nikki didn't laugh. All the other sounds—

the conversations, the rattle of quarters into cups, the yammer of the television, REM on the stereo—stopped.

"Dirty Jew. You're just a dirty stinking Jew."

Mary's voice deepened each time she said the word. She had tapped into a seam of religious and ethnic venom that she likely knew nothing about, and yet her pale face, the platinum hair down to her shoulders, the raving eyes, the anger, was an image pulled directly from Judaism's post-Holocaust collective consciousness: the German hausfrau, the Polish farmer's wife, the concentration camp nurse, the wraith who steals Jewish babies for barren European shiksas. Mary threw back her head and smiled. She probably had no idea what she was saying—but she knew it was working.

Brad had heard enough and lunged for Mary, his paw aimed at her throat. Nikki and several larger boys intervened, Mary was hustled off to another room, someone forced a beer into Brad's hand, and the whole thing ended as quickly as it began.

I don't remember anything else from that night.

—*The day you made that decision you stopped feeling Jewish in your head? You didn't think you were Jewish? I always felt Jewish. I always felt 'I'm superior, I'm a Jew, you know we run everything. . . .'*

—*Yes, but that's a bad attitude.*

—*Fuck the good or bad, I don't care about good or bad, I still felt that way. I still felt Jewish, you know? But you didn't.*

—*I don't think so.*

—*Once you decided.*

—*Once I decided that was it.*

—*That's a pretty powerful state of mind. I wish I could do that. Just make up my mind about something and it just happens.*

—*That's the way I function.*

In 1955, my mother and her parents moved from the apartment on 161st Street to a two-bedroom brick A-frame with a finished basement in Jamaica Estates. Her father, my grandfather, Gerald Glaser, was born in 1902 in a village in eastern Germany that is today part of Poland. A Jewish organization helped him come to New York on a tourist visa in 1936. After that he traveled by bus to Miami, then by boat to Havana, where he presented himself to the U.S. embassy to secure his permanent residency. He arranged for his mother and brother to come the following year. His first job in the United States was with the Easter Sausage Company, selling imported hams. After World War II he went into business with his brother, again selling imported foodstuffs, made a decent living, and retired in 1973, the year I was born. He married my grandmother, Ethel, a Brooklyn girl from Russian stock, in 1947, had two daughters, drank a beer every evening with dinner, and died when he was ninety-nine, one week after his brother passed. Grandma Ethel died of cancer when I was five. I don't remember much about her, but I enjoy looking at the photos my mother has of her as a young woman: swimming with a beau somewhere upstate; on a Sunday drive with her friends in a convertible; with my grandfather on their wedding day.

Jamaica Estates, one of New York City's first subdivisions, was built in 1904 on a patch of hardwood forest not far from Jamaica Bay. The neighborhood association's website notes, with some pride, that the city had initially considered converting the land into a large park. Ultimately, Forest Hills was selected for that, "freeing the . . . area to be developed to another vision": namely, an upper-middle-class bedroom community designed to resemble the haut-bourgeois paradise at Tuxedo Park in the Hudson Valley.

The original Jamaica Estates covenants specified that homeowners spend no less than $6,000 on home construction, land not included. The company that developed the site went bankrupt in the 1920s, leaving the

275 homeowners in a difficult position: the restrictive covenants defining the neighborhood were set to expire, imperiling the single-family-home dreams of its residents. In 1938, however, Jamaica Estates became the first neighborhood in New York City to receive a variance that limited the housing stock to detached single-family homes. Thanks to the wonders of prejudicial zoning, Jamaica Estates today remains largely free of apartment complexes and other déclassé multi-family dwellings, and, to borrow the self-congratulatory language of the neighborhood association, still resembles a "residential park."

—*You've never regretted it? You've never felt like well, here today, with me, might be the price that you're paying for it?*

—*No.*

—*Even now with me writing the book?*

—*I still think I did the right thing. I still think that it's a bad thing to be Jewish and since none of us believe in religion or God, who gives a shit?*

—*But I'm going to write this book and your friends might see it.*

—*They don't have to see the book. They'll forget about it. All they know is that you're an author and that you've got a book deal.*

—*Mom, every time they see me they'll ask. You know that, right? So what are you gonna do? Why did you tell them I was working on a book?*

—*Because I'm proud of you.*

—*I know. But there's going to be a book about your choice.*

—*I don't expect anyone to read it.*

—*It's in the first chapter, Ma. That's usually the part people read.*

—*I don't expect anybody to buy it either, and I ain't buying it for them.*

The park-like atmosphere in Jamaica Estates persists to this day, but in ways that suggest foundering urban decline rather than suburban sumptuousness. The grand Tudors survive, but they stand largely in disrepair or on the verge of collapse. More than a few appear to have been abandoned, their windows boarded up and papered with foreclosure or demolition orders. The canopy of shade trees has grown wild, with gnarled branches twisting dangerously through the power lines, or collapsing nearly down to the street. Jamaica Estates has the feel of a broken man past his middle age, out of work, and wrapped up in the bottle.

This is natural to the aging of a neighborhood that lacks a proper role. People who could afford to maintain these sorts of homes today live either in Manhattan or in a real suburb, not in Queens. The middle-class Italians and Irish and secular Jews who populated the neighborhood departed long ago. (There is a sizable Orthodox population here, part of what the *New York Times*, in 2002, called the "haredization" of the borough.) Those few who have stuck around are elderly, and their children and grandchildren live elsewhere. The first-generation immigrants who have replaced them lack both the resources and inclination to maintain the neighborhood. It has become a staging area for new Americans eager to move from first-generation poverty into the middle class. They, and perhaps the neighborhood, won't be here for long.

—*Religion is bullshit. For that it's okay to lie.*

—*No, Ma, it's never okay to lie. Don't you understand that?*

—*No.*

—*Everybody lies, but it's never okay.*

—*It's okay to decide you don't like Judaism and don't want to be Jewish.*

—*It's okay to leave the religion. It's not okay to do what you did.*

—*You have to if you're going to live among people in the South. You have to do it. I still think you have to.*

—*I don't think you're right.*

—*Well, I do.*

—*Did you ever have a specific definition of what you wanted us to be?*
—*Yeah. I wanted you to be an all-American boy.*
—*But I was.*
—*Yeah. Only if you weren't Jewish.*

We hung around for a while. I noticed that the temple down the street had been converted to a mosque. My mother found this ironic but it only seemed typical to me. I wondered if we should cross the street and knock on the door of her old house, ask the new residents for permission to look around, but I couldn't think of anything that would accomplish. The only thing we could think of to say to each other was that the house looked smaller than we remembered.

Part VI

SYNTHESIS AND SEPARATION

People will reinvent their history using specific images from a more organized moment.

—George W. S. Trow, *Within the Context of No Context*

I.

In the 1971 edition of the *American Jewish Year Book*, Charles Liebman wrote, "There is nothing incompatible between being a good Jew and a good American, or between Jewish and American standards of behavior. In fact, for a Jew, the better an American one is, the better Jew one is." Instinctively, I feel Liebman is right, and what's more, I would like nothing better than for him to be. But I know this much: He never met my mother.

Her contention that, as a Jewish boy, I could never be "all-American" gnawed at me. Had she not, in effect, restated the anxiety of identity that animates my interest in Judaism? For her, "all-American" connoted something extraordinary and mythical, an unchallenged and unified sense of self. Yet her insistence on this particularity, obtainable only through radical rejection and reinvention, at times seemed less an act of alienation than of needful hope. I am no stranger to such motivations.

As I have sifted through the fractured remnants of my genealogical inheritance, I have occasionally felt an outsider, an imposter—someone *acting the Jew*. I have never felt that way about being American. I feel all-American. I am all-American. Yet so, too, I imagine, did my maternal grandfather feel German in Berlin. And he *was*, thoroughly, from his daily beer to his sauerbraten to the removes of his Prussian formality. Unlike my mother, I see no looming anti-Semitic apocalypse in the United States. But Liebman's contention that American and Jewish identities re-

inforce each other strikes me as an exercise in folly, too. The historian
Jonathan Sarna coined a term for this particular brand of domestic self-
deception, in which this country's Jews "interweave" Judaism with "Amer-
icanism" in the hopes of fashioning a single "'synthetic' whole." He called
it the Cult of Synthesis.

Articulations of this cult, as Sarna perceived it, are long-standing, "a
central tenet" of our "civil religion." ("Anyone even remotely connected
with American Jewish life is familiar with this theme," he added; perhaps
tellingly, I had never heard of it.) They can be found in the efforts of Jewish leaders in the 1800s to prove the Native Americans were Jewish;[1] in
the assertion, by Oscar Straus (the first Jewish-American secretary of
commerce), that our system of governance had been created by the ancient Israelites ("The children of Israel on the banks of the Jordan . . . established a free commonwealth, a pure democratic-republic under a
written constitution"); in the claims made by Solomon Solis-Cohen, a
founder of the Jewish Theological Seminary in 1886, that Jews had
"striven . . . to preserve for future generations the Hebraic, the American
ideals of freedom, justice, and equality"; and in families that gave their
children such patriotic names as George Washington Cohen, Rutherford
B. Hayes Joel, and Abraham Lincoln Danziger.

This phenomenon was prevalent in the earlier stages of American
Jewish history. I think this is important. I know that Jews lived on this
continent long before Thomas Jefferson wrote the Declaration of Inde-
pendence. The first ones are believed to have arrived in 1654, when a
shipload of twenty-three Portuguese Jews from Dutch Brazil reached
New Amsterdam (now New York). By the time of the Revolutionary
War, Jewish communities existed in all thirteen colonies, though in mi-

---

1. *Discourse on the Evidences of the American Indians Being the Descendants of the Lost Tribes
of Israel*, an 1837 book by Mordecai Noah, is a forthrightly titled example.

nuscule numbers. As late as 1825, which marked the onset of a second and considerably larger wave of Jewish migration, only 6,000 Jews lived in the United States. This second migratory period, which lasted until 1880, saw a fourfold increase in Jewish numbers, mostly from Germany, and many of these Jewish immigrants settled in places like Cincinnati, Pittsburgh, and elsewhere, locales far removed from what are today considered the traditional Jewish enclaves of the Northeast. The next wave, sparked by convulsive anti-Semitic violence in Russia and Eastern Europe, began in 1881, when there were only 280,000 American Jews. By 1924, when the Johnson-Reed Immigration Act stanched the flow of foreigners to this country, that number had exploded, to 4.5 million. Significant numbers of Jews still made their way to the United States in later years, particularly after World War II, but never close to as many as during this third wave.

Nearly all of America's Jews descend from the people of the third wave. The Jews who arrived here between 1881 and 1924 were Yiddish-speaking Eastern Europeans and Russians, largely products of the shtetl life that today we tend to think of as "The Old World." In other words, this migratory wave was primarily responsible for the mainstream imagery, culture, and assumptions of American Jewry. That the Cult of Synthesis existed before this wave suggests that the Cult's impulses, the narrative of its drive toward Americanization, were different from those that spawned my mother's anti-Semitism, or Karen Bodkin's desire for fair hair, or Liebman's residual Orthodoxy. I imagined—or perhaps hoped—that these earlier synthesizers were less tightly bound to the traumas of contemporary European history, if only because they had arrived here before many of those traumas transpired. The synthesizers had to be free of the shtetl clichés and *Yiddishkeit* neuroses of their successors and cultural supplanters, the ones whose perturbations and Hebraic agita yielded the urban-American shtick of Borscht Belt comedy and smoked fish.

These other Jews, less burdened by the cultural weight under which my mother labored, would have to be different Jews. Even she, convert and iconoclast, couldn't muster the temerity to deny them their chosen all-American identity. I wondered what would have happened if she had grown up among such people. Would she have forged a different myth? What would have become of her? And of me?

II.

I had been in Kansas City for a little more than a day when Jacques Cukierkorn, rabbi of the New Reform Temple, took me out for a barbecue dinner. He chose a well-known spot in a burgeoning art gallery-and-loft neighborhood, where the hostesses wore headsets as they worried over the seating charts, the diners favored business casual, and at the bar, where we sat, mammoth flat-screens broadcast professional sports from all angles. The rabbi ordered us a platter of beef and pork ribs, along with a pile of French fries and a cheese-and-corn casserole our waitress recommended. Cukierkorn joined me for the barbecue but avoided the carbohydrates. He was on a strict and complicated diet that involved herbal remedies and near-starvation, and although the meat was a departure from the regimen, allowed in my honor, there were limits to how much he was willing to cheat.

"A truly miraculous experience," he said as he pried a ribbon of fat from one of our pork ribs. My first thought was that he was referring to the barbecue, which was extraordinary, but he meant the diet. "I've lost eighteen pounds since Yom Kippur."

He reached for a jar of seasoned salt and doused his plate with it, forgoing the selection of barbecue sauces on the table.

"I'm eating much less," he said. "But I'm much less fun company."

Cukierkorn had picked me up at the airport the day before, and along with the intricacies of his dining habits, I had gathered much biographical detail. He was Brazilian, of Polish extraction. His father, now deceased, had been a businessman who had immigrated to Rio in 1929. As a secular Jew, his father had nonetheless felt great pride at his family's lineage among the Hasidic rebbes of Eastern Europe. Cukierkorn's mother was still alive and lived in Miami ("The land of our ancestors," according to Cukierkorn). He was forty-three years old and had lived in the United States for more than twenty years, having first arrived here for rabbinical school, in Cincinnati; following his ordination, he had secured pulpits in Natchez, Mississippi, and then Joplin, Missouri. He came to Kansas City, and the New Reform Temple, which was in fact a fairly old temple, and more important, an exemplar of the Cult of Synthesis, in 2000.

The rabbi looked like an unassuming man, none too heavy, and not, in my estimation, in particular need of reduction. He had skimpy brown hair, dark appraising eyes, and a lopsided, sneering smile. His accent was a clamorous and twanging combination of Southern and Midwestern English, with hints of Yiddish, Hebrew, Portuguese, and Spanish—a linguistic road map to his genealogy and professional background. He possessed a profane manner not ordinarily associated with a religious leader. At one point I had asked him if he liked working in Mississippi, and he said he did, but that the Jews he shepherded were "medieval." Their congregation was small and rich and old; most of its thirty families traced their ancestry to Sephardim who came south to Charleston and Savannah in the 1600s. Perhaps not surprisingly, they had amassed a few antebellum eccentricities. Biblical iconography notwithstanding, they had insisted that the rabbi join them for a dove hunt.

"Some fucking Jews," he said. "The white folks hunt and the *schvartzes* bring the lemonade." He laughed. "None of them would drive a Volkswagen . . . because there's no room for a gun rack!"

Cukierkorn was irrepressible, simultaneously amused and enraged, an expert on an array of subjects both secular and divine. He lectured to me at length on the history of Reform Judaism, in Germany and the United States. He described his love of the purity of its traditions, its universal values and ethics, its rejection of rabbinical parochialism. He noted its historical openness to liberal Christianity, Mainline Protestantism, Unitarianism, and the like, and while he admired the tolerance inherent in such a stance, he had little desire to interact with his non-Jewish peers. Again and again he spoke of his love for Jews, all Jews, any Jews—he wanted to aid them, support them, lead them, make more of them. This was why he had overseen so many conversions: over 400 and counting. He reminded me of the fact that Judaism had once been a proselytizing religion, until the fourth century and the reign of Constantine the Great, the first Roman emperor to convert to Christianity. This, he said, should have killed Judaism but didn't. He ascribed the religion's survival to the dogged strength of the Jewish soul, which, he said, could be sensed via past-life regression ("A Jew is always a Jew in a past life"). He had great facility with money, knew his way around a stock option, staked out market positions short and long, and was in possession of certain real estate holdings in Leavenworth, Kansas, astutely purchased and rapidly accruing in value. Writing, on Jewish topics, was another passion. He'd published two books, all proceeds donated to Jewish charities (mostly he lost money). He grew somewhat defensive when we discussed his rabbi's discretionary fund at New Reform, which he used, in part, to finance conversion trips among the Crypto-Jews in Latin America,[1] but he insisted he could be trusted: "I may be wrong, but I never lie." He was conversant with the belief systems of the great Jewish thinkers, from Rashi to Maimonides to the Baal Shem Tov, and able to articulate their differences in

---

1. Cukierkorn is an expert on Crypto-Judaism, and I had in fact first contacted him not about the Cult of Synthesis but to discuss accompanying him on one of his conversion trips.

ways the uninitiated could understand. My experiences in Monsey and Kensington, when I spoke of them, he found dismaying.

"Those fuckers!" he snarled. "Who gives them the right to say what is a Jew?"

Of the many arguments the Orthodox offered in favor of their mode of religion, here, perhaps, was the most galling: We (meaning the Orthodox Jews) have done things this way forever, since Hashem cast aside the darkness, divided earth from sky, and declared His day of holy rest. This *stuff* we do, this holy stuff, has sustained us (meaning the Orthodox Jews), in our Diasporic exile and genocidal negation; it elevated us in the glorious epochs of the Temples, First and Second, when God's mighty favor shone brilliantly down on the (Orthodox) Israelites; in the shtetls, villages, ghettoes, *juderías*, mansions, lofts, movie sets, and therapists' offices; on the Lower East Side, in the Pale of Settlement, in Berlin, glorious Brooklyn, the darkest reaches of the Bronx, and forsaken Queens.

To Orthodox Jews, their practice was not a form of Judaism. It *was* Judaism. At one time, each Jew, each *YEED*, each schmuck, putz, *macher*, and mensch knew this; these indivisible tenets, values, and beliefs saw us through the ages not merely because they worked, but because they were *us*. By what right do Jews like Cukierkorn (and me) cast them aside? From what wellspring of shamelessness does such arrogance spring?

All of which is to say that I understood Cukierkorn's feelings about the Orthodox. We picked our ribs clean and then it was time to go. An elderly member of his congregation had died of cancer and the rabbi had to sit shiva with the family. We shouldn't be much later than we already were.

III.

The deceased had lived in a prosperous Kansas City subdivision of hushed streets and lavish lawns. The home-owner's association had chosen to observe the Halloween season by hanging strings of powder-blue lights from the ornamental shrubs lining the sidewalks. The lights cast a soothing glow and clattered pleasantly in the breeze, a sound that mixed with the white hum of traffic on a nearby freeway. The house was small for the neighborhood and a little worn, a vinyl-sided ranch with what looked like a second-floor addition. The driveway was filled with cars, so we parked across the street. Cukierkorn checked himself briefly in the rearview mirror, retrieved a yarmulke from the glove box, and we headed inside.

A woman in her fifties dressed in stretch pants and a T-shirt from a vacation destination greeted us—the deceased's daughter. Cukierkorn, altering his demeanor from his earlier manic charisma to a low-key cheeriness, asked how her father was doing and she told him not well. Her mother had, apparently, been the healthier one, until the cancer took her, and her father, who had Alzheimer's, needed full-time care.

The house had clearly been home to elderly residents. There was something in the dusty wall-to-wall carpeting, the muted colors of the family photos, the faint smells of plastic and meat. They had some Judaica about (ceramic sculptures of doves) but global trinkets from package tours predominated—tribal textiles and clay pots and lacquered chopstick sets—along with a book collection heavy on Roth and Bellow. In the formal dining room, the grown grandchildren of the deceased helped themselves to bagels and deli from a spread on the table, complaining to each other about rental prices in the cities in which they now lived.

Cukierkorn asked the daughter for permission to say the mourner's Kaddish in Hebrew. She considered it for a moment, made a joke about Jewish mumbo jumbo, and then agreed, albeit warily. This, I imagined, was an example of some of the troubles that Cukierkorn had hinted he was having with his congregation at New Reform. The older, more traditionally liberal members were uncomfortable with overt displays of religiousness, including Hebrew prayer.

Cukierkorn's real problem, he had told me, wasn't with the membership but the board of directors. We had discussed his employment contract at some length. His deal with New Reform expired in two years, and he felt that his success with the congregation, which had more than doubled during his rabbinical tenure, merited an early, and profitable, renegotiation. When he had informed the board of this, they had returned with an offer: a shorter contract term, and a 20 percent pay cut.

On this subject, Cukierkorn's sense of humor failed him, leaving only rage. The board members were a pack of anal-retentive, stubborn, stiff, hypocritical, racist, wannabe Protestants. They had made it their business to bankrupt him and destroy his position in the community. They hated the conversion trips to Latin America. If he traveled, they reasoned, then he must be neglecting his responsibilities at New Reform, even though for years he had been their servant, errand boy, and slave, taking calls at all hours, solving problems on vacation, putting out fires he hadn't started. They hated that he was so Jewish. They didn't want yarmulkes, or Israeli flags, or Hebrew. They hated that he was open to new things and new people. For what did they need the half-Jews, the gay Jews, the out-of-town Jews, the converts, the blacks, the Asians, and the Zionists? They preferred New Reform to remain as it had always been: quiet, wealthy, white, and Jewish in the most discreet way possible, a Judaism comingled with buttoned-up, tightened-down, emotionally stifled, upper-class Midwestern passive aggression.

Cukierkorn headed into the living room to check on the father. He was in his recliner, with his legs kicked up, napping in his Thom McAns. Cukierkorn stood over him for a moment, smiling; his presence must have stirred the old man, because he woke up, looking confused. Cukierkorn offered a bright hello, petted one of the old man's trembling hands, and asked if he was feeling all right.

"Where's mom?" the old man said, referring to his wife. One of his sons-in-law started at this, and rushed over to him.

"She died, Dad," he said, gently. "Did you forget?"

The old man stared at his son-in-law for a long moment, his eyes gauzy and uncertain. Then he crumpled into tears. This lasted only a few seconds, after which he relaxed again.

"I'm tired," he said.

"It's been a long day," his son-in-law said. "Let's get you to bed."

The old man struggled to his feet, and with help from his son-in-law, made his way to a motorized chair attached to the staircase in the entranceway. He glided upstairs to his bedroom, clutching his cane. Cukierkorn watched with impressive calm. I wanted to hide.

Cukierkorn asked everyone to stand for the Kaddish. He delivered the prayer, first in Hebrew, and then English, and afterward he worked the room for a while, stepping lightly, cracking mild jokes, spending a little extra time with the out-of-town children. One older woman, a blue-haired friend of the deceased, mentioned to Cukierkorn that she wasn't Jewish but Unitarian. He told her a story about how America's Reform rabbis had once grown so liberal and American and open to Christianity that they had actually considered merging with Unitarianism. He shook his head ruefully and asked her if she could believe such a thing. She had no idea what he was talking about.

IV.

I slept that night at Cukierkorn's house in the Kansas suburb of Over-
land Park, a meandering sprawl of corporate campuses, strip malls,
barbecue joints, gas stations, and six-lane roadways cut from the prairie.
It was also home to the better part of the area's 20,000 Jews, and as we
drove home that evening, Cukierkorn offered a quick tour of the local
Jewish points of interest. There, he said, was Congregation B'nai Jehudah,
one of the oldest Reform temples in Kansas and Missouri—it was
founded in 1870—and the institution from which New Reform had split
at its inception in 1967. There was Village Shalom, a gated townhouse
complex for retired Jews. Over there was the glass-encased structures of
the Menorah Medical Center. And there, last stop, was the Jewish Community Center, with an Israeli flag flying out front. Cukierkorn rolled his
eyes at this.

"Why not just hang a sign saying, 'Please bomb me!'"

Breakfast the following morning consisted of a single cracker covered
with feta cheese crumbs for Cukierkorn, and granola with milk for me.
Cukierkorn occupied himself by playing Farmville on his tablet computer
and grousing about the board. I asked him why they would want him to
go, and he shrugged. There was nothing, no good reason, he said, none at
all; although, if he were being thoroughly open and honest, he supposed
that certain leniencies he had taken hadn't helped. A particular example
could have been the wedding of a wealthy and eccentric congregant at

which he officiated. This person had, for reasons he saw no need to question—who was he to judge?—asked that her little dog be included in the wedding party, and in fact, be allowed to walk down the aisle with her, in a diamond-studded collar, and perhaps to bark a few prayers in Hebrew. He had indulged the woman, and apparently some of the old-line members of the congregation were offended. "The hypocrisy of it was insufferable," he said.

"They're so pure when it comes to me," he said. "Turn around, though, and they're all fucking each other's wives."

I suggested that perhaps, given these differences, a change of congregation might be a good idea, but he said no. Not that he had any particular loyalty to New Reform as an institution, but he liked Kansas City, he didn't want to uproot his children and wife, and really, at this point in his life, he was unwilling to be trifled with. His contract at New Reform had a non-compete clause that complicated matters if he couldn't obtain an agreement worthy of his talents, but he had a few notions on how he might get around that. He thought he might like to start a nonprofit, some kind of entity that would allow him to fund-raise and advertise his rabbinical services. Largely that would mean offering conversions or assistance with life-cycle events for non-conventional Jews. With luck, the revenue from this undertaking would allow him the freedom to travel throughout Latin America, following his passion for converting or reclaiming Jews. He mentioned in a dismissive way that his brother, who was also a rabbi, made a living performing conversions. "But he's only in it for the money," Cukierkorn said. I never met his brother, Celso, but I learned later that he lived in Florida and was the proprietor of an online business, convertingtojudaism.com. Like his brother, Celso had also written a book: *Secrets of Jewish Wealth Revealed!*

We left after breakfast so Cukierkorn could introduce me to Michael Rosenbaum, one of his allies at New Reform. Rosenbaum lived in an-

other tidy and well-heeled Kansas City neighborhood that, to my outsider's eye, appeared to be almost identical to the one we had visited for
the shiva. This house was wood shingled and painted yellow, and there
was a large plastic deer stationed in the front yard. Rosenbaum was a
slow-moving man—it took him at least five minutes to answer the
door—and very heavy, with a sickly pallor and an angry face. He was
dressed that morning in loose sweatpants rolled up to his knees, a stained
golf shirt, and he wasn't wearing shoes. His feet, I noticed, looked swollen
and inflamed, evidence of circulatory problems caused by diabetes, and
he was clearly in some discomfort.

"The Rabbit!" he cried, brightening when he saw Cukierkorn. This
was Rosenbaum's nickname for him, a nod to the easygoing nature of
Cukierkorn's rabbinical philosophy. Cukierkorn, for his part, liked to
refer to Rosenbaum as Rosen*ton*. "For obvious reasons," he said.

Rosenton was a New Yorker, from the Bronx, and had come west
with his wife, who had subsequently divorced him and took their two
sons. He lived alone now, in a cavernous and cloyingly decorated
house—a remnant, no doubt, of his marital years—cluttered with his
collection of vintage toys and the detritus of his medications. We settled in the living room and Rosenton and Cukierkorn traded insults—
bad Jew versus fat guy—something Rosenton in particular seemed to
enjoy. Then he noticed my notebook and asked what I was doing scrib-
bling down what he said. When I told him I was writing about Cukierkorn he laughed.

"Why would you want to write about this fake, pork-eating Jew?" he
asked.

I told him that I was interested in the Jews of the Midwest—he nar-
rowed his eyes skeptically at that—and that I also found Cukierkorn's
conversions noteworthy.

"All he wants to do is make more Jews," Rosenton said. "He goes to wherever the fuck it is he goes and he sprinkles these people with stardust and they deify him!"

Cukierkorn, who, when he wasn't joking at Rosenton's expense, spent most of his time checking emails on his phone, cracked a half-smile at this.

"Me, I don't want any more Jews," Rosenton said, waving at the empty house. "I want to die alone."

Rosenton told me that he liked to help Cukierkorn, with money for his conversion trips and expenses for his book. He thought very highly of Cukierkorn—"He's a very Jewish guy, the Rabbit"—and went out of his way to support him with the other members of the temple. I was curious how far that help really went, given the man's frail health, the fact he was not a particularly charming sort of person, and was, like Cukierkorn, an outsider of very different stock than the Kansas City Jewish aristocracy that effectively owned New Reform. Regardless, the quid pro quo for these efforts was Cukierkorn's friendship: The Rabbit stopped by regularly to visit, took Rosenton for meals around town, and generally provided a connection to the wider world.

Eventually, the conversation turned to Cukierkorn and the board and the lowball offer. Cukierkorn blustered, saying he was certain that he could fight for his job and win.

"They don't know who they're fucking with," he said. Rosenton seemed less sure.

"You never know where you stand with these people," he said. He paused and thought for a moment. "This discount brand of Judaism is very odd."

V.

New Reform's congregants gather for prayer in a narrow Georgian brick box in midtown Kansas City. Something about its clean-lined construction reminded me of a church. When I told Cukierkorn this, he laughed and said that it had in fact once been home to a group of Methodists. Inside I saw hints of an ecclesiastical past wherever I looked. The beige carpeting, white, cloth-backed pews, organ, and the small, bare lectern for the rabbi on the sanctuary—all of it suggested a tranquility (and blandness) of purpose that read as Protestant to me. There were no Stars of David, Israeli flags, or menorahs, no porcelain doves or eagles, no artworks of the Negev or the Old City. Even the Hebrew characters inscribed on the ark for the Torah were hard to find, obscured by a green potted plant.

This design, an exemplar of the Cult of Synthesis style, suited the founders of New Reform, a group of wealthy Jewish liberals who in the late 1960s had decided that B'nai Jehudah's Judaism had become too traditional. Many of them hailed from early Reform families, migrants of the second wave, who had come to the region in the days of the Kansas territory. For them, Judaism was the Judaism of that era, an ultra-progressive kind of Reform Judaism that is now known as Classical Reform Judaism.

"Classical Reform" wasn't a term I was familiar with prior to coming to Kansas City. I knew Reform: the Judaism of middle-class northeastern clichés, the Judaism of the yarmulke in my closet. Classical Reform was something different. It referred to the original Reform pioneered as a movement and denomination in Germany in the 1830s, and later brought to this country by German immigrants in the 1870s.[1] In "Classical Reform Judaism: A Concise Profile," Rabbi Howard A. Berman defines this variant of the Reform denomination as:

> Grounded in the Biblical tradition of the Hebrew Prophets, interpreted as the emphasis on ethical action and social justice, rather than on ritual observance or ceremonial law. Intellectually, it was an outgrowth of the modern academic, scientific study of Jewish history and philosophy that emerged in Germany in the early decades of the 19th century; culturally, it reflected the transformation of Jewish communal life at that time, in response to the Emancipation of European Jewry from the social isolation of the ghetto.

Practically speaking, Classical Reform is often defined by what it rejects rather than by what it includes. Classical Reform Jews don't wear yarmulkes, keep kosher, or offer bar and bat mitzvahs to their children (instead, they have "confirmations"). There are no light timers, no keys strapped to the wrists, no Sabbath elevators, Sabbath goy, flying chickens, or pre-ripped toilet paper. Until World War II and the Holocaust, staunch Classical Reformers rejected Israel as the Jewish homeland, on the grounds that Judaism was a religion and not a nationality.

Classical Reform temples in the United States are also replete with the trappings of the Cult of Synthesis. It would not be unusual to hear

---

1. Jewish reform efforts took place before this period, in the United States and elsewhere. But the organized Reform movement was primarily developed in Germany and transported here by immigrants.

the Pledge of Allegiance in these houses of worship, or to see the Stars and Bars flying next to the ark for the Torah. New Reform, for example, keeps an American flag on its sanctuary. Its weekly services conclude with a group rendition of "God Bless America."

At the risk of being confusing, I will point out that Classical Reform was originally known simply as Reform. Over time, though, "mainstream" Reform has incorporated a fair amount of ritual practice, Hebrew, and Zionism. Go into practically any Reform temple today in the United States and you will see men in yarmulkes, hear prayer and song in Hebrew, see young people studying for their bar and bat mitzvahs—on Saturday, not Sunday—and listen to stories about Birthright trips from the college kids. All of these things would have been wildly objectionable to the early reformers. Modern-day Reform has moved far enough away from the foundational precepts that a term like "Classical Reform" now makes sense. Any Reform congregation in this country that has been in existence for more than fifty years once espoused what would today be considered Classical Reform views. Presently, no more than fifteen Classical Reform congregations exist. New Reform, despite its name, is one of those few.

Cukierkorn had brought me to the temple on a Sunday, my last day in town. The children enrolled in New Reform's religious school had already arrived by the time we got there. They were loitering in the hallway eating bagels and drinking cups of orange juice. Cukierkorn would lead a short service for them, after which the kids would go to their Sunday-school classrooms upstairs. Cukierkorn had told me that the congregational growth he had produced stemmed largely from his openness to members from non-conventional families. That openness was reflected in the wide mix of ethnic and racial backgrounds to be seen among the children. A few adults volunteered to help with the instruction, but most parents dropped off their kids and used the school as an opportunity to steal a few free hours. According to Cukierkorn, the ones who stayed for the service and to volunteer at the school were typically from these new, less conventional, families. This irritated him to no end. The ones most likely to confront him over his methods and personality were also the least likely to be involved with the activities at the temple.

The children's services lasted about fifteen minutes. Cukierkorn delivered a hasty sermon, sped through a prayer or two, and then came down from the sanctuary, shook some hands, teased the kids, grabbed someone's baby and paraded around with her. He asked me to address the children and their parents. I told them the story of my childhood, ad-libbed a moral, and then took questions. Later, Cukierkorn complimented me on my talents as a speaker, but suggested that perhaps I was too earnest. "You need to work on your sales pitch."

Cukierkorn introduced me to one of the mothers from the congregation, a slender blonde, with blue eyes, who had converted to Judaism only a couple of years before.

"Rachel, come meet Ted," he said. Cukierkorn told me the story of her conversion, and she thanked him for his understanding and guidance. Cukierkorn brushed this aside with a laugh, and said, "I wanted you to meet him"—meaning me—"because I wanted him to see a hot, blond Jew."

Rachel blushed, but she had apparently heard this sort of thing from Cukierkorn before. She told him that she had to be getting home—the kids were late for something. Cukierkorn wrapped an arm around her shoulder and gave her a warm half-hug.

"Do other rabbis sexually harass you the way I do?"

Cukierkorn made the rounds of the Sunday-school classes, stopped in at each room, bantered amiably with the teachers, made nice with the children. Everyone seemed to react to him with a mixture of admiration and embarrassment. In one class he held forth on the Hebrew alphabet and its connection to Kabbalah. Another group—second graders by the looks of them—got a few words on the history of circumcision. The next heard about Jewish souls and past-life regression. Last was a class of teenagers who were engaged in a discussion on racism and intolerance, which Cukierkorn turned into a joking diatribe against Fred Phelps and the Westboro Baptist Church. Phelps and his followers have gained national notoriety for picketing military funerals and Jewish temples with signs reading GOD HATES FAGS and GOD HATES JEWS. They have staged protests at New Reform on three occasions. Cukierkorn said Phelps was a lesson in the Jewish ethical responsibilities in the face of evil.

"You might think that it would be okay to go out and shoot one of these Phelps people"—the teacher gave Cukierkorn a warning look, but there was no stopping him—"but good Jews aren't allowed to do this. We have a responsibility to do the right thing."

Most of the children looked bored. It was a Sunday morning and the authority figures were reminding them about Jewish victimization and superiority. One kid, an oversized boy with a fashionable mop of hair who had come to temple dressed for a Goth-metal concert, watched Cukierkorn with dead teenaged eyes. Before the rabbi could say anything else, the teacher wrested control of her class and hurried us along.

We left soon after that, for lunch at another barbecue joint. As we were eating our chicken and drinking sweet tea, Cukierkorn received a phone call. He stayed on the line for a few moments, and when he was done, he told me we would have to cut short our meal. The father of the Goth-metal kid had chewed him out over what he had told his son that morning, which had somehow been translated as "The rabbi said it was okay to kill anti-Semites." The man had threatened to leave the temple and Cukierkorn needed to go to his house and calm him down.

Cukierkorn vented angrily on the ride to the house. A problem boy, this one, emotionally stunted and strange, and the father wanted to foist the kid's issues onto Cukierkorn. Always, always, always, they wanted to fuck him. He hadn't seen the father at services in who knows how long, but still, this guy felt entitled to tell Cukierkorn how to do his job.

"Some Jews," Cukierkorn muttered as we pulled into the driveway at the man's house. "For what do I need this?"

Cukierkorn gathered himself, forced a smile, and told me to wait in the car. He returned in about half an hour, relieved but still angry.

"How did it go?" I asked.

"Group hug," he said, and he drove me to the airport.

VI.

I returned to Kansas City several months later only to discover that the amity hadn't lasted. Cukierkorn's position at New Reform, which he detailed for me as we drove around in his car, had deteriorated significantly. The board had formally withdrawn its contract offer. His contract would expire and he would be out of a job. Cukierkorn had hired a lawyer to negotiate a settlement. He wanted either to be kept on with a new contract, or to leave immediately, after being paid the balance of the money owed him. He also wanted New Reform to drop the two-year, 100-mile non-compete clause.

Cukierkorn briefed me on his plan for breaking the strictures of the non-compete. He understood that the clause barred him from accepting work as a rabbi for any congregation within the exclusion boundaries. But what, he asked, is a rabbi? What is a congregation? He couldn't take a job leading one of the existing synagogues, or start one of his own, not in any ordinary sense. But he had options nonetheless. A "Jewish learning center," for example—an academic institution, where he could teach the religion to prospective converts and to individual Jews with an interest in developing their spiritual understanding—was a possibility. It wouldn't function like a traditional temple: no Friday services and no Sunday school, no members, and no dues. Even more ambitious was his scheme to create an e-rabbi business he planned to call TheConciergeRabbi.com. Again, this would be nothing like a traditional congregation, but unlike the learning center, it wouldn't have an established curriculum. Cukierkorn would tailor his services to meet the needs of his religious consumers, and charge for services rendered. He could officiate at their weddings—dogs or no—ready them for conversion, bar and bat mitzvahs, whatever they wanted, within the flexible bounds of his Judaism. This, he said, offered the best outcome: no brick-and-mortar temple, no whiny congregation, no uptight board members who "starched their underwear."

"The idea would be to find out what people need," he said. "'How can I provide you with Judaism?'"

Cukierkorn admitted that his lawyer wasn't entirely convinced by his parsing of the law. But he appreciated the rabbi's approach.

"He respects me because he thinks I'm devious," Cukierkorn said. "He's wrong. I just have a Talmudic mind."

"I don't understand," I said to Cukierkorn. "How did things go so wrong?"

"You have to understand Kansas City," he said. "A very anti-Semitic place. Always has been. The Jews here are rich and conservative and they don't like change. They want to *pass*," he said. "And at New Reform, it's not just that they like the old system. They're the ones on top. Change can only work against them."

We reached our destination a few moments later: another ranch house, this one with a few Danish Modern touches, in yet another reputable neighborhood. Cukierkorn had brought me here to meet one of the old Jews, the ones who passed, one of Sarna's Cultish Synthesizers who also happened to be one of Cukierkorn's supporters.

Henry Marder was a frail and grumpy-looking man, eighty years old, with a rutted and leathery face, oversized rubbery ears, and a sparse, gray goatee. He was dressed in baggy blue jeans and a green flannel shirt and needed a cane to walk. He greeted Cukierkorn warmly, and nodded politely to me, brushing off my offer to help him get into the car.

"Let's get some Chinese," he said.

Cukierkorn drove us to the Pine and Bamboo Garden, a Chinese restaurant with large fish tanks and reproductions of traditional scroll paintings, the sort of place where you have to demand chopsticks. The staff all knew Marder, though, and immediately brought him the "Chinese menu." Marder ordered spicy noodles and a plate of sautéed chicken and broccoli. Then, like Rosenton, he asked me why the hell I wanted to know so much about Kansas City's Jews.

Although his family had belonged to B'nai Jehudah going back four generations, Marder had been raised in an "assimilated" household. His mother, he said, liked the idea of observance, which for her meant that when she called the kids to the breakfast table for eggs and bacon, she didn't call it bacon, but "strips." He said he had never experienced any anti-Semitism growing up, but he did concede that the city was segregated. Jews stuck together, had their own clubs and organizations and high school fraternities. Marder never liked that, though, never wanted to be an "archetypal Jew" who lived in a ghetto. His parents at one point tried to send him to a Conservative congregation to prepare for his bar mitzvah, but he refused because he thought it would set him apart as a Jew. Against the wishes of his parents, he had eloped with a "gentile girl" who refused to let him raise the children as Jews. (They eventually divorced.)

He had been among the B'nai Jehudah renegades who had founded New Reform in 1967, yet didn't view himself as an engaged member of the Jewish community. A Jew should belong to a temple, he said—he couldn't imagine *not* belonging to one—but beyond that he felt little need to mingle with his coreligionists. He was a wealthy man, gave his money to charity—over 100 different organizations benefited from his largesse each year—none, he pointed out, specifically Jewish. He had traveled to Israel once and said he "admired those people," but he never wanted to live there or even return for a second visit. I asked him if he had ever done any organized Jewish travel, and he said, emphatically, "no." He wouldn't even to go to Florida in the winter. Too Jewish, he said, although he was clearly Jewish enough to think he knew his way around a Chinese menu, which I thought but didn't say.

We discussed why the older members at New Reform seemed to react so strongly to Cukierkorn. Marder, who, like Rosenton, considered Cukierkorn a friend, said it may have had something to do with his decision to implement elements of traditional observance, like bar and bat mitzvahs, which Cukierkorn had performed since taking over leadership of the congregation. It was an aversion to such things that had motivated the creation of New Reform in the first place. At the same time, he was quick to point out that most of the old folks didn't hold strong theological opinions. Unlike the early Reformers, they had no serious ethical objections to ritual. It just made them uncomfortable. For them it was as much about *taste* as religion. Traditional Judaism, with its symbols and religious displays and swaggering Zionism and loudly self-deprecatory humor, was too showy, too overt: too Jewish.

Cukierkorn drove Marder home after lunch, and the old man invited us inside to have a look at his collection of antique canes. I tried to show as much interest in his tchotchkes as I could, but I found myself more drawn to the old black-and-white photos of Marder's father in his study. Marder senior was sitting a horse—he had dabbled in livestock until the Depression—and looked like a real cowboy. Marder seemed pleased when I told him this.

Marder's walking sticks were displayed everywhere throughout the house. They must have been valuable, because he instructed me not to touch them. I offered an obligatory guffaw at the one with a head carved to look like Bill Clinton. Marder made me guess what the head had been made from, and when I couldn't, he explained that it had been fashioned from a bull's penis.

Another one did capture my interest, though. It came from Austria, Marder told me, around 1900. The shaft was made from a single sleek piece of turned wood. The head was brass, and had been cast to depict the face of a ghoulish Jewish caricature, complete with a hooked and elongated nose, beady slits for eyes, and a shiftless, grinning, animalistic mouth. Marder had purchased it at auction, in Chicago, for $800. I asked if I could break his rules and hold the cane. He thought about it for a moment or two. The answer was no.

VII.

Rosenton's health had declined noticeably since I last saw him. He couldn't make it down the stairs to let us in, so Cukierkorn had used his own set of keys, and the three of us had our chat in the bedroom, where Rosenton was sitting in a ratty burgundy recliner, holding a plastic back-scratcher, his bulk covered with a purple afghan, except for his swollen calves and feet. A catheter snaked out from underneath the blanket. Bills, unopened junk mail, paperbacks, trade magazines, and pill bottles covered the bed and the better part of the floor.

"You have to understand," Rosenton said, "this has nothing to do with religion. For these people, a rabbi is a limo driver. That's all. If they could run the congregation without a rabbi, they would. They only have one because thirty or forty years ago someone told them they had to. That's the level of Judaism they want."

Cukierkorn had wanted me to see Rosenton again because he thought I had some misconceptions about why he was being fired. If I thought that the board wanted to be rid of him because of the Hebrew in the service, or because of the discretionary fund or the conversion trips, I was wrong. They didn't like any of that, make no mistake, and they hated the jokes, the wild statements at Sunday school, and the dog. (Rosenton said he didn't understand this one—"It's not like he brought a whore into the temple to suck his dick.") But none of these offenses, large or small, were why Cukierkorn was being fired. They wanted him gone because they couldn't control him.

"For years you were their trained monkey," Rosenton said to Cukier-korn. "Their performing seal, their prostitute, their *nigra*! And now, look at you, you come here and you're crying your eyes out."

"I never cried," Cukierkorn said.

The board and the older congregants had accepted the Rabbit's eccentricities and indiscretions so long as he was, as Rosenton put it, obedient. Cukierkorn didn't have much money when he arrived in Kansas City, and financial necessity had made him pliable. But now, with his real estate successes, his stock triumphs, and his prominence as an author and lecturer and converter of lost Jews, he couldn't be ordered around. This seemed likely, both from the way Cukierkorn had been reprimanded for his remarks at Sunday school, and the easy arrogance with which he thought he had resolved the problem. The main issue, as with most conflicts, involved control and power and ownership.

"They're angry, very angry," Rosenton said. "They're putting their dicks out on this one."

A reconciliation between the two parties no longer seemed feasible. The board had already announced to the congregation that Cukierkorn's contract wouldn't be renewed. The local Jewish paper had run a couple of articles on the situation, one of which reported that "an overwhelming majority" of the board wanted Cukierkorn to leave. The issues remaining to be resolved were when, exactly, the Rabbit would depart—Cukierkorn, if he were to leave, wanted to do so immediately—the generosity of his severance, and the non-compete clause.

Cukierkorn still held out some small hope that he could force the board to keep him on. The membership loved him, he said, even if the board didn't, and the temple bylaws stated that a two-thirds vote of the full congregation could override the will of the board. Unfortunately, Cukierkorn needed the approval of the board to move forward with a vote, which he wasn't likely to receive. Rosenton, for his part, wasn't as confident in Cukierkorn's ability to carry a majority of the congregants.

"They're going to replace him," he said to me. "With someone like what he used to be. Whether that person becomes Cukierkorn, who knows?"

Rosenton, for his part, had resigned his membership in New Reform in protest. "Only one in this whole shit pile."

VIII.

Andrew Bergerson was a professor in the history department of the University of Missouri–Kansas City. A biographical sketch on the UM-KC website described him as a "historian of everyday life . . . [whose] research focuses on the historical impact of everyday ways of being, believing, and behaving." Mostly, though, he was an expert on Germany in the first half of the twentieth century. Three years ago he joined New Reform, along with his African-American wife, and his two children. One year ago he joined the board. He was one of Cukierkorn's supporters, a newer congregant drawn to the environment Cukierkorn had created. Bergerson was supposed to be the agent of the rabbi's unlikely hopes to bring his job status to a congregational vote.

I met with Bergerson in his cluttered campus office. He was a largish man, with gentle, questioning eyes, a receding hairline, and a brownish-red beard working toward gray. He was dressed in jeans and a rumpled pink button-down, with a maroon scarf wound about his neck.

Bergerson said he was a "red diaper baby," the child of Jewish-Communist parents from back east. His family had mixed "radical atheism" with Conservative Judaism, which for them meant a Passover Seder each year, some religious education for the children, and the strong understanding that a belief in God was "silly." He had dabbled with observance while at college, but really he only liked the music. "Our faith has been kept alive by concerts," he said. He had experimented with keeping kosher but ended up becoming a vegetarian. He was spiritual but not religious. He had, at one point or another, worshipped the solstice. Eventually, he had shed all allegiance to the faith of his childhood.

"Up until a few years ago," he said, "if you asked me if I was Jewish I would always have said no."

The change came when his seven-year-old daughter asked him why they didn't celebrate Passover. He liked the holiday, and couldn't say no to his daughter, so he agreed to lead a Seder, which he discovered he was able to do, despite the years, in Hebrew. Something in this simple act of memory provoked a spiritual reckoning that sent his life careering in a new direction.

"It was such an intense Jewish experience," he said. "I found myself crying. What a connection I felt to this tradition—and I believed in it completely!"

This, he said, was not easy for him to accept. He still didn't believe in God, and the continual act of "translating" religion through the prism of his intellectualism was a struggle. His "reading of God based on Martin Buber" helped, allowed him to "embrace the contradictions in the Torah"; as did his understanding of Paul, who, he said, "Got it right more than most Jews believe." The real challenge for him, though, was that his identity had been forged from rejection—of the past, his history, his heritage. A prayer book happened to be sitting on his desk, buried beneath the textbooks and obscure journals and piles of student manuscripts. He picked it up and ran his fingers over the Hebrew characters on the cover.

"Dealing with being a Jew has been worse than when I came out as bisexual."

It had taken time for him to warm to Cukierkorn. At first, he seemed just "a snide guy," and Bergerson didn't care for his "off-color jokes." Now, though, they were close friends, someone he met with regularly to discuss religion, Torah, whatever came to mind. He preferred Cukierkorn to the older congregants, who were, in Bergerson's estimation, "too German, too Episcopal," and far too committed to an ethnic identity that he refused to embrace: white and conservative and silently Jewish. He understood their desire to be inconspicuous—"I think all Jews live in anxiety. We're always looking for a way out"—but he couldn't, and wouldn't, hide the exuberance of his return.

Bergerson acknowledged that he had only been brought onto the board to "help resolve a particular political problem," which he understood to mean bridging the divide between the old and new members. But he sounded hesitant when I asked him if he thought Cukierkorn would get his vote. There were too many oldsters on the board for that. Instead, Cukierkorn would go, he would start his new congregation, or whatever he planned to call it, and Bergerson would join him; he would resign from the board and quit New Reform. Bergerson didn't think anyone would try to talk him out of it.

IX.

The Houston's at Country Club Plaza in Kansas City skewed surprisingly upscale. The Kelly green and mustard-yellow cloth awnings and polished brass-plated front door reminded me of a pre-war hotel or serviced apartment building, minus the doormen. Inside, hardwood tables, upholstered dining chairs, and wood blinds and wood paneling gave the room a warmly formal ambience that the white tablecloths and starched waitstaff did nothing to diminish. It seemed to me a fair dose of puffery for a burger joint, but perhaps the locals saw it differently: The lunch clientele that day came dressed and primped and made-up in varying shades of wealth and semiretirement.

Cukierkorn had insisted that we meet later for lunch at another barbecue spot, so I took a table and nursed a coffee. I passed a few moments trying to tease out what it was about Henry Marder and the New Reform version of Classical Reform that bothered me. Putting aside my agnosticism, I should have found Classical Reform to my liking. It was liberal, principled, and rooted in history, and most important, free of the hackneyed stereotypes of Judaism. If one were to put to Marder my question, "Am I a Jew?" I think he would have no trouble answering "yes." But still, something bothered me.

Tom Barnett, the man I had come to Houston's to see, arrived as I was thinking about this. Barnett was the president of the board at New Reform. A reserved and dapper fellow, Barnett was sixty years old, although he looked younger. He was fit and preternaturally tanned, with the kind of weathered face one gets from excessive golfing. He was dressed in a pair of crisp slacks, a gray argyle sweater, and a light-colored oxford, the collar buttoned down and tucked into his sweater.

Barnett's father, like Marder, had been part of the B'nai Jehudah splinter group that had started New Reform. His family also had long-standing Kansas City roots: His ancestors—Germans, mostly—had been among the founders of B'nai Jehudah in 1870. Barnett owned an "incentive and promotional product" company called Mid-American Merchandising, which operated from a 60,000-square-foot warehouse built, in 1906, by his great-grandfather, who had been in the cattle-rendering business.

Barnett told me that his father had at first been reluctant to leave B'nai Jehudah. It was the oldest Reform congregation in the area, and the largest, and it had the deepest historical ties to the community. What's more, its Judaism had traditionally been the sort preferred by Kansas City's Jewish establishment: a Judaism for which the temple, Barnett explained, was less a house of worship but of assimilation. B'nai Jehudah began to change in 1960, when it hired a new rabbi who, as Barnett put it, "decided to morph into more mainstream Judaism." This meant Hebrew in the services, bar mitzvahs along with confirmations, and religious education on Saturdays instead of Sunday. This didn't sit well with people like Barnett's father.

"We liked our Classical Reform beliefs," he said. "The additional ritual and whatnot just wasn't our cup of tea."

Barnett's beverage of choice is, in many ways, a perfect example of what Reform Judaism used to be before it lost its place in the mainstream and became Classical Reform.

In 1885, a conference of America's leading Reform rabbis was convened in Pittsburgh. At the end of the meeting the rabbis issued a communiqué—"The Pittsburgh Platform"—that served as a national Reform

Jewish mission statement. Of the eight tenets in the Platform, number five seems most closely linked with the beliefs and desires of Barnett, and Marder, and their forebears:

> We hold that all such Mosaic and rabbinical laws as regulate diet, priestly purity, and dress originated in ages and under the influence of ideas entirely foreign to our present mental and spiritual state. They fail to impress the modern Jew with a spirit of priestly holiness; their observance in our days is apt rather to obstruct than to further modern spiritual elevation.

Note the confidence with which the Platform rejected tradition. It was not unusual at this time for Reform Jews to express themselves in this way. They believed—vehemently—not only in their viewpoint, but in the inevitability of its triumph.

This kind of Reform, stripped down, released from history, built on ethics—Barnett's "cup of tea"—reached its apex of national acceptance in Pittsburgh. Since that moment, Reform in the United States has seen a slow but unstinting return to the Mosaic and rabbinical traditions, marked occasionally by restatements of what the denomination was becoming. The next such restatement came in 1937, after the meeting of the Central Conference of American Rabbis, in Columbus, Ohio. A new document was put forth, this one called the "Guiding Principles of Reform Judaism." In it, Reform's leadership acknowledged the "changes that have taken place in the modern world"—the rise of Nazism, no doubt among them—"and the consequent need of stating anew the teachings of Reform Judaism." Thus, in the section entitled "Religious Life," we find:

> Judaism as a way of life requires in addition to its moral and spiritual demands, the preservation of the Sabbath, festivals and Holy Days,

the retention and development of such customs, symbols and cere-
monies as possess inspirational value, the cultivation of distinctive
forms of religious art and music and the use of Hebrew, together
with the vernacular, in our worship and instruction.

The next major document was produced in 1976. It continued the
process toward greater acceptance of ritual, declaring "private prayer and
public worship; daily religious observance; [and] keeping the Sabbath
and the holy days," fundamental aspects of the Reform denomination. For
the first time, it also openly and explicitly recognized the existence of a
Jewish nationality, in the section on the "People Israel":

Born as Hebrews in the ancient Near East, we are bound together
like all ethnic groups by language, land, history, culture, and institutions. . . . Throughout our long history our people has been insepa-
rable from its religion with its messianic hope that humanity will be
redeemed.

It is hard to determine when, exactly, Reform and Classical Reform
were no longer one and the same. But certainly this Reform would have
been impossible for people like the founders of New Reform to accept.

I asked Barnett if he recalled why his father decided to leave B'nai
Jehudah, and he said he "remembered this like it happened yesterday." He
was a teenager, a student in the one of the congregation's confirmation
classes.

"A guy comes into the class and he says to me, 'You need to go see the
cantor.' It's a relatively new cantor, and I leave the room, I go see the cantor.
I'm in his office and he hands me the *Union Prayer Book* and says, 'Read.'
And I start to read the English. And he says, 'No, read the Hebrew.' And I
said, 'I can't read Hebrew.' And he says, 'Then you can't be confirmed.'"

Barnett frowned at the memory, which, even now, seemed to sting. But it was also clear that today, as he undertook the process of firing a rabbi, he was aware that he had triumphed over this liturgical taskmaster.

"That day I got home, and I told my dad, 'The cantor says I can't be confirmed because I can't read Hebrew.'"

That did it. His father joined the splinter group, taking his family with him, and they have been members of New Reform ever since.

"If you go to B'nai Jehudah now," he said, "the Friday night service is mostly in Hebrew. There were four prayers in English at a recent one I went to. And afterward, the president of the congregation, who's a friend of mine, I walked up to him and said, 'Howard, did you understand what the rabbi was saying?' And he said, 'No, I didn't.' And I asked him, 'Well, why do you like it?' and he says, 'Well, it sounds good.'"

Nothing in this should have upset me, either, not really. It was a rational belief, and one that I shared. The problem for me was that Reform had originally started as a radical break from the stultifying ways of the past, and here, in Kansas City, it was the stultifying past. The founders of New Reform had given ground through the years—Cukierkorn did bar mitzvahs now, and there was some Hebrew—but they hadn't done so willingly. Barnett told me about the fight over transition from the old *Union Prayer Book* to the new one.

"It was overwhelmingly approved, except by one of the founders," Barnett said. "He voted against it 26 times. There were 200 people voting for it, and he kept putting deals in there to hold it up. And when you asked him about he said, 'Well, it doesn't have the old English, doesn't have the same cadence, and whatnot.'" Barnett liked this, even if he was indifferent to which prayer book they used. "It meant something to *him*."

Jonathan Sarna writes that the Cult of Synthesis began to collapse around the time that New Reform was founded, in the 1960s. Jews, like most mainstream minority groups, had become less concerned with being viewed as purely American, and the celebration of difference replaced the celebration of assimilation. "Hopes for national unity gave way to expectations of (multi)cultural diversity," Sarna writes, "and the core that once stood for America disintegrated and splintered."

New Reform has always been small. Its bylaws restrict membership to under 325 families. Barnett told me he was prepared to lose people if he fired Cukierkorn. He was comfortable with the idea of the congregation declining to 200 families, perhaps even fewer. He also knew that the old members, the founders, the ones who would vote twenty-six times for *their* prayer book, would grow old and die, and that the ones who replaced them might not share his commitment to the old way. But he didn't care. He wanted what he wanted and he would have it for as long as he could. I thought of Marder and the cane that he wouldn't let me touch. This Judaism of theirs, it was a relic, moribund, withering, and defeated. But there could be no doubt who owned it.

Part VII

THE SPARK

Some people just want to be Jewish.

—Joanne Palmer, from "A *Pintele Yid*—Stories of Conversion"

I.

Carving out space for one's spiritual autonomy—insisting on the right to accept or reject a particular god—is a fairly modern and definitely American thing to do. For some, it may appear to be a dodge: you are who you are and none other. According to that logic, there is no escape from my irreducible Jewish core, my intrinsic Jew, the one who exists independent of any desire I might have to order the world according to my preference and to my benefit. The multiple layers of upbringing, education, culture, and class imposed on me through the course of my life only conceal the true Jewish nucleus, the atomic Judaism, the Jewish *spark* that persists despite all efforts to extinguish it. That spark even has a name: *pintele yid*, which typically translates from Yiddish as the "little point of a Jew." According to tradition and argument, that "little point" is me.

The concept of the *pintele yid* seems to have its origin in biblical lore. It is written in Deuteronomy that when Moses returns from the mountaintop to address the Israelites, he explains the newly struck covenant with God:

> Ye stand this day all of you before the LORD your God; your captains of your tribes, your elders, and your officers, with all the men of Israel. . . . Neither with you only do I make this covenant and this oath;/But with him that standeth here with us this day before the LORD our God, and also with him that is not here with us this day.

Midrash *Shemot Rabbah*, one of the haggadic commentaries on the Hebrew Bible, explains that when Moses refers to "him that is not here with us," he does not mean that some Israelites were absent at Mount Sinai on that day: quite the opposite. According to Jewish tradition, Moses liberated 600,000 people—the full nation of Israelite men, women, and children—from Egypt and led them into the Negev. The midrash teaches that not only these Jews were present, but so too were the souls of *every potential Jew*, each Jew who had ever lived and who will ever live: the living, the dead, and the unborn. These other Jews were the ones Moses said were "not here," but he was referring only to their body, not to their spirit. That spirit, the *pintele yid*, was in fact there to witness the covenant, and to rejoice in God's favor.

The covenant, the souls, the indivisible mystical Jewish particles: all of it sounds to me like the storyline of a good B-movie and not a unifying principle for one's life. I have enough issues regarding Judaism without having to worry about an invisible Jew monkeying about with my id. But whether I believe the biblical tale or its Talmudic interpretation is irrelevant. Even if I divorce the concept from faith and consider it in terms of theological philosophy, I am deeply ambivalent about the *pintele yid*. To concede my soul to the spark would be to surrender the autonomy of selecting my Jewish fate. To borrow from Judith Neulander, I prefer to choose to be Chosen.

After all, if there is a *pintele yid*, of what use is my attempt to reckon with the religion? Given the spark, would I not be equally successful in answering my question if I did nothing? Eventually, without much effort on my part, wouldn't the innate Hebrew embedded in my genetic code rise—righteously angry, *payis*-clad, and Yiddish-inflected? It could be argued that my Jewish soul has surfaced already, and that this book is evidence of its undeniable essence. I am reminded of Father William Sanchez, the Crypto-Jewish priest in New Mexico who found DNA testing such persuasive indication of his *Kohanim* descent. I understand the attraction that genetics hold for those who desire a Jewish identity: It offers a way to liberate the *pintele yid* from the realm of metaphor, of smoldering religious fires, of unborn Jews amassed at the foot of Mount Sinai, and render it scientific, verifiable, inarguable. For me, the leap from the human genome to the Jewish soul is too far. But there are those who believe otherwise. As with the Orthodox, I had to make room for them in my investigation because I knew that perhaps, in the glow from their spark, I might discern some trace of my own.

II.

I met Alan Tullio for breakfast at the Yonah Schimmel Knish Bakery on the Lower East Side of Manhattan. I should point out that despite its vaunted shtetlach reputation, the Lower East Side is not, in its present incarnation, a Jewish neighborhood and has not been for more than a generation. The Jewish-immigrant ghetto-dwellers fled long ago, earning, inheriting, educating, and stealing their way of out of the mythical slum and into the mainstream. Some vestigial Jewish shops and businesses remain, for Haredi men to buy hats, and for their wives and daughters to buy dresses and shoes. There are a few sweets shops and hardware stores, too, as well as a handful of well-known restaurants, like Katz's Delicatessen, a tourist destination for pastrami, and Schimmel's, which I like for its warming, leaden potato pastries. But mostly the Jewish character is gone. Those interested in communing with history would do better to purchase a guided tour at the Tenement Museum a few blocks from Schimmel's.

Tullio, whom I had never met before, arrived a few minutes late. He was an olive-skinned man in his early fifties, with watery eyes and a prominent nose. He wore a navy overcoat, pressed black slacks, a white shirt, black tie, black leather shoes, and a black fedora.

"The hat," I asked him, "and the tie. Does that mean you're Black Hat,[1] or do you just like black hats?"

---

1. A slang term for an ultra-Orthodox Jew.

"As a matter of fact, I just like the hat," he replied, somewhat pleased at my erroneous assumption. "I am a regular attendee at a Conservative shul, but in terms of observance I'm somewhere between Conservative and Orthodox. I guess they call that Conservadox."

"But then shouldn't you be wearing a yarmulke?"

"I should," he said. "So I suppose right now I'm on the Conservative side."

Bennett Greenspan, the owner of a genetic screening company, Family Tree DNA, had introduced me to Tullio. I had learned of Family Tree because it had conducted the DNA tests for Father William Sanchez, the Catholic *Kohanim* in New Mexico. Family Tree provides genetic testing for people of every background and genealogical interest, but Greenspan, whom I had spoken to on the phone, is Jewish and takes a certain proprietary interest in the DNA of his potential coreligionists. Father Sanchez, for example, had not received his test results from Family Tree by mail or email. Greenspan had called him. "Did you know you were Jewish?" Greenspan had asked. Sanchez said he did. "And did you know you were *Kohanim?*" "No, I didn't know that." "Well, what do you do for a living?" Sanchez had replied that he was a priest, and the line went silent. "Don't worry," Greenspan had said finally. "We'll take you back."

Tullio had been raised in Bay Terrace, Queens, a neighborhood that in the 1950s, when he was a child, resembled my mother's Jamaica Estates, in terms of its significant Jewish population. Along with that demographic quirk, Tullio also seemed to share my mother's acute awareness of being surrounded by Jews, although with very different consequences. He was Catholic, born and raised, of Italian descent; his grandfather had come to the United States in 1903 from Vallecorsa, a small town southeast of Rome not much known for its Jewish character. Tullio said he suffered from "Jew envy" for as long as he could remember.

"I wanted to be a Jew. I went to Bayside High School, which had a reputation for being one of the top schools in New York City, certainly one of the top schools in Queens. My teachers were Jewish, the principal was named Sam Moskowitz. We had a Hebrew culture club, a civil rights club—it was heavily Jewish. I attended my friends' bar mitzvahs with great pleasure," he said, emphasizing the formality of the word "attended."

"You do realize that's somewhat unusual?" I said. "I mean, I went to plenty of bar mitzvahs as a kid. I found them *painfully* boring. I liked the party afterward, but the service? It was like a punishment."

"For me, it was like getting a look over the side of the fence and feeling pretty excited about it. I remember thinking that I was going to get to wear a yarmulke and saying to myself, 'Man, this is cool.'"

(In his later teenage years, Tullio discovered something else on "the other side of the fence" that he found even more intriguing: Jewish girls. "I found them exciting and intelligent and sexy. They were everything that I wanted, everything that—I hate to say it—I didn't find in Italian girls.")

Tullio's family was not particularly religious, but his mother went to church each Sunday, and occasionally he went with her.

"The Mass was always a very frightening experience for me. It was in Latin, of course, so I couldn't understand any of it. But I knew that I was afraid of the nuns, afraid of the priests."

After his confirmation Tullio asked his father for permission to stop attending Mass. Tullio made no mention of his attraction to Judaism, which was, at this point, a relatively inchoate thing, more a longing than an explicit desire to change faiths.

"Even at this age, though, you were saying to yourself, 'I think I may be Jewish. I feel a kinship with it, I'm interested in it, attracted to it?'" I asked.

"Yes. That's a simple way to put it, but yes. My father told me that if I never went to church again that was fine with him. But that I'd have to deal with my mother."

"We always do, don't we?"

Tullio said he never really believed that he would become a Jew. Italian boys from Queens, even ones with grave misgivings about their identity and spiritual center, do not convert to Judaism. He had no context for bringing that kind of change to his life. Tullio's only hope, and hope is how he thought of it, was that he could convert if he married a Jewish woman. His first wife, though, with whom he had three children, was Catholic. Perhaps not surprisingly, during the years of his marriage, he grew increasingly alienated from organized religion, although not from communities of spiritual, or at least reflective, purpose. He joined the Ethical Culture Society, but he eventually left because, he said, it felt to him more like a Jewish social group than a spiritual home, a place where lapsed Jews went to drink wine and discuss social issues.

"It was like approaching Judaism but never quite making it there," he said.

This was followed by a "twenty-year hitch" with Zen Buddhism, yoga, and meditation. He always felt that Judaism was "waiting in the wings," though, in some indeterminate way, but that there was nothing he could do to bring himself closer to it. His wife, who was resolutely secular (Tullio, for his part, was even now unwilling to go beyond agnostic when I asked him to characterize his beliefs), would never have consented to a conversion. For her, even Ethical Culture was a step too far, and Zen, well, they avoided the subject. Still, his identification with Judaism never wavered.

"People used to call me Tuluwitz."

"Because of the way you look?"

"It was my Jewish affect," he said. "I had friends who would say, 'You can't *really* be Italian and Catholic. You have to be a Jew.'"

"How did you feel about that?"

"Good. It was almost like, okay, I haven't been converted, but at least I'm being mistaken for a Jew."

Tullio and his wife eventually divorced, and in 2000, he moved to the Five Towns, a stretch of small, heavily Jewish hamlets on Long Island. I mentioned to Tullio that I had lived in the Five Towns, briefly (coincidentally, I had also lived in Bayside, as a baby), with my mother just before we moved to Mississippi.

"Then you know what it's like there on a Friday night. There's a shul on every other corner. I would see people, whole families dressed up so very well, walking together. God, I envied them. If I could have found a rabbi I would have presented myself and asked him to convert me right then and there."

What he considered to be his first concrete steps toward Judaism, however, took place not in a synagogue but in a yoga studio, when he met a woman named Mary Lynn, who went by the Sanskrit name Maji. Tullio was attracted to her, but when he asked her out she refused because, she said, although she was not Jewish, she was only interested in dating Jews. Tullio told her not to worry: he felt the same way. They were married not long after.

It took them eight years, several congregations, and a string of aborted conversion attempts before Tullio and Maji finally became Jews. The stops along the way included an interlude with a rabbi named Frank, a retired schoolteacher and converted Christian Orthodox priest, whom they met at an ultra-liberal Reform congregation in Manhattan. Rabbi Frank offered an express conversion process: He gave Tullio and Maji a copy of *Judaism for Dummies* and told them he would complete their conversion once they had read it.[1] He also suggested that rather than

---

1. Conversion processes in the United States vary depending on denomination, congregation, and rabbi. Reform is the least strict, focusing on the sincerity of the convert's desire to be Jewish. Conservative requires the adoption of an observant lifestyle for at least a year; Orthodox does too, along with Hebrew proficiency, adherence to stricter Sabbath and kosher rules, and immersion in an observant community.

ritually purifying them in a congregational *mikveh*, they could instead head to the beach, where he would perform a sacred dunking in the waters of the Atlantic Ocean. Another rabbi insisted that Maji learn to bake challah before she could be converted. They eventually opted for a Conservative rabbi, who required them to spend a full year studying, keeping the holidays, and observing the Sabbath. After that, they were officially Jews.

In 2005, Tullio's Jewish experience entered a new and unexpected phase. A friend of his, who happened to have an interest in genealogy, had recently submitted her DNA to Family Tree for testing. She suggested that Tullio, also a genealogy buff, do so as well.

"I'm a history fanatic," Tullio said. "I wanted to find out what my genes could tell me about my family history. I expected the standard story: We came out of Africa, and we went through the Horn of Africa, up into the Middle East, to the steppes of Russia, and then westward, to Europe, and then south into Italy. I never, at any time, considered the possibility that anything in my genes would have connected me with the Middle East and with Jews in particular."

"And it did," I interjected.

"It did. Genetically speaking, every person fits into a category. The most general category is called your haplogroup, and mine is known as J-1. J-1 is the haplogroup of the Jews and Arabs. So anyone who is J-1 either has Arab or Jewish background."

I knew, from some reading I had done after meeting Father Sanchez in New Mexico, that J-1 is actually a subset of the larger haplogroup J, which is considered the primary Semitic DNA signature. Of course, nothing in these genetic designations indicates religious identification or predilection. Haplogroup J members simply descend from people whose ancestors came from the Middle East.

For Tullio, though, "It was like a bombshell. I'm saying to myself, could it possibly be that my ancestors were Jewish? Could this possibly be?"

Following the testing, Tullio spent years, and a great deal of money, trying to confirm the genetic information with genealogical evidence. He hired a professional genealogist in Italy to search for public records related to his family. She was able to trace his lineage as far back as the late seventeenth century, but the archival documents she unearthed were mostly baptismal records, for people with conventional Catholic names—"Giovannis and Giuseppes and Marias and names like that"—nothing that would indicate a conversion or name change. There were hints—a distant relative who supposedly had a "secret Hebrew name"; an elderly cousin named Pasquale in Calabria who had a Crypto-Jewish narrative of hidden Jewish rituals, mutated practices, and a lineage whispered down through the generations. But there was never anything conclusive.

Tullio was not discouraged. "I'm a very traditional person, and it's important to tie my actions in with the actions of my distant ancestors, who themselves had been Jews, who perhaps had converted under duress, forced conversion perhaps. I would like at least in my own mind to be able to say, 'I set the record straight. We were Jews. We are Jews again.'"

If he lacked the tangible proof that he wished for, he believed he had something else: the *pintele yid*. He told me that he had no doubt that the spark was inside of him, although whether he understood it as a DNA signature or a metaphor for his lifelong attraction to the religion was unclear. He had tended to it, he said, carefully, in his own time and in his own way, and now, finally, it had burst into flame. "And the flame," he said, "is Judaism."

III.

amily Tree DNA world headquarters is located in a small and inevitably bland office park in Houston, Texas. The park sits next to a loud and smog-choked freeway frontage road. Its tenants, besides Family Tree, include a Zip Realty outlet, the county seat of the Democratic Party (presumably a minor operation in these parts), and an electrical-workers union. The receptionist at Family Tree ushered me to a seat in the waiting room, where I passed a few minutes leafing through the latest editions of *Ancestry* and *Family Tree* magazines. Bennett Greenspan hurried through the door about ten minutes later, offering his apologies for being late. We shook hands and I had my first look at him, unable to resist engaging in the *pintele yid* parlor game of trying to decide whether Greenspan looked Jewish. He was of average height, also olive-complected, balding, with a round face and eager brown eyes—possibly a Jew by sight, possibly not. I forced myself to stop.

Greenspan invited me into his office, and the first thing I noticed was a large and elaborate Greenspan family tree, which occupied nearly an entire wall. The genealogy was beautiful in its breadth and intricacy, the power of its historical sweep, with family branches spreading outward and down through the years and generations, with names, locations, and birth and death dates of his known relations.

"What's your first name? Just Ted?" Greenspan asked. He was seated at his desk, typing my information into his computer.

"Theodore."

Greenspan and I discussed which of Family Tree's genetic tests I should select. There were three basic options: mtDNA testing, which, for $159, would connect me with my "genetic cousins and uncover the deep ancestral origin of [my] direct maternal line"; for another ten dollars, I could have my Y-DNA tested, which would provide the same connections, but for my father's genetic lines; and for $289, I could go for the "Family Finder," a testing panel that used my autosomal DNA, the twenty-two chromosomal pairs inherited from both parents, which could then be cross-referenced against the entire Family Tree database, thus determining my "ethnic percentages"—where my earliest forebears on both sides came from—going back five generations. Each option could be upgraded, with more, and more expensive, testing available, a bewildering range of choices that quickly taxed my ability to understand the science behind the screening.

"Y-DNA testing gives a little bit better contextualization when it comes right down to it," Greenspan told me. "DNA mutates much more quickly on the mother's side than the father's. So short term, I can give you a better picture on the male side than the female side. The results are less ambiguous."

In either case, after I signed a release, my results would be entered into Family Tree's database. I could then search for individuals with similar genetic information, or a similar name, or a similar ethnic interest. For example, I might want to look for someone who shared my genetic characteristics and my surname. If I found anyone who met that basic profile, and that person, say, happened to be from the Ukraine, where my father's father was born, then there was a chance we were related. That sounded like fun to me.

The approach for someone like Alan Tullio would be different. He would search for people with genetic matches but different surnames, ones that "sounded" Jewish. If his DNA matched a plenitude of Cohens, Levines, and Rubensteins, perhaps even some from Italy, then Tullio might—reasonably or not—take this as confirmation of the *pintele yid* sparking from the test tubes.

"I think I should do my mother's side," I said, thinking that a peek into the mtDNA might offer my mother a genetic out. "Let's see if there are any Cossacks in her background instead of Jews."

"You wouldn't find that," Greenspan said. "The likelihood is that any Cossack raping a Jewish woman would be a man. Which means that the Y-chromosome would have been passed on to those women's sons but not to their daughters."

Bennett handed me a DNA test packet and a release form allowing the company to enter my particulars into its database. I opened the packet and inserted the scrape device, a thin plastic dipstick with tooth-brush bristles on the end, into my mouth, and began brushing the in-side of my cheek. The kit instructions suggested a vigorous scrape ("A great scrape gives us a great sample!"). I followed the directions with perhaps too much enthusiasm. When I removed the scraper from my mouth I noticed that it was covered in a thin film of blood. Greenspan chuckled—"You really want to know, eh?"—and he handed me the sec-ond scraper.

Greenspan occupied himself at his desk as I scraped, riffling through the names and markers of Jewish people in the company database. I stood over him at his computer screen, moving the scraper carefully inside my cheek and watching as he scanned the reams of names and data and an-cestral regions, mostly J-1s (and more specific designations from people who had chosen to pay for it), from Israel, Brooklyn, Ireland, Latvia, any-where.

"Wait. I want to make sure I understand this," I said, the scraper choking me slightly as I spoke. "Someone comes in and gets tested, shares

the data, and his name ends up here cross-indexed with these other people. What does that mean?"

To explain, Greenspan typed in Alan Tullio's name and waited until
his matches appeared on the screen.

"It means that when I compare all of his markers to everyone else in
the database, these . . ."—he pointed to a long list of names—"are the
closest guys genetically."

Most of the names seemed to be Italian, but there were a few that
could reasonably be Jewish.

"They're related to him?" I asked.

"They're related to him. Distantly, within a few hundred years, okay?"
he said. "And this guy"—Tullio—"claims that he has found that he is of
Jewish descent." (This was a reference to Tullio's discovery of Cousin
Pasquale, with the Crypto-Jewish rituals.)

Greenspan pointed the mouse at one of the names on the list of his
genetic relations.

"Look at *him*. I would assume that with a name like that this guy is
of Jewish descent."

He scrolled down to another name.

"This one here, I remember him. He paid for his cousin to be tested
as well. I think both of them are Jewish. Bottom line, Alan's closest
matches are to some guys who are Sicilian-Italian. That's clear. But look
a little bit farther away genetically, a little bit farther back historically, and
his only matches are to Jews." He smiled. "Do I think this guy has a Jewish
ancestry? Absolutely."

Greenspan tapped on his watch: no more scraping necessary. He took
the stick and placed it in a secure container, and then offered me a third
stick. He had decided to throw in the Y-DNA test for free.

"Use the other side of your mouth," he said.

"My Jewish side?" I replied.

Greenspan took me on a tour of his laboratory. He had me put on a white coat and a hairnet before we entered the clean area. The laboratory was in the back of the office and housed a number of complicated-looking machines, each manned by technicians hunched over their equipment and performing various operations.

"This is where we sequence the DNA and take a look at it," Greenspan said, pointing at a machine with the words "ABI 37 Sequencer" printed on the side. "We're going to have your DNA run here, in our express lab. I'm going to rush your results." (Family Tree also has a commercial laboratory facility at the University of Arizona.)

Greenspan walked me through the facility, offering brief explanations for each station, most of which I had a hard time following. He chatted up the lab technicians as we went, made a few remarks to one fellow about lab security protocol, and looked very much the part of the boss giving a tour. We finished up at the laboratory's coffee station, where we each drank a cup of instant coffee in our coats and hairnets.

Greenspan had drawn his first family tree in 1965, when he was twelve years old. His grandmother had passed away, and at the funeral his father had walked him around the cemetery. He wanted his son to see the graves of the people in his family. This had a big impact on the young Greenspan. There was something moving for him in seeing this concrete representation of his family's past, and it kindled an interest in finding and documenting his historical connections that has never waned. As a teenager, during the Cold War, Greenspan traveled to Poland. He hoped to find his family's ancestral village, and perhaps locate any relatives still living in the area, or if not that, then records related to his family, anything from his genealogical past that would add detail to his continuing efforts to fill out the family tree. "There wasn't anything

to find, of course. The Germans had done a very effective job of extermi-
nating my family."

At a genealogical dead end, Greenspan tabled serious work on the
family tree for many years. In the mid-1990s, though, he found himself
with the free time to return to it. Having sold the photographic supply
company that he had owned and operated for twenty-five years, he was
financially comfortable and bored.

"I was puttering around the house a lot, volunteering to do things for
my wife, you know, like helping to reorganize her cupboards, because they
seemed to be a little disorganized." He laughed. "After a while, she told me
I needed to pick up golf, or go back to my genealogy. Either way I needed
to get the hell out of her kitchen."

Greenspan returned to his family tree. His research now included
forays onto the Internet, where he discovered the Jewish Genealogical
Database, an online meta-search engine funded by the Museum of Jewish
Heritage. As he was searching for potential relations to his maternal
great-grandfather, a Ukrainian man with the surname Nitz, he discovered a group of people by the same name living in Buenos Aires, Argentina. This was an exciting and unexpected find. Any basic genealogical
search requires interviewing all known family members and asking them
about their relations. No one in Greenspan's extended family had ever
heard of anyone migrating from Europe to South America. Yet Nitz was
far from a common name, and he suspected that there was a link between
the Argentine Nitzs and his branch, which hailed from Omaha, Ne-
braska. The only problem was that conventional genealogical research
provided no way to determine if they were in fact connected.

Then Greenspan had what he called his "eureka moment." He had by
this point already founded Family Tree DNA. It was a small company,
which he ran from his garage, selling test kits for paternity and genetic
disease recognition. A genealogy application had never occurred to him.

He realized that if he could obtain a Y-DNA sample from a male Nitz in Argentina and compare it to his own Y-DNA, he could determine with a fair measure of certainty if they were related. He contacted the Nitzs in Buenos Aires and found someone willing to send him a sample.

"That's how we started this. I saw the results and learned that this guy in Argentina had the same Y-chromosome as me. I realized that this was a great exclusion or inclusion tool. Every genealogist was going to want it."

Greenspan was able to improve the system dramatically several years later.

"I was reading all the scientific papers that were coming out, and I saw that there was a connection between what are called the STRs, short tandem repeats, which we use for matching purposes, and the haplogroup. The haplogroup is the branch of the tree of mankind that someone descends from, and we can use those STRs to predict the branch of the tree you're on. Now I could tell people not only if you, Mr. Goldstein over here, are related to you, Mr. Goldstein over there. I could also tell you if your DNA was Semitic and was typical of people who came out of the Middle East, which would mean that you were probably deported by the Tenth Roman Legion, 1,900 years ago, after the Judeans made a terrible mistake and decided to tug on Superman's cape in an inopportune time in history."[1]

This innovation allowed Greenspan to expand his business, out of the garage and into the office park. Today, Family Tree is one of the largest DNA-testing companies in the world. While Greenspan seemed rightfully proud of his achievements as an entrepreneur, it seemed to me that he derived more satisfaction from being able to add new branches to his family tree.

---

1. He was referring to the destruction by the Romans, in 70 c.e., of the Jewish Temple in Jerusalem.

"If we have the same Y chromosome and we have the same last name, then we are related somewhere along the line," he said, still somewhat struck by the fact that he had solved this genealogical puzzle. "Logic demands it."

———

Logic has its demands, to be sure, but so, too, do religion, history, genetics, and genealogy. More often than not the clamorous emotion they produce will overwhelm the more metronomic rhythms of rational thought. Something about the shortcomings of logic in this realm reminded me of a strange experience from college. My class was studying a novel written by a Palestinian author, and it came up during a discussion one day that I was Jewish. The professor, for reasons I still do not entirely understand, seemed to expect me to account for all actions taken by the Israelis in the Occupied Territories (he probably would have pinned the Crucifixion on me, given the opportunity). The other students, sensing the direction the professor wanted everyone to go, piled on. It was a long hour and a half. At the end of class, though, a gorgeous young woman, whom I had never before worked up the nerve to engage in conversation, stopped by my desk and told me not to listen to the other students. She had always wanted to be Jewish. When I asked her why she would want such a thing, she said, "Then I could be *rich*."

Greenspan laughed when I told him this story.

"As I understand it, after the circumcision you get the gold," he said.

I had recounted this anecdote for Greenspan because I was curious if he encountered, if not similar, then comparably irrational, motivations in the people who came to him to determine if they were Jewish.

"Most people who come to me to do a DNA test are looking for one thing: family. But then they find something else, which for them is interesting or scary, and they start investigating that. Whether they eventually start to put on, you know, black hats and start looking like Poles or Hasidic in Brooklyn, I don't know. But I do find a number who think they have Jewish ancestry, or who wonder if they have Jewish ancestry, or for one reason or another have decided they want to go the opposite direction of your mother. They want to be Jewish, and who knows why? Maybe they have a martyrdom complex, or they are just dissatisfied with Christianity and are looking or searching for something else. There's a phenomena today of Americans converting to Islam, you know. Scary, but that seems to be the case."

Greenspan said that these philo-Semites made up only a small fraction of those who used Family Tree for testing.

"This isn't a revolution, Ted. It's not a mass movement or wildebeest crossing the river in Kenya. It's not thousands and thousands and thousands of animals lined up on the shore waiting to swim across to the Holy Land. It's individuals, who for one reason or another feel some sort of unexplainable kinship with Jews. Is it from their soul? As a non-religious Jew I don't deal with that. But I do have people who explain to me that they woke up in the middle of the night as if a shotgun had gone off outside their bedroom window, and they're wide awake and they can't go back to sleep, and they say 'By God, I think I want to visit Israel.' Or they find themselves, consciously or unconsciously, making a wrong turn on the way to work, and they drive by the only synagogue in their city, and they feel a tug, and they want to go in, but they don't know if they're allowed to go in or not. They want to but they don't know if they can or if they should or if they are able to."

He paused, as if uncertain whether to make his next point.

"You also find some people, not a lot of people, but some people, who are kind of constricted emotionally, intellectually, and philosophically, and they find themselves drawn to a religion that they don't know a lot about. In fact, maybe they know more about Judaism from its detractors than its proponents."

I had thought of this, too. I think it is fair to say that outsized professions of respect and admiration for Jews can have a palpable anti-Semitic element. Often the traits most admired by philo-Semites, when stated explicitly, are in fact anti-Semitic, with the thoughtlessness of my money- and Jew-loving classmate serving as a prime example. I am reminded of an old joke, recounted in a scholarly work on the subject, *Philosemitism in History*: "Q: Which is preferable—the antisemite or the philosemite? A: The antisemite—at least he isn't lying."

I had asked Greenspan if he could think of examples of people haunted by the *pintele yid*, the disturbed sleepers, synagogue lurkers, the Judaically compelled. He returned to his database again, and when he found a name that fit, he searched his emails for messages from these people (of course, I couldn't see their email addresses). Here, he said, was one from a Muslim convert to Christianity, an Algerian who suspected— hoped—he might be Jewish and wrote to see if Greenspan would waive the fee for a Y-DNA test (Greenspan said he probably would). There was another one, from a woman whose mother was Puerto Rican and her father Muslim ("my father is not a friend of the Jews"). She had been tested, and despite "all this Jewish wanting," had learned that she had no genetic connection to a Jewish past. She still planned to convert, though. ("When I die I want to ask God why he made me this way.") There was one from a woman who thought she might have Jewish ancestry, not because of her testing, which was inconclusive, or because she had converted, or because she planned to convert, but because *her daughter* had converted: "She felt a pull," the woman wrote. She indicated in her message that her daughter's "pull" might represent the subconscious call of a higher genetic truth. She wanted to know if there was more testing she could do. Another one was from a man who had been tested and whose results had also shown no genetic link to Judaism. He wanted Greenspan to know, however, that his (very Lutheran) grandmother had just died, and among her possessions he had discovered a *tallit* bag. He did not know if this meant his grandmother was Jewish, but as it turned out, his mother had converted to Judaism, which raised certain questions for him. He conceded that his mother knew nothing about the bag when she converted, but he, too, thought unseen Jewish forces were at play. Perhaps this religious artifact might throw his test results into a new light? Greenspan showed me the note from another man, whose results had confirmed a genetic form of Jewish descent. The man had converted as a result, and he wanted to recount his struggle to adapt to a Jewish identity. ("I didn't know where to stand, when to bow, didn't know the songs or the *Shema*, and the books were freaking backwards!") Fortunately, in time he had grown accustomed to the Jewish way of things. Now his new faith was like a "nice pair of shoes that just needed to be broken into."

Admittedly, these examples do not necessarily indicate anything about the existence of the *pintele yid*. Contemporary society offers a nearly unlimited array of potential identity crises, hidden Jewish souls or no. But the narratives were odd and moving to read nonetheless. Were these Jew-loving anti-Semites? Perhaps. My inclination, though, particularly for the converts, was to give them a pass. These were people who had looked for Judaism and found it, in whatever way they understood it. Their discovery resulted from an act of will and I respected that, even for those who learned, to the degree that genetic testing proves anything, that they were not in fact Jewish. But I reveled in the specificity of their need.

"What if you looked up my name?" I asked Greenspan. "There must be a lot of Rosses. Or how about Rosenzweig?"

Greenspan tapped rapidly on his computer.

"There you go. We have ten J-1s with that name in the database: Michael, Marcus, Franz, he's a German, this guy's not Jewish—"

"Julius, he could be. Oh, wait, of course he is: he's in Teaneck, New Jersey."

"Yeah, come on. That's too easy. There's Peter in Hamburg, and Ivana, and Lauren. . . ."

"Not a lot."

"No, not a lot, but that's only under that exact spelling of Rosenzweig, without variants."

Greenspan navigated to Family Tree's Rosenzweig DNA project. Family Tree's customers can create projects correlating the genetic and genealogical information in the database. I could, say, start my own Rosenzweig project, but limit it only to J-1 Rosenzweigs who identify as Ashkenazi. There are several Crypto-Jewish genetic projects, including one started by Father Sanchez.

"This has a wider range. Let's look at what the results there show. You see this? This is a Jewish line," Greenspan said. "These are not. This one is probably . . . hmm . . . this guy is a Viking. And these guys right here, these guys, well, probably not Jewish—nope, not Jewish."

"Now I really want to see my test results."

"We're going to process them. You should match some of these people."

"I know this is your business, Bennett, but this is also your big toy, too, right? You must spend a lot of time poking around here."

"The most fun that you can have with your clothes on. And I believe that, I say that in crowds, and sometimes I get laughs, but not always."

Before I left that evening, Greenspan showed me one last email. This one was from a woman who wanted to thank him for helping her discover and confirm her Jewish roots. One line in particular struck me, with its echoes of the unborn souls at Mount Sinai: *History inscribes, and all that is left is the body.*

IV.

The St. Edwin Parish church is located on the south side of Albuquerque, New Mexico, on a dusty and countrified street in the Atrisco valley. The neighborhood around the church is spare and still and populated almost exclusively by the city's large Mexican working class. The housing stock consists primarily of Pueblo Revival cottages, many of them in states of advanced decline, with their side- and backyards given over to crop gardens. The *acequias*, irrigation channels that have supplied water to the region since the days of the Spanish Empire, are still in evidence, dry on a late winter day but for a brown and brackish trickle.

I had returned to New Mexico to see Father William Sanchez, who was about to start a weekday Lenten Mass. I took a seat in the pews, and was one of the few Anglos in a church filled with Hispanic cowboys and cowgirls and their children. Father Sanchez was seated next to the altar in a wooden chair wide and sturdy enough to support his considerable bulk. His eyes were closed as he listened to a young woman open the service with a hymn in Spanish. The song ended, and he opened his eyes and walked slowly to the pulpit, revealing the design carved into the back of his chair. It was a large and quite unmistakable Star of David. I took note of the other Jewish objects Father Sanchez displayed in the church. On the altar, next to the Communion plate and chalice—sanctified objects—was a menorah. A mantelpiece on the wall behind the altar held a shofar; beside that a smartly carved Staff of Aaron rested in a display stand, a gift, Sanchez had told me earlier, from one of his elderly congregants.

The service was brief. Father Sanchez called the congregants up for Communion, offered prayers for "all the people of Libya, Iraq, and Afghanistan," and said, "we will have generations and generations of healing to do for all these wars." He prayed for the recently deceased of the congregation, and made a special supplication for the soul of the actress Elizabeth Taylor, who had passed a few days earlier. He concluded the service with a selection from Psalms: "Happy are those who follow the law of the Lord Adonai."

Over the years I have had some occasion to attend Christian religious services. Surprisingly, the urge to participate, which I succumbed to as a child, to shuffle forward for the heavenly flesh and blood, remains strong. I managed to stay in my seat that day, although when the collection plate came around, I could not resist making a contribution.

After the service, Father Sanchez invited me to his office. He took a seat at his large pressboard desk, mopping his brow and struggling to catch his breath, fatigued by his godly labors. He had a few posters and paintings of Jerusalem on the walls, trinkets from a trip he had led to Israel with other members of his congregation. These were hung next to a liturgical calendar and two hand-carved-and-painted santos, statues of New Mexican patron saints.

In Houston I had learned that Father Sanchez had inserted himself into an academic conflict involving Bennett Greenspan and an anthropology professor named Wesley Sutton, the author, along with Judith Neulander and others, of the 2006 study in the *Annals of Human Biology* questioning the genetic evidence of Jewish ancestry in New Mexico. In the conclusion of the study, Sutton claimed to have "refute[d] the popular and widely publicized scenario of significant crypto-Jewish ancestry of the Spanish-American population." Greenspan, who strongly supported the

Crypto-Jewish claims, had conducted his own study challenging Sutton's, and had returned with diametrically opposed results. The disparities between the two seemed to arise primarily from the differing size and quality (according to Greenspan) of the DNA samples used for their respective studies. Sutton had collected DNA from 139 unrelated Spanish-American-identifying males living in a few remote towns in northern New Mexico and southern Colorado. Greenspan had used samples from a much wider source: his database. He was able to find 1,500 participants, drawn from New Mexican and northern Mexican projects started at Family Tree. The people in his pool could be related or not, Spanish-identifying or not.

"Think about it," Greenspan had told me. "You go out to nowhere, New Mexico, and you start stopping people and saying, 'I'm from New York and I'd like to get your DNA'"—Sutton was a doctoral candidate at NYU when he conducted his study—"except say it with your New York accent, Ted. How well do you think that's going to go down? Do you think they were able to test all of their desired candidates?"

Greenspan provided much more detail demonstrating why his study was superior to Sutton's—variances and "down-weighting" and the like—most of which I am in no position to judge. The important thing is that Greenspan considered the sanctity of his population sample to be paramount. ("I wanted to be holier than the Pope. I wanted my numbers to be so reasonable, my methodology to be so . . . uh, religious, so to speak, that no one could say 'he was overstretching.'")

Unfortunately, Greenspan's papal ambitions had brought him into conflict with Father Sanchez, who had administered his own informal study, via Sanchez's project at Family Tree. Greenspan, in order to avoid charges of methodological or sample bias, had decided not to use DNA from Father Sanchez's pool, a choice that Father Sanchez had interpreted as proof that Greenspan did not believe in the veracity of the New Mexican Crypto-Jewish claims.

Greenspan, for his part, felt Father Sanchez's research methods with-stood scrutiny no better than Sutton's. "You call up your uncle Fernando, and you say to him, 'Primo, I'm doing some DNA testing on, you know, *la família.*'" He shook his head. "Father Sanchez is upset because he spent a lot of time on his personal project and I didn't include it because I was *trying to prove his point.* Sometimes, if you want to defend someone you send them out of the room because it's not savory to have them in the room when you're eviscerating their competitor, okay? Because it doesn't look right. Because you're not trying to sell *them* but the other hundred people in the room."

Father Sanchez merely saw it as a slight against the truth of his Jew-ish ancestry, which he often had to defend to others, and about which he was fiercely proud.

"It's about being honest about what's inside of us," he said, pressing a hand to his chest, just below the Star of David he wore around his neck. "We have the Torah. You can't deny it."

Nor would I. The saga of the dueling studies was not the main reason why I had come to see Father Sanchez. Before I flew to Albuquerque, I had received an email from him:

> Are you ready for this one? My niece had her baby last week.
> I phoned to Santa Fe and spoke with her fiancé, and the
> first thing he tells me: "Uncle Bill. When Jacob was born, the
> first words of the Doctor delivering him were, 'This baby was
> circumcised in the womb.'"

"He was born without foreskin," Father Sanchez told me. "Moses was born that way, too. Read Exodus. Read Deuteronomy."

I did in fact do some reading, and discovered something called apos-thia, a rare congenital abnormality in which a baby is born lacking a pre-puce. I reviewed my Old Testament, too, but was unable to find anything definitive relating to Moses's member, be it cut or uncut. One of the Talmud tractates, the *Avot d'Rabbi Natan* ("The Kings, According to Rabbi Nathan"), does mention the blessed state of the Mosaic phallus, noting that not only was Moses *bris*-ed in the womb, so too were Adam, Seth, Noah, Shem, Jacob, Joseph, David, Zerubbabel, and even Balaam "the wicked." Nevertheless, the evidentiary style of the tractate, which is delivered as a series of poetic homilies, is not entirely compelling. Consider this example, offered in support of the purity, at birth, of Shem's penis. "Shem, too, was born circumcised, for it is said, 'And Melchizedek king of Salem' (Gen. 14:18)." In the words of one of my old teachers at Christ Episcopal: "Clear as mud. Twice as thick."

We left Father Sanchez's office and walked behind the church to the rectory. Father Sanchez lived in a spacious salmon-colored stucco cottage with a gravel front yard. A boxer's training bag stood on a stanchion in the yard (Father Sanchez was trying to lose weight). As we went inside, Father Sanchez pointed to the mezuzah in the doorframe, a gift, he said, from another priest, this one a Jewish convert to Christianity.

Father Sanchez had clustered practically all of the contradictory elements of his religious pursuits in the entranceway to his home. There was a Torah on a small table, and a menorah, and *Shabbos* candles, and an Elijah cup (used at a seder for the cup of wine set aside for the prophet Elijah—a practice, interestingly enough, not often maintained by Sephardic Jews), and a *tallit*. The shawl, Father Sanchez told me, was only for display.

"I keep mine in here," he said, pointing to a small ornamental box.

The same table held a small ceramic statue of Our Lady of Montserrat, an Our Lady of Seville, an Our Lady of Lourdes, and a plaster-and-gesso figure of the San Ysidro, along with Easter candles, and several works of Native American folk art.

The living room was decorated with a few oil paintings, including one of Covenant Rock, the mystical point of "convergence" I had visited with Father Sanchez on my first trip to the Southwest. The bookshelves were filled with history books and family photos, including several of the putatively miraculous young Jacob. Father Sanchez switched on the radio, to a jazz station.

Father Sanchez was a fluent conversationalist, and I gave him free rein to lead me through his maze of religious, social, and spiritual associations. He saw connections between Liberation theology, Mexican identity, Native American identity, and Jewish identity; he discussed the value of his experiences in Freudian psychoanalysis ("If you ever have the opportunity, you should do it"), which had taught him "to listen, to be respectful of dreams." He detailed his conflicts with the Catholic hierarchy. His superiors, he said, tended to find his political views, particularly those related to Jews and the Middle East—"I give money to J Street. I would fight for Jerusalem. I would die for her. But I won't kill Palestinians"—decidedly objectionable. His willingness to discuss the Church's sexual abuse scandals in public was, obviously, a more serious problem. This last, he said, had resulted in his being transferred by his bishop from a wealthy congregation in Santa Fe, where his family lived, to St. Edwin's. "This is my exile," he said. "The bishop told me that I was going to die in Albuquerque."

I asked him if his allegiance to the Jewish world compromised his position in the Catholic one, and he expressed his frustration, and increasing fatigue, with trying to fit neatly into either.

"People always tell me I must be schizo. 'How come you can't choose?'"

He said that occasionally he thought about leaving the Catholic Church altogether and living as a Jew full time, perhaps even becoming a rabbi. In particular, he could see himself "closing the circle," and finding a Jewish congregation in Toledo, Spain, where his ancestors once lived and were forced to leave the religion.

I chose not to discuss the *pintele yid* with Father Sanchez. Neither did I mention my test results from Family Tree, which had arrived before I made my way west. I am, apparently, J-1, which means something or nothing, answers a question or poses a series of new ones, breathes new life into the spark submerged in my deepest heart or extinguishes it forever. It is information, a data point on Greenspan's fascinating and ever-growing graph of humanity, heavy with meaning but featherlight in its lack of context. I was free to accept it now, later, or never.

"I don't really see much difference between being a Catholic priest and a rabbi," Sanchez said. "Life is like choosing between a series of doors. But behind each door is God."

Part VIII

UNIQUE POPULATIONS

Suppose the stolen offspring of some mountain tribe brought up in a city of the plain, or one with an inherited genius for painting, and born blind—the ancestral life would lie within them as a dim longing for unknown objects and sensations, and the spell-bound habit of their inherited frames would be like a cunningly wrought musical instrument, never played on, but quivering throughout in uneasy mysterious moanings of its intricate structure that, under the right touch, gives music. Something like that, I think, has been my experience.

—George Eliot, from *Daniel Deronda*

I.

The Jewish Agency office in Manhattan is located in a building noteworthy mainly for its adamant discretion. A grayish-blue steel tower, sheathed in tinted glass, the building had all the requisite elements of corporate anonymity: a stifling lobby teeming with dazed businesspeople and sullen support staff; a kiosk for buying newspapers, bottled drinks, and junk food; and the obligatory Art Deco posters, generic as flowered wallpaper, dominating the walls. This seemed to me the necessary ambiance for an institution devoted to facilitating migration to Israel, and whose name is so insidiously opaque as to seem ripped from the pages of the *Protocols of the Elders of Zion*.

I submitted to a brief but thorough identification check at the security desk, after which I was allowed to proceed to the elevators with a freshly printed guest pass adhered to my chest. I had been informed that the Jewish Agency was on the twenty-first floor, but I wasn't prepared for the labyrinthine layout when I exited the elevator. I wandered around the warren of blind turns and narrow spurs leading to locked bathrooms for several moments, stopping at different doors, most of which were unmarked and possibly janitorial closets, or bore the names of enterprises that gave little indication of their line of work. Finally, I noticed a sign for the Bank of Israel, followed by the New York State office of the Department of Homeland Security. I figured I was moving in the right direction.

The Jewish Agency predates the Israeli state, having come into existence in 1929 at the World Zionist Congress, a gathering whose name also seemed designed to stoke the fears of anti-Semitic conspiracy theorists. The Agency served as a quasi-official government-in-waiting, and it was recognized by the League of Nations as the legal representative of a country that did not exist. After the creation of Israel in 1948, the Agency relinquished most of its responsibilities. Its senior leadership, including David Ben-Gurion, Israel's first prime minister, left to join the new government. Today, the Agency is a non-governmental organization that receives its financial support from charitable donors, mostly the Jewish Federations of North America. The Agency's primary area of operation revolves around aliyah. For example, American (and Canadian) Jews interested in claiming Israeli citizenship do so first by submitting an application to the Jewish Agency, which functions as the official go-between and gatekeeper to the Israeli Ministry of Immigrant Absorption.[1]

The entrance to the Jewish Agency office is secured by a keypad and monitored via surveillance camera. Next to the door, a young, light-haired and blue-eyed Israeli sat at a desk behind a thick pane of what I assumed to be bulletproof glass.

"Are you planning on making aliyah today?" he asked, his voice slightly distorted by his microphone.

I was not. Given my background and my mother's conversion, I was not even certain that I could. Was I eligible? How would I prove it? Could I present a copy of my results from Family Tree? Show them my photocopy of my grandfather's Nazi-era passport, stamped *Juden*? Is a Jew, as defined in the United States (to the extent that it is), the same as one in Israel? To my surprise, I discovered that the right to aliyah was important to me, even if I knew that I would likely never exercise it. It was one thing

---

1. Absorption: the trump card in the sinister terminology game, besting Jewish Agency, Zionist Congress, and Department of Homeland Security.

to choose not to claim my Israeli citizenship; but to be unable to do so, well, that was something quite different. I was reminded of the old Groucho Marx line—*I don't want to belong to any club that will accept me as a member*—only I wanted membership in the club that would not have me.

I informed the receptionist that I planned to keep my U.S. passport for the time being, but that I had an appointment with a public relations officer named Jacob Dallal. The receptionist made a series of phone calls, his Hebrew sounding sterner by the moment. I had, apparently, mistaken the time of my appointment and shown up two hours early, an oddity that the security-conscious staff found suspicious. Eventually, after assuring the young man that I was carrying neither weapons nor explosives, I was allowed inside.

In his office, Dallal waved away my apologies and presented me with a stack of Jewish Agency promotional pamphlets. He was about my age, a former military spokesperson originally from Chicago. He had agreed to walk me through the mechanics of the migration process, and after that he would take me to see the Jewish Agency's CEO and president of international development, a man named Misha Galperin, who would discuss aliyah and Jewish identity in more expansive terms.

"We have a presence in about sixty countries," Dallal said, as I flipped through the marketing materials. "Emissaries, educators—all over. The idea is to build a sort of Jewish-Israel identity, which climaxes, in some instances, with immigration to Israel."

Subsequent to that climax, Dallal explained, each *olim* (migrant) would receive a "basket of services" from the government, benefits generous enough to make an American progressive green with envy. These included: a cash payment of approximately $5,000 for a single migrant (families receive more); full coverage under the Israeli health care system; two months of free housing; a longer-term rental subsidy; favorable mortgage rates; free Hebrew-language instruction; a one-way airline ticket to Israel; and even a free taxi ride from Ben-Gurion Airport in Tel Aviv.

The Agency also offered a selection of "absorption packages" tailored to the varying needs of its newest citizens. This might mean a stay in one of several "absorption centers" located throughout Israel: There were singles centers for single migrants, centers for families, and still other centers oriented around the migrant's level of religious observance. Those accustomed to the highest levels of migratory service could opt for the "Aliyah on a Red Carpet" package, which promised to assuage the inconvenience of transit, mitigate the complexities of the bureaucratic ordeal, and, as the pamphlet put it, "bring everything to you!"

Prior to enjoying such packaged splendor in Israel, the proposed migrant would of course undergo a security screening, background check, and most important, an interview, arranged by the Agency, with a *shaliach* to determine one's qualifications under Israel's Law of Return. This last, I told Dallal, seemed the key issue for me. Would my complicated family history be an obstacle to meeting the legal requirements of Jewish-ness, as defined by the Israelis?

"Are both of your parents . . . ?" he asked.

"Both of my parents were born Jewish."

"So you're no problem. By religious law, you're completely Jewish."

The details of my life story were irrelevant, provided I could give the Jewish Agency certified proof of my Judaism, which, in this case, meant demonstrating that at least one of my grandparents was a Jew. Israel's Law of Return, which was first enacted in 1950, originally defined a Jew as anyone who was "born of a Jewish mother" (or who had converted), but the law had been amended in 1970, broadening the definition to include the "grandchild of a Jew."

A fundamental aspect of the American national character rests on the belief, however mythical, of the special place afforded here to immigrants, newcomers, and refugees. That belief is as old as the country, and exists even in this current era of politically charged anti-immigrant hostility. With obvious and notable exceptions—Native Americans, to name but one—each American family comes from somewhere else. We did not begin as Americans: we had to *become* Americans. Israel, again with obvious and notable exceptions—Arabs—offers a similar migratory ideal, with one key difference. Embedded in the idea of (Jewish) Israel is the understanding that aliyah is not a process of *becoming*, as in America, but of *return*. Those making aliyah do not become Israeli. By virtue of their Judaism they already are Israeli.

A comforting sentiment and true as far as it goes, which, if one is Palestinian, is not very. What's more, the idea that no Jew can be turned away, while no less valid today than in the aftermath of the Holocaust, has become less necessary. Jews no longer confront determined existential threats to their faith and person. Anti-Semitism exists, of course, and, yes, there is Iran and its centrifuges, and al Qaeda, and a host of other dangers, but most Jews in most places are safe most of the time. Israel remains the guaranteed land of final refuge for all Jews. But the *necessity* for it to do so has, thankfully, lessened, a fact that can be demonstrated in the aliyah statistics. Israel absorbed 171,000 Jews per year, on average, in the first four years of its existence. In the last four years, that rate has averaged just 17,000 people. This makes sense, given world events, and not surprisingly, the Jewish Agency had adapted its approach to aliyah to reflect the current reality.

"In the pre-state era, and in other decades during the post-state period, in order to ensure a strong Israel you needed to get more people to Israel," Dallal said. "That was the main focus. Today, though, anyone who wants to go to Israel can. It used to be if you were behind the Iron Curtain, you may have wanted to go, but you just couldn't. So it's a different situation now. What remains today, in terms of aliyah, is that it is almost 100 percent a process of choice."

What I took this to mean was that it was no longer enough for the Jewish state to merely embrace its newest citizens who, marked by the *pintele yid*, were already citizens. Israel had to compete, with absorption packages, global Zionist educational programs, and even aliyah applications for the iPhone (iAliyah).

"The state of the Jewish people, and the state of Israel, has evolved a lot," Dallal said with a shrug. "We don't build kibbutzim anymore, either, because, well, Israel doesn't export oranges."

———

With migratory evolution, the extinction of the kibbutz, and the official approach to aliyah explained, it was time to see Misha Galperin. Unfortunately, Galperin appeared rather unenthusiastic to see me, for reasons I had encountered on occasion in my Jewish travels. He, and others, seemed to have considered my question already, in contexts both more relevant and more interesting than my own, and, having pondered its ramifications at length, exhausting its metaphysical, logistical, and spiritual potential, he—and they—evinced an almost lethal boredom about the subject. Galperin, a dapper and intense-eyed Ukrainian with a graying mop of curly hair, nonetheless agreed to soldier on. I also sensed that speaking to me wasn't really a burden for him. He had worked as a psychotherapist before coming to the Jewish Agency and clearly liked to talk.

"The unique thing about being Jewish is that it's not very clear to most people, including Jews—maybe more so for Jews than others—what exactly that means," Galperin began, delivering his remarks while reclining in his desk chair. "Depending on who you ask, and depending on what time it is, and depending on where it is, it will mean being members of a certain religious grouping, or it will mean members of a certain ethnic group, or residents of a particular place and space in time."

Galperin's eyelids drooped lower with each phrase, his posture one of weary intellectual ennui. He punctuated his last statement with a shrugging "etcetera, etcetera, etcetera" that concluded with him practically losing consciousness.

"The notion of Jewish people being something distinct and separate is something that people have been thinking about and writing about recently," he said. "But the real question is: Does it require a boundary of any sort? Is there such a thing as boundaries to being members of this group? If so, what are they, and, if not, what makes this a group?"

Galperin started to talk about the "unique populations" in Israel as an example. The unique populations comprised Jews from locales not traditionally associated with Judaism: Ethiopia, India, Congo, South America, China, the Amazon, and elsewhere, many of whom have been recognized by the Israeli government as *Zera Israel*, or the "Seed of Israel."[1] The Seed of Israel refers to individuals and communities of Jewish descent, who, for reasons that might include duress or historical dislocation, had converted from Judaism or only discovered in the modern era that their ancestors had done so. Approximately 120,000 Jews of Ethiopian extraction currently live in Israel. That migrant population, which first began coming to the country in 1984, can be divided into two distinct groups, although they all believe themselves to be descendants of the Lost Tribe of Dan. The first group consists of Ethiopians who have lived, historically and in the modern era, as Jews (at least according to the Israeli government; as with all lost-tribe Jewish communities, the truth of these claims remains a subject of debate). This group was allowed to make aliyah under the Law of Return.

The second group has a different history. In the latter part of the nineteenth century, British missionaries operating in Ethiopia had unexpectedly encountered Jews among the natives and converted many of

---

1. Notable for its exclusion in this category are the American Crypto-Jews.

them to Christianity, possibly under duress. These converts did not completely join the larger Christian world, and they lived in Ethiopia as a separate group of former Jews—not entirely accepted as Christian but no longer Jewish (similar to the *cristianos-nuevos* in Inquisition-era Spain). These Christian-Ethiopian Jews have also been allowed into Israel, though not under the Law of Return but via the *Zera Israel* legal concept. They enter the country with the agreement that they will convert "back" to Judaism.

I had always known that I would travel to Israel. In truth, though, I was never entirely certain as to why. Israel was for me only a place and not the promised, and perhaps even genetic, repository of my Jewish dreams and aspirations. Or perhaps it was and that *still* wasn't enough for me to create an emotional connection. Nevertheless, I would go to Israel, whether I understood why or not, perhaps because the *pintele yid* made it inevitable, or from a desire to investigate the puzzling boundaries Galperin had described for me, or perhaps because I would only understand why I was there once I was there.

"Jewish identity has some individual elements and a collective aspect," Galperin said. "Part of it is identifying as part of this group, which, in effect, is an extended family called the Jewish people. You are part of this collective, part of this extended family, and it is a purposeful thing. That's what our religious heritage is. We have a purpose in the world and we've been called upon to persevere and survive because of it. Whether you believe in God or in mysticism or whatever it is that you believe in, it's hard to understand the survival of the Jewish people without understanding that there is some purpose."

I wasn't sure if I was prepared to accept that premise, but Galperin was ready to end our discussion. He had other appointments. Before he could escape, I asked him a final question, one that I resisted asking most people.

"So tell me, what do you think?"

"About what?"

"Am I . . . ?"

He shrugged.

"Why not?"

II.

In the weeks after my visit to the Jewish Agency, my mind kept returning to those "unique populations." I was, of course, familiar with this kind of Jewish narrative from my time in New Mexico and Texas, but I think comparisons between the American Crypto-Jews and these other groups are not necessarily helpful. Both might very well be "lost Jews," with all the tragedy, mythology, and implied demographic potential embedded within the term. But it seems possible that the migratory motivations of a proposed Israeli from Manipur or Addis Ababa might be radically different from one from Albuquerque or El Paso. Many of the Crypto-Jews I met in the United States were poor, at least when judged by this country's very high standards, but even in this awful economic moment, American poor is not third world poor. Aliyah for the latter group could involve an economic calculation in a way that it would not for the former.

During this period, I happened to receive an email from my cousin Greg asking me to accompany him to an event at the Jewish Enrichment Center (JEC) in Manhattan. He had included an electronic flyer detailing the evening's enrichment: "An Evening with Shavei Israel: Discussing Lost Tribes and Hidden Jews." Shavei Israel ("Israel Returns") was a nonprofit whose work, as it happened, involved the same unique populations that were on my mind at the time. (From its website: "Shavei Israel strives to extend a helping hand to all members of our extended Jewish family and to all who seek to rediscover or renew their link with the people of Israel.") The primary goal of that work was to locate, religiously educate, and assist those unique populations in their efforts to make aliyah.

The event was held at the JEC building in Greenwich Village, in a small, fluorescent-lit classroom on the second floor. Perhaps thirty people filled the rows of folding chairs, post-Birthright types mostly, drowsy from work and the night's chill, along with a few retirees, comatose from their heavy layers they were wearing and the extra helpings of sandwiches and wine on offer. A young woman from the JEC went to the microphone at the front of the room, tapped it cautiously once or twice to see if the sound was on, and then launched into the introductions.

Michael Freund, the founder of Shavei Israel, was an American migrant to Israel, and had previously been a press spokesperson for Benjamin Netanyahu. He was a pale and fatigued-looking fellow with brown hair and thin lips, dressed in an ill-fitting blue business suit, wire-rimmed glasses, and a multicolored yarmulke that he pinned securely to the back of his head. Tzvi Khaute was the evening's representative from the unique populations. A compact and dark-skinned man with South Asian features, Khaute was powerfully built for his size, with a stern face and an erect, almost military posture. He was dressed in black pants, leather shoes, a yarmulke, and a thick navy-blue peacoat. He looked cold and ill at ease.

The JEC woman stumbled through a brief history of Khaute's people. The Bnei Menashe, as they are called, believe themselves to be one of the Lost Tribes, in this case the Manasseh. The Manasseh are descended from a relatively obscure Israelite ruler of the same name, whose presence in the Bible largely concerns his acts of idolatry, military defeat at the hands of the Assyrians, forced exile to Babylon, and final repentance to God. Bnei Menashe have been migrating to Israel from their homeland in Manipur since 1984. One thousand seven hundred have successfully made aliyah so far. An additional 7,000 remain in India waiting for the opportunity to migrate. The woman from the JEC repeatedly lost her train of thought as she spoke, struggling to keep herself from staring at Khaute. Khaute silently accepted her furtive gaze without any change in his expression.

"I think this is a really fascinating topic," she concluded. "I'm so happy and so excited that all of you have come tonight. It's going to be a great event. This is really great, sexy, *National Geographic* stuff!"

Freund stepped to the microphone after that, stopping for a moment to glance in Khaute's direction, perhaps to see if he had understood this last bit of exuberance. Thankfully, it seemed that he hadn't.

"From a Jewish perspective, New York is not a diverse place," Freund began. "White, Ashkenazi, everyone has seen *Fiddler on the Roof*: all the same. But there is a much wider world out there. We are one nation with many faces. That is the beauty of our people."

According to tradition, Freund continued, the Bnei Menashe path of exile from the Holy Land led eastward and north into China, where they settled for several centuries. At some point, and the tribal history is unclear, an evil Chinese king or emperor began to persecute them, possibly on religious grounds. They fled again, to the southwest this time, until they reached a remote and mountainous region of what is today northeastern India. Here, largely isolated from outside influences, they continued to practice a form of biblical-era Judaism, a variant of the faith that is free of the rabbinical influences and legalistic interpretations implemented in later centuries. In practical terms, their Judaism would not include things like Hanukkah or Purim, both of which are based on events that occurred after their exile. They kept the Sabbath, but their koshering practices were far simpler than the version refined over time by observant Jews who were following the rabbinical definitions. As a result, when British missionaries and military officials first reached Manipur in large numbers in the nineteenth century, they discovered a local minority who worshipped a single God, possessed oral traditions whose stories were reminiscent of those in the Bible, and whose faith included strictures that mirrored Christian practice. Most Bnei Menashe converted to Christianity during this period, but a few managed to hold out. In 1948, when word of the creation of Israel reached them, some of them packed their bags and began moving west.

"Even though they were lost to us, the Bnei Menashe never forgot who they were," Freund said. "They have been writing to Israeli prime ministers asking to be recognized at least since the time of Golda Meir."

Freund, whose organization works with Jews from China, Spain, Portugal, Italy, Poland, Russia, the Amazon, and elsewhere, received one such letter when he worked in Netanyahu's government. At first his interest in the Bnei Menashe had less to do with history than with demographics.

"We are a small people, growing smaller all the time," he said. "I believe it is in our interest not to ignore this phenomenon but to embrace it. If we are wise enough to cultivate them, it can only strengthen us demographically."

I had heard echoes of this language before, in the lamentations over the National Jewish Population Survey, in Rabbi Stephen Leon's grand designs for the Southwestern Crypto-Jews, in the Orthodox seductions at the *ba'al teshuvah* Sabbath table, even in the meta-Jewish conceptualism of the Rebooters. In each case, though, the language of the population cure tended to be phrased with a more delicate touch. Whether for the lapsed Jew, the lost Jew, the hidden Jew, or some yet-undiscovered other Jew, the return is expressed in terms of the best interest of the one returning, and not that of the extant Jewish nation. That is, the revival of a lost Jew is supposed to redound to the benefit of the individual. It has a value that exists independently of the impact on other Jews and on Israel: Lost Jews must be allowed to return because it is good for *them*, not because it is good for the greater world of Jews. If their reintegration serves to grow the Jewish population, well, so much the better, but it is presented as a happy demographic byproduct and not as a motivation. A desire to see Jews go forth and multiply by means other than procreation would fall into the ethically questionable province of Christian crazies and outright cultists.

This means that although Rabbi Leon may very well have wanted to pack the better part of El Paso off to the Old City, he never actually said it. Roger Bennett reached out to Jews, but he also insisted that he was not motivated by demography, numbers, and growth. Rabbi Klatzko never directly stated that he wanted more people to be Orthodox.

Any outreach organization associated with a religion will want, at least in part, to generate adherents. It will also take pains to frame the effort to do so as beneficial for the new member. Christian evangelicals tell prospective rebirthers (my term, thank you) that accepting Jesus Christ as their savior is good for them. Buddhism offers greater cosmic perspective, equanimity, and who knows what else. All religions do this and Jews should not be held to a different standard. So long as they practice what they preach without coercion or lies I see nothing wrong with it. In fact, I expect and even prefer the rhetorical dance that Freund omitted. When Shavei Israel refers on its website to "The Need" (the desire for lost Jews to return) as "a tremendous opportunity" for Judaism "to reinforce its ranks," I am decidedly ill at ease.

On reflection, though, I wondered whether I was making a cultural misjudgment. From a Zionist perspective, as opposed to a Jewish-American one, expressing a desire to see more Jews in Israel is normal, if not entirely agreeable to all parties. Presently, just 40 percent of the world's Jews live in Israel. Another 40 percent are in the United States, with the remaining 20 percent spread across the globe, and no more than 4 percent in any one country. Jews, as a percentage of the Israeli population, peaked in the late 1950s and have been in decline ever since, primarily because of increased Jewish security and prosperity in other countries, as well as higher fertility rates among the non-Jewish populations in Israel. The largest pool of potential Israelis exists in the United States, but, as Jacob Dallal explained to me, those Jews tend to like it here: in 2010, only 4,000 Americans made aliyah, a figure that actually represented a significant increase over recent years. That migration rate will do little to alter demographic trends in Israel, and anyone committed to a Jewish majority in Israel may want to consider Jews from other parts of the world.

The discussion of "unique populations" and "Lost Tribes" takes on a different, and possibly exploitative, character when viewed in this context. The desire to maintain a specific demographic balance in the Middle East leaves me with a distinct feeling of discomfort. I detected such a program in the slick material presented to me at the Jewish Agency, the cheery assurances of my prospects for acceptance by Israel, and Freund's remarks about the Bnei Menashe.

I am not suggesting a nefarious plot to manipulate the world's poor into believing they are Jewish so that they might make aliyah. In my experience, the Jews who dedicate themselves to this sort of thing do so *because they really like Jews and wish there were more of them.* Shavei Israel's website, for its part, calls the return of lost Jewish people "a deeply personal decision," one that "cannot be imposed from the outside." And Freund, after he concluded his remarks and took questions from the audience, said that his approach to communities and individuals "is always one of skepticism. We always say, 'show us the evidence, show us the proof.'" I thought about quizzing Freund about that proof, but chose instead to watch Tzvi Khaute, wondering to what extent he understood—or had perhaps used to his advantage—his latent demographic potential. He stood like a statue next to Freund, his hands clasped tightly in front of him.

III.

A few months later I was in a taxicab in Jerusalem, on my way to visit Michael Freund. The driver, a Palestinian man in his late forties, was an amiable and unshaven chain-smoker with a cousin in Michigan, which helped account for the colloquial English he shouted at high volume as we swerved through traffic—pedestrians were assholes, other drivers, *motherfucks*. When he learned that I was American he smiled and said, "You are like a man standing on a fault line. Soon the earth will swallow you whole and you will die." This doom was, I think, intended for the United States in general and not me personally, but to be safe I tipped him when I got out.

I decided to sit for a few minutes at a small water fountain in a dingy plaza around the corner from Freund's office. I was jet-lagged still and needed a moment to collect my thoughts after the cab ride. Besides, it was pleasant to listen to the water and the traffic, and to watch the procession of Haredi women, European tourists, Palestinian workmen, and young Israeli soldiers strolling along the thoroughfare. Across from the plaza was a crumbling apartment building, a sandstone heap assembled in the Soviet-bloc-meets-Old-Testament style so favored by Jerusalem's architects. I noticed a banner hanging from a balcony on one of the upper floors, with an image of an aged and sad-looking American Indian chief. Beneath him was a slogan that read, in English: ASK ME ABOUT LAND FOR PEACE.

As I struggled to interpret this slogan, I was reminded of the surge of emotion Jews are said to experience in Israel, the sense of an emptiness filled, of completion, acceptance, of epiphanies and catharses. I felt none of this. I admit to some disorientation at the sight of so many people who looked, dressed, and sounded American but who spoke Hebrew; and it was odd to see large groups of Orthodox Jews in traditional garb—folks who seemingly exuded deep ties to this land—and then, when they spoke, hear strong New York accents. But I might have the same thoughts in certain parts of Brooklyn or Paris or Moscow, or any country influenced enough by American culture to contain such dislocation. Yet I was not immune to the pressure to have an *experience*, to read something significant into the banner, or into every prayerful maniac at the Wailing Wall, every ingratiating Arab T-shirt salesman, every falafel stand. Jerusalem! City of Portent!

My expectations were silly. Things happen when they happen and most moments are only moments. So I laughed along with my humorously bloodthirsty driver, and I made no effort to puzzle out the meaning of the banner with the chief and his exhortation. Likewise, I resolved to give Michael Freund the benefit of the doubt.

"I made aliyah back in 1995," Freund told me in his office. "A year later, after Prime Minister Netanyahu was elected to his first term, I went to work for him. David Bar-Illan, of blessed memory, was the communications director, and I was David's deputy. The bulk of our work was dealing with the foreign press, speech writing, press releases, and things of that sort. One day, though, a letter arrived from this community in northeastern India, the Bnei Menashe, that I had never heard of before. They claimed to be the descendants of a lost tribe of Israel, and they were pleading with the Israeli government to allow them to come back to Zion after twenty-seven centuries of wandering."

Freund admitted that he did not at first believe the Bnei Menashe were who they claimed to be. "Initially I could not believe the whole lost tribe bit, but I was very taken with them at a human level, at a personal level, by their sincerity and their desire to be Jews and to live in Israel," he said.

"You didn't believe that they were Jews but you were impressed by the fact that they wanted to be Jews?"

"Right. And I figured, nowadays, if someone is crazy enough to want to *join* us, then why should we put obstacles in their path?"

With that thought in mind, Freund took his first steps toward advancing the interests of the Bnei Menashe with the Israeli government. He was able to negotiate a special migration quota for the Bnei Menashe, which allowed 100 *olim* into Israel each year, under tourist visas, with the agreement that they convert to Judaism once they arrived. Freund left government in 1999, when Netanyahu stepped down, and committed himself full time to helping the Bnei Menashe. He soon expanded his aliyah interests to include other far-flung groups, most notably the Jews of Kaifeng, China, who are considered another lost tribe. Eventually, like so many people I had met along the way, he came to believe in the Bnei Menashe and their lost-Jew confreres: These were real Jews, they could be identified, and they had a right to return. Freund's desire to bring more Jews to Israel and his belief that these Lost Jews were in fact Jews in no way strikes me as incompatible motivations. One supports the other, neat as can be.

"I'm a Zionist," Freund said. "I believe that we need more Jews in Israel, and I myself have made the personal decision to tie my fate to this country and the fate of my family and my children and my descendants to this country." Demographics, he contended, were but one part of a "much larger puzzle" that had as much to do with satisfying the spiritual needs of these Jews as it did with satisfying the population needs of the Israeli state.

Not everyone in Israel accepts Freund's assertions. Nearly all of the returnees practice Orthodox Judaism, which, in a society struggling to balance the demands of the observant and the expectations of the secular, makes return its own form of demographic expansion. Most of the Bnei Menashe also settled in locales of great value to the Orthodox: the settlements. Taken together, these points meant that the issue of lost Jews was not limited to the Jewish sincerity of a particular "sexy, *National Geographic*" population. It tracked along the spectrum of conservative-liberal, observant-secular conflict, and could be linked to politics. In 2003, the newly appointed interior minister, Avraham Poraz, a representative of one of Israel's secular parties, ended the special arrangement for the Bnei Menashe, stating, in rather bald fashion, that Israel had no business "scouring the Third World to find Jews." His action was an indictment of people like Freund, because it implied that their efforts were a concealed attempt to advance the interests of the religious right.

Freund, who is Modern Orthodox as well as politically right wing, was undeterred. A year after the Bnei Menashe special arrangement was stopped, he convinced Israel's chief Sephardic rabbi to dispatch a rabbinical court to Manipur to investigate the Bnei Menashe. The court found that the Indian Jews were indeed *Zera Israel*, and a conversion court was then sent to Manipur, with the aim of converting the entire tribe en masse. In 2006, more than 215 Bnei Menashe converted and were able to make aliyah. Preparations were under way to continue the conversions when Freund encountered another problem. The Indian government objected to the presence of Zionist proselytizers making off with large numbers of its people. The in-country conversions were halted. Two hundred and thirty people who had already converted in India were allowed into Israel in 2007, bringing the country's current population of Bnei Menashe to 1,700. The 7,000 remaining in Manipur are still waiting to depart, while Freund, and others, attempt to negotiate a new arrangement (or possibly sue the government). Freund explained that the issue of right-wing interests, particularly the settlements, complicated matters for the Bnei Menashe both politically and with the larger secular public.

"In the early years, most of the Bnei Menashe went to Jewish communities in what are commonly referred to in the Western press as 'the settlements,'" he said. According to Freund, this was neither ideological nor political but practical. The conversion process in Israel took a full year, a period during which the migrants, who had not actually begun the aliyah process, were not eligible for government services.

"We had to find communities that would be willing to take them in knowing that they would not receive any budgetary support. In principle, everyone was happy to take in new immigrants, but in practice, the only places that were ready and willing to take them were the Jewish communities in Judea and Samaria, and I say that to their credit."

Understandably enough, the converts, who had found shelter in Orthodox communities, tended to remain in those communities after they became citizens. This, Freund said, and not a subversive program to settle Jews on contested land, explained the high concentration of Bnei Menashe in the settlements.

"Certain voices on the left objected and argued or asserted that the Bnei Menashe were being brought here to strengthen the settlements. Everything in this country is over-politicized and often hyper-politicized. I continue to believe, perhaps naively, that there are some issues that should be above and beyond politics. Aliyah is one of them."

Freund understood, however, that clustering the Bnei Menashe in the settlements harmed his larger goals. In the end, and not without regret, he changed tactics. Subsequent Bnei Menashe have been encouraged to settle in less politically sensitive areas, with help from Shavei Israel.

"Personally, I don't have any problem if the Bnei Menashe choose to live in [the settlements]," he said. "Ideologically I have no objection to that. But that's not what this is about." By encouraging the Bnei Menashe to relocate, Freund could argue that he had "shown that there is no political agenda, neither overt nor covert."

He seemed satisfied with that response. Although my instinct was not to believe him, I thought about my cabbie and the banner and my reluctance to judge. I knew little of the dynamics of the Israeli political world, and in truth, I was not sure I could truly understand them even if Freund could be trusted to explain them to me without his own spin. I held my tongue.

IV.

The Mevasseret Zion Absorption Center sits atop a sunny and tree-lined hill in a suburb thirty minutes west of Jerusalem. The Romans built a fort here to control the road to the city that their Legionnaires would one day destroy. The Crusaders maintained a stronghold as well; and much later, an Arab village stood on this ground, too, but now it is long gone. In the 1950s, a settlement for immigrants from Iraqi Kurdistan, who labored in a nearby quarry, was established at the foot of the hill. The workers raised fruits and vegetables on the slopes. Today the town is small and Jewish and pleasant enough in its way, although the farms and gardens are no more, replaced with wide streets, a big-box mall with a kosher McDonald's and a European cheese shop, and an ever-widening perimeter of upscale, gated neighborhoods with new townhouses and expensive cars: a taste of Los Angeles in the Middle East.

I was supposed to meet a representative from the Jewish Agency who would show me the Absorption Center, but I had exited the bus from Jerusalem at the wrong stop, which meant I conducted my own tour. I bought a cappuccino and pastry at the mall, and then I plunged into the grid of manicured lawns and clean sidewalks, silent and empty on a mid-week morning. The atmosphere changed noticeably when I neared the Absorption Center. Children were running about in all directions, as teenage girls put colorful laundry out to dry. Their fathers and uncles smoked cigarettes, keeping a close watch on me. This was a tense place, wary of strange faces (or at least my strange face; also, I was jotting things down in a notebook) and likely made uncomfortable by a strange man wandering about their neighborhood. An elderly woman in traditional Ethiopian garb, her face wrinkled like a raisin, pushed a toddler behind her skirts as I passed. An older man ignored my small wave as I hailed him while he stood on his front stoop. I stopped another man to ask for directions but he shook his head and kept walking.

The Center, which opened in 1970, stretches over several square blocks and was completed before the wealthy neighborhoods surrounding it. Its age shows, in both the concept and the condition of the housing stock and the apartment buildings—Levittown design gone to seed. The squared-off street corners and the blight, juxtaposed against the anonymous wealth of the bedroom communities, suggested to me the stark inequalities one often finds in U.S. cities. One thousand seven hundred Ethiopians cycle through Mevasseret Zion in two-year stretches, learning Hebrew, acculturating, and finally converting and becoming Israeli citizens.

The first Book of Kings includes a passage that recounts the meeting in Jerusalem of the Queen of Sheba and King Solomon. News of Solomon's wealth and wisdom had reached the queen, and she had traveled to the Holy Land to meet the king and "test him with hard questions." (The biblical verse makes no record of the queen's questions or Solomon's replies, but we can safely assume them to have been satisfactorily Solomonic.) The queen praised Solomon and showered him with gifts of gold, exotic spices, precious stones, and "great quantities of *almug* wood," the last of which was used to build the steps to the Temple. She then gathered her attendants and guards and returned home.

In Ethiopia, which is believed to be the location of the historical realm of Sheba, this tale is told with significantly greater detail. In both versions Solomon greeted the queen and accepted her flattery and her gifts. In the Ethiopian version, however, the queen did not return home with the same alacrity. Solomon was attracted to the beautiful queen and requested the pleasure of her company in his palace. She consented, but only on the condition that Solomon not touch her without her permission. Solomon considered this and countered with a condition of his own: The queen's person would be sacrosanct so long as she did not take any of the king's possessions without permission. In the event that she did, Solomon would be free to demand something of hers in return.

That evening Solomon held a feast in the queen's honor, and this being a Jewish meal, the chef had a heavy hand with the salt. Later that night, the queen retired to her bedchamber to sleep, only to wake in the middle of the night, extremely thirsty. Solomon, crafty as well as wise, had commanded a pitcher of water to be placed beside her bed, and the queen drank from it. Solomon appeared not long after, saw the empty pitcher, and demanded his due. Then, as in the Bible, the queen returned home, only now she was with child, making her son Menelik the first Ethiopian Jew.

A final wrinkle to the Ethiopian legend: The queen would later send young Menelik to Jerusalem to be raised and educated in his father's palace. Menelik lived with Solomon until he reached his majority, at which point he set out for home with his retinue.[1] One Friday evening on the journey home Menelik's party reached a river, which some of his followers crossed in violation of the Sabbath; some did not. Those who forded the river abandoned Menelik's faith and became Christians; those who obeyed the Sabbath strictures remained Jews. That mythological schism has an analog in the modern era. When Protestant missionaries from England arrived in Ethiopia, they were, as in Manipur, relatively success-

---

1. Menelik, too, is believed to have taken something from Solomon without asking: the Ark of the Covenant. According to legend, and the concluding moments of *Raiders of the Lost Ark* notwithstanding, the Ark is currently in the hands of Christians at the Church of Zion, in Axum, Ethiopia.

ful in their proselytizing efforts among Ethiopia's Jewish natives. Those who renounced Menelik's faith and crossed the river into Christianity are referred to as the Falash Mura, a derogatory term in Amharic that loosely translates as "stranger." The ones who resisted, observing the Sabbath along the riverbank, are known as the Beta Israel.

The Ethiopians in the Mevasseret Zion Absorption Center today are Falash Mura, although the majority of the approximately 110,000 Ethiopian Israelis are Beta Israel. Most Beta Israel arrived in 1991, as part of Operation Solomon, during which 15,000 Beta Israel were airlifted, with much drama, into Israel in advance of a civil war. An earlier, large-scale Jewish-Ethiopian egress—Operation Moses—occurred in 1984, when 8,000 Beta Israel fled Ethiopia on foot and attempted the arduous trek into secret refugee camps in Sudan (Sudan didn't want its neighbors to know it was cooperating with a Mossad-funded program). Subsequent migrations of Beta Israel continued fitfully and only after much debate in Israel over how to determine the total number of bona fide Ethiopian Jews. The Christian-Ethiopian Jews began coming to Israel in 1999 after the Beta Israel migration was complete. Unlike the Beta Israel, the Falash Mura were not allowed in under the Law of Return, but as *Zera Israel*. Since then, the flow of Falash Mura, as with the Bnei Menashe, has picked up or slowed depending on political trends in Israel.

I finally located my Jewish Agency minder, a South African named Michael Jankelowitz, in the Absorption Center's dusty interior quad, which was surrounded by prefab trailers housing a school, maternity clinic, and administrative offices. He had disembarked at the proper bus stop and was waiting for me outside the mother's clinic where a group of women with infants strapped to their backs were being harangued into a proper line by an Israeli social worker. Jankelowitz was a portly fellow, with a prominent belly, stubby legs, and a light-brown mustache. He greeted me with a tip of his battered navy-blue Kangol cap.

"Here to see the natives, eh?" he said. "Come along. Let's have a look, shall we?"

Jankelowitz shepherded me through the buildings. We interrupted a Hebrew class for adults where the students—young men, very shy—quizzed me on American sports and culture, asked me what exactly a journalist does, and wondered why, if I spoke no Hebrew, I wasn't required to study it as they were. I came up with answers only for the sports questions. In the day care, the children were busy with an arts-and-crafts project, and the teacher, an Ethiopian woman who had herself come through Mevasseret Zion years earlier, greeted our presence with some irritation. Outside, we stopped at one of the Absorption Center's two "model reconstructed homes," replicas of Ethiopian huts built by the migrants. Israeli schoolchildren were often brought to the Center on field trips, and the homes provided an inkling of what life in Ethiopia had been like. Jankelowitz rolled his eyes when he described this to me, suggesting in an offhand way that the Ethiopians found the homes condescending and perhaps insulting, although these replicas were considered necessary nonetheless.

"We have visitors here every week," he said. "The days of people"—by which he meant Americans: funding for the Absorption Center comes from the Jewish Agency, which administers the site, and which is in turn largely funded by Jewish-American charities—"just writing checks are gone. The younger generation wants accountability, programming, studies. Nothing like their grandparents." I don't think Jankelowitz meant that donors should simply give money away, but rather that "accountability," as defined by visits to model homes, was a farce.

On our way to another building to sit in on a teaching seminar, we noticed a small camera crew unloading its gear. Jankelowitz recognized them as from one of Israel's Ethiopian television stations.

"Must be here for the new arrival," Jankelowitz said.

A Falash Mura family had arrived at the Absorption Center that week after waiting for permission to migrate for nearly ten years. The crew was here to document how they were adjusting to their new life. Jankelowitz approached the camera crew and began chatting in Hebrew with the on-air reporter, a slender and very handsome Ethiopian man with short dreadlocks, wearing Diesel jeans and a tan sports coat with the sleeves pushed up to his elbows. One of the cameramen, also a fashionably dressed Ethiopian, greeted me in halting English and we spoke for a few moments as Jankelowitz negotiated with the television personality to let us come with them.

The cameraman, whose name I never learned, was Beta Israel and had come here as a child during Operation Solomon. He told me that he had lived in a different Absorption Center, though he was quick to point out that his family had left after much less than two years. Speaking with gentle disdain, he described what he saw as an increasing reliance of more recent Ethiopian migrants on government services. Better instead for the Israeli government to push the Falash Mura into society as quickly as possible. Unlike his generation, the new Ethiopians were being "coddled."

The on-air personality said something to the cameraman in Hebrew and the young man told me he had to go. Jankelowitz came back and said we had permission to accompany the crew when they went to film the new arrivals. I mentioned what the young man had said and Jankelowitz nodded and, as we continued our walk, offered some context. The two communities of Ethiopians in Israel are, as dark-skinned people in a predominantly light-skinned country, thrust into close contact. Unfortunately, their history and divergent experiences mean that each group has little affinity for the other. One point of contention seems obvious: The Falash Mura converted and the Beta Israel did not. But there are less apparent issues that were reflected in the cameraman's opinion. The Operation Solomon migrants arrived in Israel in large numbers and with almost no infrastructure in place to meet their needs: They were black, didn't speak Hebrew, and had few if any skills useful in a modern, technologically advanced society. As a result, those early Ethiopian migrants struggled in Israel, with high rates of poverty and crime, and an alarmingly high rate of depression and suicide. Also, some argued that certain elements within Israeli society had exploited the newcomers. The primary evidence can be found in the disproportionate number of Ethiopians in Israeli military combat units. The Falash Mura faced these issues as well, but because the support system was more advanced, and perhaps because white-Israeli society had become somewhat more attuned to people of color, there is a sense among the Beta Israel that the Falash Mura have had it too easy.

Demographics also complicated matters in ways I had not anticipated. Beta Israel migration commenced in 1984 and essentially concluded in 1999, when the Falash Mura began to be brought to the country. It is believed—although this is open to dispute—that all Beta Israel in Ethiopia who wanted to migrate have already done so. This is a population of 45,000 people, excluding children born in Israel after migration. Already, some 35,000 Falash Mura have entered Israel, and they are continuing to come in. This creates a scenario in which the Christian-Ethiopian Jews may one day outnumber the Jewish-Ethiopian Jews, despite the fact that, after conversion for the Falash Mura, they are *all* Israeli-Ethiopian Jews.

Unraveling the strands of discord—there were more, Jankelowitz assured me—occupied my mind until we reached the house issued to the newly arrived Falash Mura family. We squeezed inside along with the television crew, which included the host, two producers, two cameramen, and a man holding a microphone boom and light. The house was cramped and drafty, but the walls were freshly whitewashed, and the space was clean. The bedrooms had no doors and the new residents had strung up bed sheets for privacy. The new family had relatives who had already settled in Israel, and the women and children had congregated in the kitchen, cooking *injera* flatbread on a round ceramic griddle that Jankelowitz said practically all the migrants brought with them from Ethiopia. Pots of spiced lentils and stewed meat burbled away on the stove, their scent competing with the odor from a carafe of strong Ethiopian coffee. I noticed that one of the women had a crucifix tattooed on her forehead. Jankelowitz explained that this was a Falash Mura practice that was originally adopted to demonstrate the sincerity of earlier Christian converts, but it was now done as a semi-tribal affectation. In the hallway, the television host was interviewing a shy and wiry Falash Mura man with a goatee. He seemed overwhelmed by all the strangers and provided his answers in an Amharic whisper, which the television host repeated in Hebrew for the camera. Jankelowitz translated for me.

The man had been a nurse in a small village outside of Gondar, Ethiopia, and had come with his parents, he said, gesturing to an elderly couple in one of the back bedrooms. I looked in on them. The old man was dressed in a weathered suit and his wife wore a white robe. They sat on the bed in stunned silence, not meeting my gaze.

The crew finished its work and departed, leaving the migrants to their absorption process. The young cameraman seemed a little confounded by the encounter with his brethren. Inside, I had watched him as he watched—with pity or revulsion, I wasn't sure which—one of the women puzzle her way around a light switch. Jankelowitz escorted me down the hill to the bus stop, where I would take the bus back to Jerusalem. He clearly cared for and about the Ethiopians—Jewish, Christian, and otherwise—and he railed against the political obstacles to the process of bringing them here. He also understood the difficulties the Ethiopians faced in Israel, and was not optimistic about the prospects for the family we had met.

"Many of them are still living in the Bronze Age. They have to be shown everything: how to use the lights, the stove, everything." He turned to look up the hill at the Absorption Center. "It's not easy."

V.

Jankelowitz played tour guide for much of the rest of my stay. He took me to dinner at an Ethiopian restaurant tucked into a back alley in the center of Jerusalem. He chaperoned me around the Knesset, introducing me to important political figures that I should have known but didn't. In the parliamentary cafeteria I ate falafel and rice and interviewed an Ethiopian member of parliament (only the second so far elected), an intensely charismatic man named Shlomo Molla, who said it would take a generation for the Beta Israel to accept the Falash Mura as Jews.

I spent an evening at the home of a family of young Orthodox American expatriates engaged in a sort of reverse *Rumspringa*: instead of allowing themselves a year or two away from the strictures of traditional society, they had immersed themselves more deeply *within* it, which in this case meant a Jerusalem enclave of ultra-Orthodox *Yeshivists*. I had tea with an Israeli archaeologist digging up relics buried beneath contested land, interviewed an Israeli anthropologist who had published a children's book on the Jews of the Amazon, and visited a museum dedicated to a family of pre-1948 settlers who had spied for the British during World War I and were thwarted by the Turks because of an incompetent homing pigeon. I had coffee at a bus station with a Chinese Jew working as a travel agent. I was invited to a *Shabbos* dinner party where I met an Israeli journalist, an engineer, an actor, the sister of an American celebrity, and a student, all of whom seemed thrilled and amused at my project. I bantered with the manager of my hotel, a Palestinian man with a long brown beard and extensive knowledge of American football. I wandered the Old City, immersed in its swirl of mysteries, spiritual attractions, and clichés. I watched at sunset as the throng of ecstatic Jewish supplicants stuck scraps of paper—holy requests for blessing, sufferance, or remembrance—into the cracks in the Wailing Wall. I moved aside as two middle-aged Asian women trudged through the Christian Quarter lugging a massive wooden cross on their shoulders. I bought strawberries and dates from a Palestinian boy pushing a wheelbarrow down a dark alleyway off the Cardo. I enjoyed myself at the falafel stands, shawarma stands, hamburger and pizza joints, bagel spots, coffee shops, tea stalls, and kiosks for purveyors of incense and spices and confections and treats. I heard the voice of the muezzin carry through the Muslim Quarter during the calls to prayer. I took note of the priests, the imams, the rabbis, the tourists, the businessmen, the soldiers, the pilgrims, people from every corner of the globe, speaking every conceivable language, who had come to this fundamental (and fundamentalist) city for myriad reasons and who invested it with diverse and often contradictory powers. I had ample opportunity, I think, for realizations, understanding, clarity, certainty, and life-altering determinations made in the shadow of the Dome of the Rock.

Yet nothing came. Mostly I felt exhausted, by my project, and by the weight of not only coming up with an answer but also deciding what I wanted that answer to tell me. I had not come to Israel with high expectations. I had told myself again and again that it is a place like all other places and that it would provide no solutions and solve no riddles. I understood all of that, but I still felt I had earned the right to some disappointment at having crossed continents to find something I knew wouldn't be there only to confirm that it wasn't.

Part IX

AN ANSWER

I.

In time, my mood lightened. Having had my false expectations dashed in the Holy Land even proved beneficial, I think. The reality of Israel forced me to dismiss the tempting solutions of compelled inclusion and easy citizenship. I returned home and lost myself in the research and reading and daily routines. The weeks and months fell away almost without my noticing it, until one day I realized that almost a year had passed since Sukkot.

Directly following my night with Roger Bennett and the Rebooters in Union Square, I had flirted with the idea of purchasing my own sukkah (my construction skills are such that I never considered building one). I resisted the impulse, though, with what at the time seemed to be good reason. My life has not been entirely without Jewish religious holidays. I've celebrated Hanukkah, for instance, and my father's family has held a Passover seder every year. As an adult, I've even hosted a few seders of my own. These two observances comprise the outer limits of my Jewish practice, however, and I have taken great pains to rationalize the Judaism out of them: Hanukkah is about gifts (for me when I was young, and now for my children); Passover is a chance to eat European comfort foods, drink sweet wine, and to see relatives. My focus never strayed from the secular aspects of the holidays, allowing me to view them as not substantially different from, say, Thanksgiving, or the Super Bowl. (In fact, there have been years when I skipped Passover, Hanukkah, and Thanksgiving—but never the game.)

Sukkot was different. Even with Reboot's exhortations ringing in my ears, I wasn't particularly inclined to bring Roger Bennett's idea of "lifting up a festival" into my home. Largely this was due to an aversion to the sukkah itself. The hut, symbol of the shelters used by the Israelites in the desert, was an inescapably religious and spiritual artifact. To use a sukkah with any sincerity required an acknowledgment of things I wasn't comfortable acknowledging: God, prayer, spirituality, the soul. I understand that Sukkot is not demonstrably different from the two holidays I keep, and that the menorah and the seder plate are religious symbols of no less import than the sukkah. But because Hanukkah and Passover are so firmly associated for me with family and entertainment, I can ignore the liturgical elements. With Sukkot, that was impossible. My inexperience with the sukkah meant that I would find no secular escape. There was no way to talk myself out of its religiosity. To take on the sukkah would have been a contrived act of Judaism, false and ridiculous.

That was how I felt the year before. Yet with the holiday approaching again, I began to feel differently. Not about the religious aspect, mind you: I continue even now to find the sukkah to be an alien religious artifact, one to which my connection is uncertain and uneasy. The change is that my antipathy toward religion no longer seemed something I could simply take for granted. The sukkah, despite my discomfort with it, or perhaps *because* of it, was now something I needed to reckon with, an object that might even embody the distance I had come since I had first considered my question. Judaism—whether understood as faith, identity, or ethnicity—would never come to me. I would have to move toward it, and the sukkah could serve as evidence, however scant, of that movement, of a shift in my life. Or maybe it wouldn't. But I needed to find out for myself, instead of dismissing a whole swath of Jewish experience out of hand.

All of which helps to explain how I found myself one bright early fall day, standing in front of the Sukkah Center in Borough Park, Brooklyn.

There was a small grocery across the street that sold the sort of baked goods that my mother, despite her Jewish misgivings, had raised me to enjoy. I stopped off for some rugelach, which I downed before heading inside the "showroom," which was really a grime-covered, windowless warehouse, anonymous but for a small banner with the company name and phone number: 1-800-227-SUKA.

A handwritten sign on the door directed me to a steep and narrow staircase. A young Orthodox woman carrying a baby in a sling and holding hands with a toddler was descending as I started up, so I backtracked and held the door for her. She returned my brief acknowledging smile, which pleased me. Here I was, a Jew, doing what Jews do, buying the stuff that they buy—normal stuff, not ridiculous at all.

The showroom was crammed full of sukkahs. Dominating one corner of the room was a "panel sukkah" the size of a single-wide trailer, with an aluminum frame, veneer wall panels, and a door with a handle and a latch. Next to it stood a "snap sukkah," so named because the steel beams that form its frame snap together. This one, about half as large as the panel sukkah, would offer comfortable shelter for perhaps ten well-fed Negev wanderers. There were several smaller ones made from nylon or canvas, vertical tents, really, designed for standing or sitting instead of lying prone. Two cardboard boxes, one filled with bamboo mats and poles for the sukkah's roof, the other with a selection of religious-themed posters, sat beside them. A large display of accessories, parts, and decorations had been set up in another part of the room. There were fluorescent lightbulbs and a variety of light fixtures; clamps, brackets, and other fittings; pom-poms, tinsel, garlands of plastic grapes; and an assortment of complete decoration sets. A television anchored to a platform above the showroom floor played a short sukkah-assembly demonstration video on a loop. Every five minutes an Orthodox man erected a large panel sukkah with great efficiency, his movements, which were accompanied by peppy electronic music, a choreographed display of religious carpentry. Congratulatory shots of the completed sukkah were followed by a few seconds of black screen, and then the video restarted and the man began his project again.

A modestly dressed woman with her head covered by a light-brown wig sat at a cluttered desk logging orders on an ancient computer. Behind her, separated by a Plexiglas-and-particleboard wall, were four dour and heavyset bearded men busily making notations in various ledgers, penciling things onto forms, and punching at the keys of oversized receipt calculators.

"And may I help you?" the woman asked.

"Yes. I'd like a PopUp sukkah."

I had done some research online before heading to the Sukkah Center, and the PopUp sukkah seemed the cheapest and simplest sukkah available, although in truth, I had other reasons for wanting one. The product description on the PopUp sukkah's website, which I found both amusing and persuasive, explained that since the days of "the wonderful Cloud of Glory Sukkah in the desert," Jews had searched in vain for the perfect holiday shelter. The PopUp, which came to market in 1999, "after 3311 years of ambitious attempts and close copies," was to date the only sukkah to offer biblical-era quality. "Good lookin', movable, light, bright and comfortable," the PopUp weighed just seven pounds, collapsed down to a single inch in width, and required no tools for assembly. The Sukkah Center was listed as an authorized retailer. Done and done!

The woman summoned one of the men from behind the glass partition to ask if they had any PopUps in stock. The man, whom I immediately recognized as the skilled sukkah builder in the video, came out, inspected me with some curiosity, made a few mental calculations, and then told me I didn't want a PopUp.

"I don't?"

"No. This thing isn't durable at all," he said, idly fingering his beard. "Not what you want. You really are going to want a pop out sukkah."

"Pop *out*?"

"Yes. Pop out."

"Does it come . . . complete?" I asked. "I mean, is it, uh, fully, you know, kosher?"

"Fully kosher?"

"Yes, I mean, do I have to buy anything else to, uh, you know, *use* it?"

He assured me that the pop out sukkah came ready for operation, both in terms of religious design and construction materials.

"Schlock, too?" I asked.

This question was a setup. The Sukkah Center website clearly stated that sukkah *schlock*—which was the term for a rain tarp—was sold separately. But I liked the word, and I wanted to know why it was used in this unexpected context.

"Why do they call it that?" I asked.

"Call what what?"

"Schlock. Why do they call schlock 'schlock'?"

He seemed confused. "It's the covering. That's what it is. In Yiddish."

"Yeah, I know. But I thought it meant something else. Like cheap, or flimsy. Right? Low quality?"

He retreated to the office without answering and launched into a discussion with his colleagues. They began bickering heatedly in Yiddish and I riffled through the box of posters while they struggled to reach a consensus. I selected one with a nature theme (deer, a rushing waterfall, flowers) that also happened to be 3-D. It came with a pair of paper viewing glasses and cost ten dollars. The pop out sukkah arrived from the stockroom a moment later. A sullen teenager wearing a yarmulke had lugged it upstairs, struggling with the awkwardly shaped cardboard box.

I noticed that he had a small Post-it Note stuck to the back of his shirt. It read: HEY! DON'T FORGET TO TIP!

Finally, the men seemed to have resolved their linguistic differences and the man marched back to the showroom floor to render their decision. He was, I saw, smirking ever so slightly, and his brethren seemed to be trying not to laugh.

"It's a—what do you call it?—a *multi-tasking* word," he said.

II.

I took a walk one afternoon in October, pushing my daughter in her stroller. On the short trip from our home to Prospect Park, I passed upward of five or six sukkahs. The majority were prefabricated structures purchased from the Sukkah Center or its competitors. Others were more personalized and elaborate. The sukkah outside Congregation Beth Elohim, a prosperous synagogue in a stretch of historic brownstones and expensive townhouses, was a high-modern specimen, crafted from blond wood, bent rebar, and Spanish moss. I learned later that it had been designed by one of the winning architecture firms from Sukkah City. The one at Chai Tots, a Jewish preschool, was more homespun, its walls made from two-by-fours covered with bed sheets and a ceiling of fresh cedar sprigs. Inside, children were eating cookies and sipping juice with their parents and teachers. We passed one street on our walk that had been cordoned off for a Sukkot block party. The participating families had hired a rock band, which was belting out 1970s-era southern rock in Hebrew. The children, when they weren't running in and out of the sukkahs in front of the homes, enjoyed ice cream from an ice cream truck, had their faces painted, and gobbled down hummus and pita.

I returned home a few hours later and dragged the cardboard box with my sukkah into the backyard and opened it with a pair of pruning scissors. Inside were two zip-up carrying cases, the first containing the sukkah frame and nylon wall covering, and a smaller one with the *schach*—the bamboo mat and poles. The *schach* came with a sheet of paper that confirmed that it had received a "Kashrut certification" from a suitable rabbinical authority. As with everything I have assembled during my adult life, there were items included in the box—two thin metal strips—whose use I could not fathom. I rested them on the top of the barbecue.

The pop out was simply designed: its frame "popped out" to its full height, about seven feet, with minimal effort. The nylon wall, which actually consisted of two layers, a rugged and rain-resistant outer shell and a thin interior mesh dotted with small pouches for storage and hooks for decoration, had to be strapped lengthwise around the frame. It was somewhat difficult to attach, but only because I velcroed it on upside down at first and had to remove it and start over. I climbed atop my picnic table to put the bamboo poles and mat in place. Then I entered the sukkah and sat cross-legged on the ground.

It was cool and damp inside, the ground littered with leaves and bits of toys discarded by my children that summer. Light from the late-afternoon sky filtered through the bamboo slats. Birds and squirrels chattered in the trees, their complaints competing with a party some doors down. I heard the whine of a fire engine, the bleat of car horns, the screech of a passing jet, the garbled voices from a television broadcasting a football game. I let the aural distractions intermingle, forming a soothing and remote wall of noise.

Sukkot is, in part, a commemoration of homelessness, and of the perseverance of a lost people wandering in a desert. It is a reminder of the luxury of permanence, of refuge, of home. My mother had, in her way, subjected me to a metaphorical homelessness. She had taken us from the home of our identity and imposed something new and tenuous. I could, if I chose, allow the sukkah to represent the return to my original home. At the very least it could signify my right to claim shelter in this particular structure.

Yet I was not sure how far I wanted to push that idea. I need, as all people do, shelter, succor, and protection, but I still find it difficult to think of the sukkah, or Judaism, as a home, the Promised Land found after the era of dislocation.

That does not mean that my question will go unanswered. I am a Jew. I believe that. I am entitled to believe that. I could not make it otherwise even if I wished. My resistance, then, stems not from the decision to accept or reject this as my answer, but from the impossibility of fully understanding what it entails. I will never exhaust the potential inherent in my question. I will never be content with my knowledge of how it intersects and diverges from the broader American project, of which I am a product and a part. I will never find the proper balance between the demands the question makes and the benefits it offers. Nor do I desire to. For me both question and answer represent a process of continual, conscious, purposeful *becoming*.

I stood up and stepped from the sukkah. I have asked the question. I will continue to do so. That will have to be enough.

End.

Brooklyn, New York. 2011.

AN ACCOUNTING

I feel it only right to recognize those individuals who helped this work become whatever it has ultimately become. I do so not only from a deeply held sense of gratitude and respect, but also from the sincere belief that blame, too, must be apportioned as merited. In that light, a short list of those most responsible: Meghan Stevenson, Jim Rutman, Jennifer Szalai, Ben Metcalf, Roger Hodge, Rabbi Yehuda Sarna, Shulem Deen, Ben Austen, Ryann Liebenthal, Alexander Kelly, Ben Gottlieb, Ryan Healey, Caroline Sutton, John Fagan, Liz Keenan, Ashley Pattison, Jaya Miceli.

SELECTED BIBLIOGRAPHY

Abel, Richard. "Contested Communities." *Journal of Law and Society*, 22:1 (March 1995).

Adler, Frank J. *Roots in a Moving Stream: The Centennial History of Congregation B'nai Jehudah of Kansas City, 1870–1970*. Kansas City, Mo.: The Temple, Congregation B'nai Jehudah, 1972.

Ament, Jonathon. "American Jewish Religious Denominations." United Jewish Communities Report Series on the National Jewish Population Survey 2000–01, February 2005.

Ariel, Yaakov. "Hasidism in the Age of Aquarius: The House of Love and Prayer in San Francisco, 1967-1977." *Religion and American Culture*, 13:2 (Summer 2003).

Armstrong, Karen. *History of God: The 4,000-Year Quest of Judaism, Christianity, and Islam*. New York: A.A. Knopf, 1993.

Baum, David. *The Non-Orthodox Jew's Guide to Orthodox Jews*. New Jersey: Veracity Press, 2010.

Bayer, Barbara. "NRT, Rabbi Cukierkorn Go Separate Ways." *The Kansas City Jewish Chronicle*, April 11, 2011.

Bechofer, Yosef Gavriel. *The Contemporary Eruvin: Eruvin in Modern Metropolitan Areas*. Jerusalem; New York: Feldheim Publishers, 1998.

Beinart, Peter. "The Failure of the American Jewish Establishment." *New York Review of Books*, June 10, 2010.

Berger, Joseph. "Judaism Takes Different Turns; In Places, Blocks of Orthodoxy." *The New York Times*, September 27, 2002.

Berman, Lila Corwin. "Sociology, Jews, and Intermarriage in Twentieth-Century America." *Jewish Social Studies: History, Culture, Society*, 14:2 (Winter 2008).

Berman, Howard A. "Classical Reform Judaism: A Concise Profile." *Issues* (Winter 2007).

Blutinger, Jeffrey C. " 'So-called Orthodoxy': The History of an Unwanted Label." *Modern Judaism*, 27:3 (October 2007).

Blustain, Sarah. "A Paradoxical Legacy: Rabbi Shlomo Carlebach's Shadow Side." *Lillith*, 23:1 (March 1998).

Brodkin, Karen. *How Jews Became White Folks & What That Says About Race in America*. New Jersey: Rutgers University Press, 1998.

Bronfman, Edgar M. "Opening our Tent." *The Forward*, December 17, 2010.

Carroll, Michael P. "The Debate over a Crypto-Jewish Presence in New Mexico: The Role of Ethnographic Allegory and Orientalism." *Sociology of Religion*, 63:1 (Spring 2002).

Cohen, Steven M. and Kelman, Ari Y. "The Continuity of Discontinuity: How Young Jews Are Connecting, Creating, and Organizing Their Own Jewish Lives." 21/64, 2007.

Cooper, Alanna E. "Conceptualizing Diaspora: Tales of Jewish Travelers in Search of the Lost Tribes." *Association of Jewish Studies Review*, 30:1 (2006).

Diamant, Anita. *Choosing A Jewish Life: A Handbook for People Converting to Judaism and for Their Family and Friends*. New York: Schocken Books, 1997.

Freehof, Solomon B. "Reform Judaism in America." *The Jewish Quarterly Review*, 45:4 (April 1955).

Fox, Marvin. *Interpreting Maimonides: Studies in Methodology, Metaphysics, and Moral Philosophy*. Chicago: The University of Chicago Press, 1990.

Gitell, Seth. "The Case for Jewish Outreach." *The Forward*, January 19, 1996.

Gitlitz, David M. *Secrecy and Deceit: The Religion of the Crypto-Jews*. Albuquerque: University of New Mexico Press, 2002.

Goldberg, J. J. "America's Vanishing Jews." *The Jerusalem Report*, November 5, 1992.

Goldberg, J. J. "A Jewish Recount." *The New York Times*, September 17, 2003.

Griessman, Eugene B. "Philo-Semitism and Protestant Fundamentalism: The Unlikely Zionists." *Phylon*, 37:3 (Fall 1976).

Halevy, Schulamith C. "Manifestations of Crypto-Judaism in the American Southwest." *Jewish Folklore & Ethnology Review*, 18:1–2 (1996).

Halevy, Schulamith C. "Anusim in North America: The Ingathering." *Traditions*, 30:1, (Fall 1995).

Hershenson, Roberta. "Telling the Story of Ethiopian Jews." *The New York Times*, July 7, 1991.

Herz, Cary. *New Mexico's Crypto-Jews: Image and Memory.* Albuquerque: University of New Mexico Press, 2007.

Hordes, Stanley M. *To the End of the Earth: A History of the Crypto-Jews of New Mexico.* New York: Columbia University Press, 2005.

Howe, Irving. *World of Our Fathers: The Journey of the East European Jews to America and the Life They Found There.* New York: Harcourt Brace Jovanovich, 1976.

Idov, Michael. "Clash of the Bearded Ones: Hipsters, Hasids, and the Williamsburg Street." *New York*, April 11, 2010.

Kaplan, Dana Evan. "Reform Jewish Theology and the Sociology of Liberal Religion in America: The Platforms as Response to the Perception of Socioreligious Crisis." *Modern Judaism*, 20:1 (February 2000).

Kamenetz, Rodger. "Has the Jewish Renewal Movement Made It Into the Mainstream?" *Moment*, 19:6 (December 1994).

Kertzer, Morris N. *What Is a Jew?* New York: Touchstone, 1994.

Klaff, Vivian. "Defining American Jewry from Religious and Ethnic Perspectives: The Transitions to Greater Heterogeneity." *Sociology of Religion*, 67:4 (Winter 2006).

Kunin, Seth. "Juggling Identities Among the Crypto-Jews of the American Southwest." *Religion*, 31:1 (January 2001).

Kurzweil, Arthur. *From Generation to Generation: How to Trace Your Jewish Genealogy and Personal History.* New York: Morrow, 1980.

Kutz, Jack. "New Mexico's Mystery Stone." *Desert*, August 1974.

Liebman, Charles S. "Orthodoxy in American Jewish Life." *American Jewish Year Book 65.* New York: American Jewish Committee, 1965.

Liebman, Charles S. "Reconstructionism in American Jewish Life." *American Jewish Year Book 71.* New York: American Jewish Committee, 1971.

Lopatin, Asher. "The Dos and Don'ts of Re-heating on Shabbat: Important Standards of Shabbat Food Preparation for the Anshe Sholom Community." September 15, 2000.

MacDonald, G. Jeffrey. "What Does 'Jewishness' Mean?" *Christian Science Monitor,* September 15, 2004.

Maimonides, Moses. *The Guide for the Perplexed.* London: Routledge & Kegan Paul Ltd., 1904.

Mintz, Jerome. *Hasidic People: A Place in the New World.* Massachusetts: Harvard University Press, 1985.

Montefiore, C. G. "Liberal Judaism." *The Jewish Quarterly Review,* 20:3 (April 1908).

Myers, D. G. "The Judaism Rebooters." *Commentary*, July 2009.

Naim, Asher. *Saving the Lost Tribe: The Rescue and Redemption of the Ethiopian Jews.* New York: Ballantine Books, 2003.

"National Jewish Population Survey, 1990." New York: United Jewish Communities, 1991.

"National Jewish Population Survey, 2000–01." New York: United Jewish Communities, 2003.

Neulander, Judith. "The New Mexican Crypto-Jewish Canon: Choosing to Be 'Chosen' in Millennial Tradition." *Jewish Folklore and Ethnology Review* 18:1 (1994).

Norich, Samuel. "Anomie Plaguing Jews in Diaspora." *The Forward*, February 3, 1995.

Ochs, Vanessa L. *Inventing Jewish Ritual.* Philadelphia: Jewish Publication Society, 2007.

Perry, Peña. *Beyond Crypto-Judaism.* Lulu.com, 2006.

Philipson, David. "The Beginnings of the Reform Movement in Judaism." *The Jewish Quarterly Review*, 15:3 (April 1903).

Philipson, David. "The Reform Movement in Judaism. II." *The Jewish Quarterly Review*, 16:1 (October 1903).

Philipson, David. "The Breslau Rabbinical Conference." *The Jewish Quarterly Review*, 18:4 (July 1906).

Philologos. "An Essential Point." *The Forward*, November 24, 2006.

Quirin, James. "Oral Traditions as Historical Sources in Ethiopia: The Case of the Beta Israel (Falasha)." *History in Africa*, 20 (1993).

Rakoff, Joanna Smith. "The New Super Jews." *Time Out New York*, December 4–11, 2003.

Robinson, George. "American Judaism at the Crossroads." *The New York Times*, August 15, 1993.

Ross, James R. *Fragile Branches: Travels Through the Jewish Diaspora.* New York: Riverhead Books, 2000.

Rushkoff, Barbara. *Jewish Holiday Fun . . .For You!* New York: Universe, 2004.

Rushkoff, Douglas. *Nothing Sacred: The Truth About Judaism.* New York: Three Rivers Press, 2004.

Sacks, Jonathan. "Beyond the Cult of Survival." *The Jerusalem Report*, March 10, 1994.

Sands, Roberta G. "The Social Integration of *Baalei Teshuva.*" *Journal for the Scientific Study of Religion*, 48:1 (2009).

Santos, Richard. "Chicanos of Jewish Descent in Texas." *Western States Jewish Historical Quarterly*, 15 (July 1983).

Sarna, Jonathan D. "The Secret of Jewish Continuity." *Commentary*. 98:4 (October 1994).

Sarna, Jonathan D. *A Great Awakening: The Transformation That Shaped Twentieth Century American Judaism and Its Implications for Today*. New York: Council for Initiatives in Jewish Education, 1995.

Sarna, Jonathan D. "The Cult of Synthesis in American Jewish Culture." *Jewish Social Studies*, 5:1–2 (August 1998–Winter 1999).

Sasso, Sandy Eisenberg. *Abuelita's Secret Matzahs*. Cincinnati: Emmis Books, 2005.

Saxe, Leonard. "U.S. Jewry 2010: Estimates of the Size and Characteristics of the Population." Maurice and Marilyn Cohen Center for Modern Jewish Studies, December 20, 2010.

Schain, Ruchoma. *All for the Boss: The Life and Impact of R' Yaakov Yosef Herman, A Torah Pioneer in America: An Affectionate Family Chronicle*. Jerusalem; New York: Feldheim Publishers, 2001.

Schiffman, Lawrence H. *Who Was a Jew? Rabbinic and Halakhic Perspectives on the Jewish Christian Schism*. New Jersey: KTAV Publishing, 1985.

Schrank, Bernice. "'Cutting Off Your Nose to Spire Your Race': Jewish Stereotypes, Media Images, Cultural Hybridity." *Shofar*, 25:4 (Summer 2007).

Siegel, Richard, Michael Strassfeld, Sharon Strassfeld, eds. *The First Jewish Catalog: A Do-It-Yourself-Kit*. Philadelphia: Jewish Publications Society, 1965.

Teltsch, Kathleen. "Scholars and Descendants Uncover Hidden Legacy of Jews in Southwest," *The New York Times*, November 11, 1990.

Walker, Rebecca. "Love Child." *Heeb*, 13, July 2007.

Waxman, Chaim Isaac. "From Institutional Decay to Primary Day: American Orthodox Jewry Since World War II." *American Jewish History*, 91: 3–4 (September, December 2003).

Wertheimer, Jack; Cohen, Steven M.; Liebman, Charles S. "How to Save American Jews." *Commentary*, January 1996.

Whitfield, Stephen J. "Enigmas of Modern Jewish Identity." *Jewish Social Studies*, 8:2/3 (Winter–Spring 2002).